D1766588

University of Hertfordshire

Learning and Information Services

College Lane, Hatfield, Hertfordshire, AL10 9AB

For renewal of Standard and One Week Loans,
please visit the website: http://www.voyager.herts.ac.uk

This item must be returned or the loan renewed by the due date.
The University reserves the right to recall items from loan at any time.
A fine will be charged for the late return of items.

4827/KM/DS

Cambridge Studies in Romanticism 6

KEATS, NARRATIVE AND AUDIENCE

CAMBRIDGE STUDIES IN ROMANTICISM

This series aims to foster the best new work in one of the most challenging fields within English literary studies. From the early 1780s to the early 1830s a formidable array of talented men and women took to literary composition, not just in poetry, which some of them famously transformed, but in many modes of writing. The expansion of publishing created new opportunities for writers, and the political stakes of what they wrote were raised again and again by what Wordsworth called those 'great national events' that were 'almost daily taking place': the French Revolution, the Napoleonic and American wars, urbanization, industrialization, religious revival, an expanded empire abroad and the reform movement at home. This was an enormous ambition, even when it pretended otherwise. The relations between science, philosophy, religion and literature were reworked in texts such as *Frankenstein* and *Biographia Literaria*; gender relations in *A Vindication of the Rights of Woman* and *Don Juan*; journalism by Cobbett and Hazlitt; poetic form, content and style by the Lake School and the Cockney School. Outside Shakespeare studies, probably no body of writing has produced such a wealth of response or done so much to shape the responses of modern criticism. This indeed is the period that saw the emergence of those notions of 'literature' and of literary history, especially national literary history, on which modern scholarship in English has been founded.

The categories produced by Romanticism have also been challenged by recent historicist arguments. The task of the series is to engage both with a challenging corpus of Romantic writings and with the changing field of criticism they have helped to shape. As with other literary series published by Cambridge, this one will represent the work of both younger and more established scholars, on either side of the Atlantic and elsewhere.

KEATS, NARRATIVE AND AUDIENCE

AUDIENCE

The Posthumous Life of Writing

ANDREW BENNETT

University of Aalborg

CAMBRIDGE
UNIVERSITY PRESS

CAMBRIDGE UNIVERSITY PRESS
Cambridge, New York, Melbourne, Madrid, Cape Town, Singapore, São Paulo

Cambridge University Press
The Edinburgh Building, Cambridge CB2 2RU, UK

Published in the United States of America by Cambridge University Press, New York

www.cambridge.org
Information on this title: www.cambridge.org/9780521445658

First published 1994
This digitally printed first paperback version 2006

A catalogue record for this publication is available from the British Library

Library of Congress Cataloguing in Publication data

Bennett, Andrew, 1960-
Keats, narrative and audience: the posthumous life of writing / Andrew Bennett.
p.   cm. – (Cambridge studies in Romanticism)
Includes bibliographical references.
ISBN 0 521 44565 5 (hardback)
1. Keats, John, 1795–1821 – Criticism and interpretation.
2. Authors and readers – England – History – 19th century. 3. Reader-response criticism.
4. Romanticism – England. 5. Narration
(Rhetoric) I. Title. II. Series.
PR 4837. B45 1994
821′. 7 – dc20
93-24773 CIP

ISBN-13 978-0-521-44565-8 hardback
ISBN-10 0-521-44565-5 hardback

ISBN-13 978-0-521-02442-6 paperback
ISBN-10 0-521-02442-0 paperback

For
Michael Ayres

Contents

Acknowledgements

This book has benefited from the advice, interest, encouragement and criticism of a number of people who have read and commented on individual chapters or the whole book at different stages in its development. I would like to thank Maud Ellmann, Barbara Hardy, John Dixon Hunt, Anna-Maria Hämäläinen, Philip Martin, Nicholas Royle, Victor Sage, Jennifer Searle, Stuart Sperry and Peter Womack, as well as various anonymous publisher's and journal readers, for their help. Between 1989 and 1992, I was fortunate to work closely with Nicholas Royle at the University of Tampere in Finland: our collaborations in both teaching and writing have made a significant difference to the final version of this book.

Earlier versions of parts of this book have been published in *Keats-Shelley Journal* (Chapter 5), *Style* (Chapter 6), *Word and Image* (part of Chapter 7), and *Criticism* (part of Chapters 2 and 9). I would like to thank the editors of these journals for permission to reuse this material.

Abbreviations

All quotations from Keats's poetry are from *The Poems of John Keats*, ed. Jack Stillinger (London, Heinemann, 1978).

BL   Samuel Taylor Coleridge, *Biographia Literaria*, eds. James Engell and W. Jackson Bate (2 vols., London, Routledge and Kegan Paul, 1983)

CL   *Collected Letters of Samuel Taylor Coleridge*, ed. Earl Leslie Griggs (6 vols., Oxford University Press, 1956–71)

CN   *The Notebooks of Samuel Taylor Coleridge*, ed. Kathleen Coburn (6 vols. to date, London, Routledge and Kegan Paul, 1957–) [Referred to by note number]

EY   *The Letters of William and Dorothy Wordsworth: The Early Years, 1787–1805*, ed. Ernest de Sélincourt, 2nd edn., rev. Chester L. Shaver (Oxford University Press, 1967)

Heritage   G. M. Matthews, ed., *Keats: The Critical Heritage* (London, Routledge and Kegan Paul, 1971)

KC   *The Keats Circle: Letters and Papers, and More Letters and Poems of the Keats Circle*, 2nd edn., ed. Hyder Edward Rollins (2 vols., Cambridge, Mass., Harvard University Press, 1965)

LB   William Wordsworth and Samuel Taylor Coleridge, *Lyrical Ballads*, eds. R. L. Brett and A. R. Jones (London, Methuen, 1968)

Letters   *The Letters of John Keats, 1814–1821*, ed. Hyder Edward Rollins (2 vols., Cambridge, Mass., Harvard University Press, 1958)

LY   *The Letters of William and Dorothy Wordsworth: The Later Years*, ed. Ernest de Sélincourt, 2nd edn., rev. Alan G. Hill (4 vols., Oxford University Press, 1978–88)

MY   *The Letters of William and Dorothy Wordsworth: The Middle Years*, ed. Ernest de Sélincourt, 2nd edn., rev. Mary

Moorman and Alan G. Hill (2 vols., Oxford University Press, 1969–70)

Prose   William Wordsworth, *Selected Prose*, ed. John O. Hayden (Harmondsworth, Penguin, 1988)

Reiman   Donald H. Reiman, ed., *The Romantics Reviewed: Contemporary Reviews of British Romantic Writers* (9 vols., New York, Garland Publishing, 1972) [Part no., vol. no., and page no. given, e.g. A2, p. 132]

Works   *The Complete Works of William Hazlitt*, ed. P. P. Howe (21 vols., London, Dent, 1930–34)

[The text of Keats's letters is reproduced exactly from Rollins's editions of *KC* and *Letters*, including the use of square brackets ([]) for editorial corrections and other insertions, curly brackets ({}) for insertions which fill gaps caused by tears, etc., and angled brackets (⟨ ⟩) to designate letters or words cancelled in the manuscript.]

Journals

ELH	*English Literary History*
JEGP	*Journal of English and Germanic Philology*
KSJ	*Keats-Shelley Journal*
KSMB	*Keats-Shelley Memorial Bulletin*
MLN	*Modern Language Notes*
MP	*Modern Philology*
NLH	*New Literary History*
PMLA	*Publications of the Modern Languages Association of America*
PQ	*Philological Quarterly*
SEL	*Studies in English Literature, 1500–1900*
SiR	*Studies in Romanticism*
SP	*Studies in Philology*

Introduction: figures of reading

What makes the poetry of John Keats so compelling, at once so disturbing and so seductive, are its uncertain but irreducible and scandalous instabilities. What may most fundamentally be identified as the 'character' of Keats's poetry involves the uncontainable intensities of an inundation of figures, such as oxymoron, enjambment, neologism, and an adjectival distortion and syntactical dislocation, by which 'thought' – the ideational or 'thetic' – is apparently subsumed within the suffocating sensuousness of 'language'. At the same time, such intensities themselves generate an unmatched intertextual complexity, conceptual scope and intellectual force: Keatsian 'solecism' is produced by the interlocking and conflicting energies which displace and redefine oppositions between beauty and truth, mortality and immortality, thought and feeling, dreaming and wakefulness, passivity and activity, life and death. These are some of the uncertain polarities which generate form out of the sparks which fly from an intense conjoining and unsettling of incommensurable differences. These are the constitutive energies of Keats's poetry, energies of solecism met by the uneasy responses which the poetry continues to elicit.[1]

The instabilities of Keats's poetry are nowhere more evident than in the way that stories are formed, constructed, shaped and directed towards readers and towards audiences. Narrative may be said to produce the fundamental uncertainty of Romantic poetry, the uncertainty of audience. In narrative is inscribed the inescapably public dimension of poetry, a dimension which produces an awakening from the Romantic Dream of poetry (the Dream of lyric poetry) isolated from – both antagonistic and determinedly insouciant towards – its audience. Without stories – but there are only and always stories – Romantic poetry would be able to dream of a text with no reader, a speech-act with no addressee. But stories are

inescapably oriented towards and written *for* readers: the irreducible
ground of narrative *is* audience. This is why narrative can be defined
in terms of 'communication', as 'someone telling someone else that
something happened'.[2] The unavoidable production of audience by
the very existence of narrative results in the Romantic solecism which
is the Keatsian solecism before all others: the solecism of lyric poetry.
The Romantic Dream of texts without readers (which is the Dream
of texts without stories) is also the Romantic Dream of lyric poetry
(the Dream of poetry without audience because it is without
narrative).

In this study, I suggest that Keats's poetry engages, above all, with
the figure of solecism. In this respect it is important to recognize ways
in which solecism itself inhabits, infects and violates the opposition
between the poet and the audience, the private and the public.
Solecism is an impropriety of language, a violation of the rules of
grammar or syntax, a breach of good manners or etiquette, a social
blunder, an error, incongruity or inconsistency (*OED*): in each case
there is a collision between incompatible codes, between the private
or personal and the public or social.[3] Poetry, specifically the poetry of
Keats, is grounded in solecism because of its distortions of and within
language. For poetry, the decorum of grammar is violated, conventions are disrupted, language itself is 'tortured'[4]: words must be
stretched, misplaced, collided incongruously with other words,
dissected into etymology, fragmented into paronomasia, semantically
voided, and then bombarded with meaning.

Keats would seem to be eminently suited to such transgressive
dissolutions of the decorum of language. The story goes like this:
'cockney', widely but indiscriminately read and with a limited
classical education, vulgar, jejune, visceral, Keats's torsions of
language may be understood – in terms of class, cultural literacy or
education – as an attack on the decorum of poetry.[5] Reading Keats
we are faced, again and again, with the problem of reading solecism
– generic, historical, aesthetic, social, mythological, lexical, syntactic,
narratorial – almost as a structuring device in his poetry: the endless
questing for romance in *Endymion*, the historical error over who
discovered the Pacific Ocean in the Chapman's Homer sonnet, the
impropriety of shrill political denunciation in 'Isabella', the explicit
sexual consummation which disturbed his publishers in 'The Eve of
St Agnes', the scandalous reappropriation and internalization of a
classical myth in 'Ode to Psyche', the lexical breaking of 'happy' in

stanza three of 'Ode on a Grecian Urn', the syntactical incompletion of 'To Autumn', the self-parody of narrative form in the clichéd opening of 'Lamia', and more generally the 'humanizing' embarrassments discerned throughout his work by Christopher Ricks and the 'enlightening' vulgarity described by John Bayley. These are just some of the ways in which the poetry presents us with the problem of reading solecism. In each case, what is articulated is a fault-line, a 'faulture' (a Keatsian neologism/solecism from *The Fall of Hyperion*) between private and public. Solecism constitutes the necessary faulture of poetry, the inescapable friction of the 'personal' with the 'social'. Solecism, in other words, is reading.

In the present study it is the pervasive faulture of narrative poetry that we shall examine most intensively: narrative as faulture, as solecism, because of its fracturing of the privacy demanded by the Romantic lyric. As a number of critics have shown, narration begins in instability, in unresolved tensions, most generally in a gap or opening in the finished surface of causality, reason, understanding or desire.[6] Such instabilities may be understood to inhabit the space between text and audience: the instability produced by an unfinished plot is not just the product of an irreconcilable friction within a narrative, but is constituted by the uncertainty of the reader in the text. It is possible to describe such uncertainties in terms of what might be called, after Jonathan Culler, the 'double logic' of narrative. Culler uses the phrase to describe the way in which the relationship between 'story' ('a sequence of events') and 'discourse' (that which 'orders and presents events') is constituted by *aporia*. To put it simply, Culler suggests that narratology must confront the paradox that while in any account of a narrative it is possible to show that story determines discourse, *at the same time* it is also possible to show that discourse determines story.[7] I suggest that this recognition of, finally, the impossible (double) logic of narrative, should also be framed in terms of audience. It is in reading, or in what Paul de Man calls the 'impossibility' of reading, that the double logic of narrative operates.[8] Culler's double logic of story and discourse is, in fact, only one of the double logics of narrative. Others include the paradox of what Paul Ricoeur has described as the 'progressive contingency' and 'retroactive necessity' of narrative: if narrative is founded on the possibility of causal relations between events, this causality progresses from contingency to necessity within the temporal space of reading itself.[9] Another double logic is that of the friction, or what Jean

Ricardou has called the 'belligérance' of narration and description: in order to tell a story a narrative must include description which is, by definition, an interruption of narration.[10] And, related to this, we might also refer to the antagonism of an aesthetics of lyric timelessness towards narrative temporality, and the apparently paradoxical sense in which narrative constitutes what Barthes has called the 'espace dilatoire', or what, in speaking of the Romance mode, Patricia Parker has characterized as a digression towards the end.[11] In each case, the double logic of narrative is also a problem of reading: to the extent that the Romantics wrote narratives, they were dealing with what I shall term an 'anxiety of audience'.

One element of the Romantic anxiety of audience may be accounted for, then, by a recognition of the problematics of narrative 'logic' together with the apparently constitutive incompatibility of narrative with lyric and its necessary engagement with audience. However, a number of social, economic and technological developments may be understood to have produced a historically specific anxiety at the turn of the nineteenth century. The eighteenth and early nineteenth centuries witnessed a number of advances in print technology, an increase in the market for books, in literacy and in the spread of print media generally, together with a decline in patronage and a subsequent professionalization of the writer.[12] One major consequence of this change in the role of the writer was an increasing division between poets and their audiences. At the beginning of the nineteenth century, writers found themselves in the predicament of what Jean-François Lyotard calls 'modernity', a predicament in which the writer 'no longer knows for whom he writes'. Rather than 'networks of reception', the published book is controlled by 'economic networks': 'as to what may happen to the book, what its actual reception may be, no one really knows'.[13] In this respect, it comes as no surprise that one of Wordsworth's unanswered and finally unanswerable questions in the 1802 Preface to the *Lyrical Ballads* is 'To whom does [the Poet] address himself?' (*LB*, p. 255). The possibilities and dangers of this situation can be graphically illustrated by referring to a few sales' figures: while Byron's *The Corsair* is said to have sold 10,000 copies on the day of publication,[14] a letter written by Keats's publisher delightedly records having sold seven or eight copies of *Endymion* (*KC*, vol. 1, pp. 52–3), and the first edition of the *Lyrical Ballads*, despite its eventual relative success, was remaindered. In a letter, Shelley estimated the total readership for

Prometheus Unbound to be only five or six.[15] With the examples, not least, of Scott and Byron, the Romantics were aware of and eager to exploit the possibilities offered by a vertiginously expanding reading public. At the same time, however, in the face of their uncertainty of audience and of what was taken to be contemporary neglect, the reception of their poetry by *future* generations of readers, in posterity, became crucial to the Romantics.

The historical configuration of the Romantic audience, then, may be said to account for certain fundamental aspects of Romantic writing – most generally the conflict between the private and the public nature of poetry. Romantic texts might be understood to be largely generated from an anxiety of the private as public, or poetry published: in this sense, publication is itself a solecism, a showing forth of that which should remain hidden, secret, private.[16] Thus the very relationship between Keats and audience might be framed in terms of the notion of solecism, and one way of conceiving solecism is as a form of Freud's 'uncanny', the revelation of that which should remain hidden, such that the strangeness of the uncanny is constitutive of Keats's poetry.[17] This complex of ideas – audience-solecism-uncanny – might be further elaborated and related to censorship. In this respect, censorship should be understood as an attempt to police the scandal (ethical, legal or social) of that which is at once public (written, published) and 'private' (that which should remain unwritten and unpublished). In a recent essay entitled 'Keats Reading Women, Women Reading Keats', Margaret Homans has begun to position Keats in terms of gender and censorship. Homans argues persuasively that Keats's position with regard to his female readers involves a defensive reaction to their implicit power over his poetry: Keats 'needs women to want him and his books, yet he resents women's power in the literary marketplace as much as he resents their sexual power over him'.[18] In particular, Homans discusses Keats's revisions to 'The Eve of St Agnes' and his arguments with his publishers over these revisions. In a well-known drama of censorship recorded in a letter written by Richard Woodhouse, a literary adviser to Keats's publisher, Keats is said to have altered the ending of the poem in order to 'leave on the reader a sense of pettish disgust' and to 'play with his reader, & fling him off at last' (*KC*, vol. I, p. 91), and to have altered the climax to make its sexual suggestiveness more explicit. Woodhouse claims that these changes 'will render the poem unfit for ladies'. For Keats, however, this is beside the point (or precisely the point) because 'he says he does not want ladies to read his poetry' (*KC*, vol. I, p. 92). Keats's publisher, John Taylor, responded angrily to the poet's rejection of a major section of the reading public, pointing out that if Keats had 'known truly what the Society and what the Suffrages of Women are worth, he would never have thought of depriving himself of them' (*KC*, vol. I, p. 96). Of this exchange, Homans comments that 'Keats has not so much made his poem uninteresting to women readers, as made it necessary as well as pleasurable for male readers to control its distribution'.[19] This is an intriguing idea, which I would like to develop by suggesting that just such a drama of censorship is exemplary for Keats's poetry. According to Homans, the pleasure of the Keatsian text involves the double pleasure of scandal and censorship: the male reader (or writer or editor) is empowered by the poem to experience both the (erotic) pleasure of reading the forbidden text and at the same time the (again, potentially erotic) pleasure of forbidding that pleasure to women. Homans rightly focuses on the implications of this for the construction of gender in Keats's letters and poems. More generally, however, the structure of the scandal implicit in the pleasure of censorship might be understood to be fundamental to Keats's poetry. That is, Keats's poetry – and not only at moments of embarrassment, scandal, 'vulgarity', or 'badness' – may be understood to be structured by an unstable oscillation between privacy and publicity, between scandal and censorship. Reading Keats is figured as the solecism of reading not only that which should but, in an important sense, that which *does*, remain hidden.

This may account to some extent for various conflicts in Keats's texts, conflicts ultimately resulting in a reception which both reads and resists their figures of reading. The focus at various points in this study on what I refer to as Keats's 'figures of reading', involves a recognition of the importance of representations of readers and reading within Keats's poems. I propose that representations of reading or readers in the poems themselves constitute, fundamentally, the site of reading. This is not to suggest, in any simple sense, that the poems are 'self-reflexive'. Rather, I would point to a more radical recognition of the importance and difficulty of reading representations of reading. Figures of reading are necessarily both responded to and resisted, both read and, as instruments *of* reading, elided.

A similar point was made some time ago by Paul de Man in his discussion of Proust in *Allegories of Reading*, when he suggests that 'the allegorical representation of Reading ... [is] the irreducible component of any text'. De Man then discusses the impossibility of reading reading:

All that will be represented in such an allegory will deflect from the act of reading and block access to its understanding. The allegory of reading narrates the impossibility of reading ... Everything in [*A la recherche du temps perdu*] signifies something other than what it represents, be it love, consciousness, politics, art, sodomy, or gastronomy: it is always something else that is intended. It can be shown that the most adequate term to designate this 'something else' is Reading. But one must at the same time 'understand' that this word bars access, once and forever, to a meaning that yet can never cease to call out for its understanding.[20]

In one sense this can be understood to result in the fact that the reception accorded Keats's poetry overwhelmingly repeats the reading figured in the texts themselves without attempting to read those figures. In as much as the critical reception of Keats's poetry involves, for example, assertions of enthralment with respect to 'La Belle Dame sans Merci', or aesthetic questioning and desire in relation to 'Ode on a Grecian Urn', this reception repeats the figured reading of Keats's poems without attempting to read its own reading as a figure of repetition. In this sense, 'figures of reading' designates the site of what Jonathan Culler calls the 'transference' which splits the identity of the literary text. In a recent essay which considers the question of the formalistic privileging of moments of 'self-reference', Culler suggests that such moments 'may be the marks of a situation of transference. The critic who claims to stand outside the text and analyse it seems hopelessly entangled with it, caught up in a repetition that can be described as discovering structures in the text that (unbeknownst to him) repeat his own relation to the text, or as repeating in his interpretation a relation already figured in the text'.[21] As Timothy Clark comments in a consideration of Culler's essay, however, far from questioning the identity of the literary text – as Culler proposes – this mode of argument 'generalizes' reflexivity 'into a structure whereby the poem (in a parody of the Hegelian system) includes within itself its own readings'.[22] Rather than putting into question the limits of the literary text, Culler's notion of reflexivity simply expands them to include the text's reception. By redefining 'reflexivity' as 'figures of reading', I would like to suggest

that the determination of reading by reflexive or embedded representations of reading is accepted only on condition of what de Man
would call the 'impossibility' of such reading. Most fundamentally,
but also most tentatively, I shall suggest that the end-point of figures
of reading in Keats, and in the Romantics more generally, is a
reading after death – the 'posthumous life' of writing, but also the
posthumous life of reading.

As I have indicated, the present study attempts to situate such
problematics of reading within the terms of the more specifically
historical question of the audience for Romantic poetry. I explore
ways in which Keats's poetry is related to the complex conception of
audience developed by various writers in the early nineteenth century
– in particular, by Wordsworth – in order to account for the
fractured, problematic relationship between their poetry and their
audiences. Over the last few years, critics have shown considerable
interest in Romantic responses to, and productions and representations of, its readers or audiences (all of which may be suggested by
the phrase 'figures of reading').[23] These considerations may be
divided into a number of sub-categories. In the first place, there has
been work, influenced primarily by Wolfgang Iser, on the role of the
reader, on strategies adopted by hypothetical or 'implied' readers
with respect to poetic language: rather than engaging with a
historical analysis of the social construction of reading, such
discussions are presented as a kind of grammar of reading.[24] Secondly,
there are studies of the rhetorical intentions of the poet, studies which
recognize – despite Shelley's nightingale singing to please itself and
John Stuart Mill's poetry overheard – ways in which the Romantics
were profoundly and quite explicitly concerned to *affect* their
audiences, consistently expressing a concern both with how readers
read and with how poets can manipulate the response of readers (to
ethical, social or aesthetic ends). In these studies critics have been
more interested in the notion of the poet's engagement with his or her
audience than with the responses of those audiences *per se*.[25] The third
major mode of critical engagement with Romantic reading also
involves the reader *in* the text: colluding in some ways with both of
the first two categories, a number of critics have sought to examine
ways in which embedded, framed, or inset readers function, and ways
in which such readers might affect, presuppose or manipulate the
responses of empirical readers.[26]

The present book owes much to these studies of Romantic readers and reading. In as much as they elide a number of theoretical and epistemological problems which beset the criticism of Romantic poetry and poetics, however, critics have tended to delimit their project to the terms either of showing that a poet was concerned with audience, or showing how attention to the role of the reader helps to elucidate the poet's technical control over poetic form.[27] Frances Ferguson has stated that 'it seems... impossible to talk about an audience for Wordsworth's poetry without talking about reading':[28] I would suggest that once we start to talk about the intricate and contingent strategies of reading, the monolithic, autonomous, and homogeneous concept of 'audience' is fractured and disrupted. At the same time it is precisely this 'audience' which impels Romantic texts and which therefore undermines any examination of the complexities of reading separated from a consideration of the rhetorical compulsions of texts.

In this study I attempt to elaborate the problematics of reading and audience in Keats's poetry through a reading of his canonical texts. I suggest that the relationship between readers and audiences is inherently unstable: reading, in both senses, is subject to the incommensurability of the private and the public, reading as figured and figures of reading, the impossible temporality of reading (involving a teleological projection forward and an anterior reversal or rereading from the end), the conflict between the empirical and the hypothetical or ideal, between the living and the dead. It is my contention that such conflicts are ultimately incorporated into the crucial Romantic notion of 'posterity', a notion which might be glossed as the Romantic invention of reception infinitely but undecidably deferred to the future. Although the desire to 'live on' or 'survive' in one's writing goes back at least to Horace's *aere perennis*, and is a particularly notable feature of the Renaissance – in, for example, Shakespeare's sonnets – the Romantic period makes of posterity *the* major trope of reading. This 'invention' involves a refiguration of posterity as the necessary ground of artistic production and has important consequences, not least for strategies of reading and authorial presence. Both writing and reading become problematic because both involve a kind of 'posthumous life'. Writing 'lives on' after the death of the author, in posterity, a posthumous supplement of a life. Reading is thus understood to be textually necessary but, founded on the death of the author, it can never be present to itself. Put simply, once posterity becomes necessary to writing, the attempt by reading to return to the originary act of inscription is interrupted by the absolute barrier of death itself. The originary moment of inscription which reading desires – under the guise of, for example, the attempt to 'understand' authorial intention or meaning – is displaced to a time *after*, a time which, in 'Tintern Abbey', Wordsworth calls 'after years'.[29] And this time, this after time or posthumous life which 'survives' in writing, is itself inscribed in the originary moment of reading. Reading, then, can only ever be other to itself, constituting *itself* as a kind of remainder or supplement of writing, while Romantic writing calls for an impossible coincidence of reading with the event of inscription.[30] Romantic writing inscribes reading as both a remainder – that which occurs or survives in a time radically posterior to the event of writing – and itself originary. The repercussions of this description of writing and reading in Romantic poetry result in an undecidable play of difference – suggested by the reciprocal notions of the 'posthumous life of writing' and 'the death of the reader' – which the work of, for example, Jacques Derrida, both responds to and results in.[31]

The question of posterity in Romantic poetry, the attempt to remain in one's remains, is the subject of a study which I hope to publish in the future. Let it remain for now with one or two examples of configurations of posterity, of posthumous writing and of the radical absence of the addressee in canonical Romantic poems. Coleridge tends to figure his addressee as mentally absent: in the conversation poems, the addressee tends to be sleeping or in a 'pensive' trance, and the effect of the Mariner's tale in 'The Rime of the Ancient Mariner' is to 'stun' the Wedding Guest. In Shelley's *Adonais*, the poet-reader dies in response to Keats's poetry, his 'Ozymandias' ends with a scenic devastation, a disintegrated monumentalization, from which the reader is excluded, while 'A Defence of Poetry' presents reading as a form of haunting by the unreadable, the unspeakable and the immemorial. Shelley also seems fascinated by the possibility of writing *after* his own death: in a letter, for example, he refers to Moses writing 'the history of his own death',[32] and his second volume of poetry constituted just such a fiction in its title – *Posthumous Fragments of Margaret Nicholson* – while the Advertisement to *Epipsychidion* declares that 'The Writer of the following Lines died at Florence'.[33] Similarly, the problem of remains, of how to remain in one's writing, is itself an object of explicit concern in Romantic poetry and poetics, a concern most notably expressed in Wordsworth's question in *The Prelude*: 'Oh, why hath not the mind / Some element to stamp her image on / In nature somewhat nearer to her own? / Why, gifted with such powers to send abroad / Her spirit, must it lodge in shrines so frail'.[34] Similarly, 'Tintern Abbey' may be read as an elaboration of the problem of how it is possible for the poet to remain in his remains – the mansion of Dorothy's mind, her memory – after his death. In his essays, Hazlitt repeatedly returns to the question of posterity and in such texts as 'On Posthumous Fame, – Whether Shakespeare was Influenced by a Love of it' (from *The Round Table*), 'On the Living Poets' (from *Lectures on the English Poets*), and 'On the Feeling of Immortality in Youth', he refers to the writer 'living on', 'outliving himself', and 'surviving himself'. Keats himself frequently refers to the importance of a future reception in his letters and poetry – in poems such as 'Oh Chatterton! how very sad thy fate', 'To my Brother George' (lines 67ff.), 'Sleep and Poetry' (lines 81–4, 358–9), 'Great spirits now on earth are sojourning', 'Bards of passion and of Mirth'; and in comments in letters such as the statement that 'I think I shall be among the English Poets after my death' (*Letters*, vol. I, p. 394), or more commonly his despair that 'If I should die ... I have left no immortal work behind me' (*Letters*, vol. II, p. 263) and his wish that his tombstone should carry the words 'HERE LIES ONE WHOSE NAME WAS WRIT IN WATER' (*KC*, vol. II, p. 91).

One way in which posterity is figured in Romantic poetry, then, is in terms of the posthumous life of writing. The most economical and powerful formulation of such a 'death' may be read in Keats's enigmatic fragment-poem 'This living hand':

> This living hand, now warm and capable
> Of earnest grasping, would, if it were cold
> And in the icy silence of the tomb,
> So haunt thy days and chill thy dreaming nights
> That thou would wish thine own heart dry of blood
> So in my veins red life might stream again,
> And thou be conscience-calm'd – see here it is
> I hold it towards you – [35]

The poem is an exemplary expression of the posthumous life of writing. But it also suggests some of the paradoxes of such a 'life'. In particular, it announces the death of the reader. Distracted by the word 'wish' in line five and by the conditional tense in line two, most critics have read the poem as suggesting that readers might *desire* to die so that the poet can live. In fact, however, if we take the words 'literally' we find that the life of the poet's hand *entails* the death of the audience: in order for the hand to live, the reader must transfuse his or her blood into it. Furthermore, the deictic assertions of presence – 'This living hand' and 'see here it is / I hold it towards you' – suggest that the hand does indeed live, which, according to the logic presupposed by the poem, means that the reader must have died. To the extent that the poem's empirical audience would want to refute the assertion of their own death, however, the poem would have to be read 'metaphorically' or 'figuratively': the text is 'only' a poem, and the words 'only' figurative. By this strategy of reading the audience refutes the logic of reading established by the poem, and to this extent excludes itself as an audience for the poem. In excluding itself from the poem's logic, however, the audience has not escaped the power of the poem's earnest grasp because, in refusing the logic of reading promulgated by the poem, the audience has become a non-audience – for this poem at least, the audience has died. In order to escape this mortal double-bind, the audience might attempt to traverse a reading somewhere between the 'literal' and the 'figurative' readings sketched above. But such a reading would seem to be kept in perpetual limbo, constituted by an icy indeterminacy of how to read – a reading which, like the construction of the Romantic audience as 'posterity', is structured around indefinite deferral. Finally, the 'reader' might point to the conditional tense of line two and assert that (at the moment of inscription, at least) the hand and the poet do indeed live. To do so, however, would only be to repeat, against the 'evidence' of our 'senses', the gesture which the poem prefigures, and to assure the poetic hand of its posthumous life. The poem suggests, then, that inhabiting the Romantic theorization of audience is a logic of reading which involves an indefinite deferral to a time after the reader's death. While Shelley's *Adonais* mythologizes the poet as destroyed by his readers (the reviewers), Keats's poem has already reversed this mortal thrall. As such, Keats's 'This living hand' is an exemplary Romantic poem because of its explicit engagement with, and implicitly, its presupposition of, the death of its reader.

A 'rational' explanation for what I term the 'death' of the reader might involve the following argument: in recognition of the fundamental absence of the addressee, the Romantics reinvented response as deferred to a time after the poet's death. In this sense, response becomes a form of remaining, and the fundamental impulse for writing becomes the desire to remain. Once one becomes dependent for one's remains on others, however, then the death of the other takes on a crucial significance and there is a slippage from a concern about one's own death and remains to a concern with the death of one's readers, in whom one can, potentially, 'live on'. (This pathos of remaining is most clearly and explicitly described at the end of William Hazlitt's essay 'On the Feeling of Immortality in Youth'.[36]) In this sense, Keats's poem may be read as an attempt to short-circuit or prefigure this disastrous but inescapable logic of remains, and the inevitable event of the death of the reader.

Brooke Hopkins is right, in a recent essay on 'This living hand', to discuss the poem in terms of the uncanny because in doing so he reveals an important element of Keatsian solecism:[37] poetry in Keats involves, as I have suggested, a showing forth of that which should remain hidden, secret, private, unpublished. It is not necessary to consider one possible intended destination of 'This living hand' – Fanny Brawne – and its supposed origin as a love-poem; nor is it necessary to consider that the poem remained hidden, unpublished, until 1898; nor, indeed, is it necessary to remind ourselves that it is only in the last decade that the poem has been read with the scrupulous intensity for which it calls:[38] the solecism of the uncanny inhabits the poem's engagement with the reader's death. And it is this figuration of reading which Hopkins arrives at as the poem's 'most uncanny feature': 'the reader is placed in the position of sacrificing his own life in order that the hand in front of him ... might become "warm and capable / Of earnest grasping"'.[39] But this reading is hedged by the concluding sentences of Hopkins's essay:

It appears to threaten the life of the reader as well, making him wish his 'own heart dry of blood' so that the same blood can flow in the veins of another. It is as if the poem *itself* has become the poet's body, something that can be reanimated only through a transfusion of life from the reader, the reanimation of the words on the page. Once alive in the act of writing, those words are now dead and can only be brought back to life by the reader in the *act* of reading. But that only serves to recall the reader to a consciousness of his own dying. And it is from that recollection, a version of Freud's *Nachträglichkeit*, that the uncanniness of Keats's poem ultimately springs.[40]

'It appears ... making him wish ... It is as if ... But that only serves to recall ... from that recollection ... ' One hundred and seventy years after a living hand pulsing with warm blood flowing through a diseased body, a mortal body which was to last less than 'a thousand days', inscribed the words of 'This living hand', Hopkins produces a reading which goes as far as may be conceived to transfuse life into the hand of the poet. But Hopkins finally resists the assertion of what we must all by now know: the solecistic, uncanny logic of 'This living hand' allows for no other reading than that of and, crucially, that in, the death of its reader.

'This living hand' produces an indefinite deferral of reading in posterity. And we have already begun to read the intransigent complexities of the (trans)figured audience in Keats's poetry. We might take this poem as the end-point of a teleological trajectory of the Keatsian corpus, the body of work which ends in, or with, the death of reading. But, as this suggests, the death of the reader will be recognized most intensively in Keats's later poems: as such, the present study will itself be seen to be impelled by the inescapable teleological pathos of the Keatsian biography which, in ineluctable metamorphosis, becomes the thanatological trajectory of a posthumous life.

The present book elaborates, nevertheless, a reading of the poetry of Keats – poetry which, as Paul de Man has commented, seems to be 'haunted by a dream that always remains in the future'.[41] In this study I would like to propose a fundamental redescription of poetry so haunted, and of what it means to 'remain' in the future. Indeed, the body of the book is precisely a return, once again, to those most enthralling, most haunting and intriguing of texts, the major poems of Keats. Before beginning the ultimately self-defeating task of 'reading' Keats's poetry, however, I shall attempt to specify what is at stake in questions of narrative, reading, and audience in the early nineteenth century. In Chapter 1 I discuss ways in which narrative and audience are presented in writing at the turn of the century generally, and in Chapter 2 I focus on Keats's letters to examine ways in which Keats himself theorizes reading and audience in his prose. From then on we shall be more or less alone with the poetry of John Keats in the finally undecidable solitude of reading.

CHAPTER I

Narrative and audience in Romantic poetics

What is the status of narrative in the poetics of the early nineteenth century? What are the problems and questions raised by stories, narrative poems and novels, and how do writers and critics frame such questions in relation to audience and readers? How are readers and audiences 'figured', generally, in Romantic prose? These are some of the topics which I would like to consider in order to suggest ways in which narrative and audience constitute a fundamental locus of anxiety for Romantic poetry. It is my suggestion that narrative, and the relationship between narrative and audience, provided important and troubling sources of generative energy for early nineteenth-century poetry. In this chapter I shall discuss – briefly and schematically – three interrelated questions: firstly, the question of what Romantic writers understood as the necessary elements of a narrative; secondly, very generally, the relationship between narrative and audience or readers in the early nineteenth century; and thirdly, the way in which Wordsworth, in particular, re-invents posterity as the deferral of reading. My recognition of the problematic relationship between narrative and audience in Romantic poetics is based on the view that, in the most fundamental if contradictory sense, narrative both presupposes and necessitates the construction of an addressee, and that for the Romantic writer the status of the audience, the addressee, is radically uncertain. The question for the Romantics, then, becomes: how can narrative operate within the terms of an undecidable and forever-absent addressee? In the first part of this chapter, I shall discuss ways in which narrative is a site of irreducible conflict in Romantic poetics.

Narrative is most often distinguished from 'non-narrative' in terms of its presentation of temporally and causally related events or 'incidents'. The Romantic distrust of narrative is, in this sense, most clearly evident in Shelley's distinction between a 'story' and a 'poem' in 'A Defence of Poetry': 'a story is a catalogue of detached facts, which have no other bond of connexion than time, place, circumstance, cause and effect; the other is the creation of actions according to the unchangeable forms of human nature, as existing in the mind of the creator'.[1] Similarly, Coleridge states in a letter that 'incidents are among the lowest allurements of poetry' (CL, vol. 1, p. 566).[2] Such 'allurements', however, are not only attractive but, as Coleridge implicitly recognizes, functions of reading. This recognition is made rather more explicit in a notebook entry when Coleridge comments on *Paradise Lost*, Books Eleven and Twelve: these two books are less interesting 'owing in great measure to the habit of reading Poetry for the Story – . If read in connection as the History of mankind nothing can be finer' (CN, 4495). Narrative, then, is a function of reading – for Coleridge, a bad habit of reading. In fact, however, Coleridge is not alone in condemning such reading, which was often understood to be a result of the increasing popularity of the novel. This is made clear in an anonymous review, in *The British Critic*, of Wordsworth's *The Waggoner*: 'there are too many readers in whom, if we could analyse the pleasure which they derive from poetry, we should find that it was precisely the same as that which a novel affords them; they read as a boy reads Tom Jones, skipping the introductory chapters, for the story only' (Reiman, AI, p. 176). In Coleridge's opinion, this habit is akin to 'gaming, swinging, or swaying on a chair or gate; spitting over a bridge; smoking; snuff-taking; tete a tete quarrels after dinner between husband and wife; conning word for word all the advertisements of the daily advertizer in a public house on a rainy day, &c. &c. &c'. (BL, vol. 1, p. 49). Similarly, in the 1800 Preface to the *Lyrical Ballads*, Wordsworth echoes countless contemporary critics and reviewers when he complains of the 'savage torpor' of the modern mind caused (in part) by the reading of 'frantic novels, sickly and stupid German Tragedies, and deluges of idle and extravagant stories in verse' (LB, p. 249).[3] Underlying such attacks is the recognition of a fundamental opposition between the events of a narrative and 'poetry'. Wordsworth is objecting not simply to sensationalism, to a 'degrading thirst for outrageous stimulation', but to narrative itself. This point is suggested by the causal relation which he establishes between history and story, between 'the great national events which are daily taking place' and 'a craving for extraordinary incidents' as a result of the homogenizing influence of urbanization: for Wordsworth, the sensational eventfulness of contemporary writing constitutes a mimetic response to the contrast between the narrativization of world history and the tedium of everyday life.

As attempts to 'counteract' such influences, many of the poems in the *Lyrical Ballads* may be read as repeatedly undermining the readerly desire for 'events' and 'incidents' by producing narratives which go nowhere, or which evaporate as they are read. Thus, for example, 'Simon Lee' is a tale which tests the reader's ability to 'find / A tale in every thing' – even in 'Simon Lee'; similarly, the narrator of 'Hart-Leap Well' resists the potential sensationalism of narrative by claiming that 'The moving accident is not my trade, / To freeze the blood I have no ready arts', and that he writes for 'thinking hearts' (lines 97–100); 'We Are Seven' produces a repetitive, inconclusive and apparently pointless allegory of what Lyotard would call the '*différend*', an irreducible incommensurability of discourses;[4] 'The Thorn' presents a study in loquacious refusal to narrate; 'Old Man Travelling', a narrative moving in its immobility, is about the unmoving mobilities of grief, about 'A man who does not move with pain, but moves / With thought'; 'A Slumber Did My Spirit Seal' is a narrative of death remarkable for its presentation of the event of death only as an absence, the event of death as the unsaid or unsayable; 'Nutting', a parable of pathological destruction, is also a parable which remains, finally, resistant, blank, to allegorical reading; and so on.[5]

Wordsworth's comments on narrative are, in fact, more or less conventional: narrative poetry is usually understood to inhabit a space of irreducible difference in which telling a good story conflicts with an attempt to fill the verses with description, pathos, sentiment, or moral reflection – thus John Gibson Lockhart, for example, on Shelley's *The Revolt of Islam*:

It will easily be seen, indeed, that neither the main interest nor the main merit of the poet at all consists in the conception of his plot or in the arrangement of his incidents. His praise is, in our judgment, that of having poured over his narrative a very rare strength and abundance of poetic imagery and feeling – of having steeped every word in the essence of his inspiration. (Reiman, CI, p. 103)

A similar opposition is evident in a review of Leigh Hunt's *The Story of Rimini*: 'We wish indeed that the story had moved on a little more rapidly; but we are not unwilling to loiter among the beautiful descriptions, and enjoy the fresh diction of Mr Hunt' (Reiman, CI, p. 324). The rhetoric of ambulation is also evident in one of Coleridge's letters, in which the poet comments that in reading Bürger, an 'idea was so striking, that it made me *pause, stand still* and *look*, when I ought to have been driving on with the horse' (*CL*, vol. I, p. 565). Similarly, attempting to define poetry in the *Biographia Literaria*, Coleridge puts into question the teleological imperative of narration when he suggests that, in reading, the reader 'should be carried forward, not merely or chiefly by the mechanical impulse of curiosity, or by a restless desire to arrive at the final solution; but by the pleasurable activity of mind excited by the attractions of the journey itself' (*BL*, vol. II, p. 14). In another definition of poetry, Coleridge seems to be attempting to reconcile a linear or narrative conception of poetry with a lyric, timeless, 'organic' one, a narrative without (artificial, external) 'narrative': 'The common end of all *narrative*, nay of *all*, Poems is to convert a *series* into a *Whole*: to make those events, which in real or imagined History, move on in a *strait* Line, assume to our Understandings a *circular* motion – the snake with it's [*sic*] Tail in it's Mouth' (*CL*, vol. IV, p. 545). The passage attempts to negotiate narrative and non-narrative in a way which foreshadows more recent analyses of narration: Paul Ricoeur, for example, points out that plot '"grasps together" and integrates into one whole and complete story multiple and scattered events, thereby schematizing the intelligible signification attached to the narrative taken as a whole'.[6] But what this suggests is a resistance to narrative within narrative, a resistance to the arbitrary or circumstantial which narrative necessarily produces: as Tilottama Rajan comments, for Shelley, 'Narrative ... being rooted in the circumstantial, is a disfiguration of poetry'.[7]

By contrast with such uncertain questionings of the value of narrative, however, explicit valuations of poems precisely for their narrative force are also very common. Charles Lamb, for example, values Homer for the ways in which, in reading him, 'you want to go on, to have more of his agreeable narrative'.[8] Coleridge himself complained when he found that the contemporary poetic story-teller *par excellence* neglected narrative. Referring to Sir Walter Scott's *Lady of the Lake*, Coleridge complains of tedium ('between a sleeping Canter and a Marketwoman's trot') due to the slow story: 'I never remember a narrative poem in which I felt the sense of Progress so languid' (*CL*, vol. III, p. 291). The same assumption – that some poems need a strong story-line – seems to be behind Francis Jeffrey's surprise when he finds that the first two cantos of Byron's *Childe Harold* please him even though they have 'so few of the ordinary ingredients of interest or poetical delight. There is no story or adventure – and, indeed, no incident of any kind', to which he added the comment, at the end of the review, that '[i]ts chief fault is the want of story, or object' (Reiman, B2, pp. 836, 840). Similarly, of Canto Three, he remarked that 'it does not belong to a sort of poetry that rises easily to popularity. – It has no story or action' (Reiman, B2, p. 851).[9] Indeed, Jeffrey defined a crucial element in the popularity of Byron's 'Tales' when he spoke of the poet's 'unparalleled rapidity of narrative' in *The Corsair* and *The Bride of Abydos* (Reiman, B2, p. 851). As Scott pointed out in a review of Jane Austen's *Emma*, 'such is the universal charm of narrative, that the worst novel ever written will find some gentle reader content to yawn over it, rather than to open the page of the historian, moralist, or poet'.[10]

Narrative, then, is crucial in terms of a poem's reception. Similarly, and in spite of their distrust of narrative, the Romantics recognized the *aesthetic* importance of story in their poems: when 'a friend' of Wordsworth suggested that in 'The Idiot Boy' the poet should have distinguished the particular type of idiot depicted, for example, Wordsworth countered in a letter that he found it impossible to describe the character of the boy because 'the narration [in] the poem is so rapid and impassioned that I could not find a place [in] which to insert the stanza without checking the progress of it, and [so lea]ving a deadness upon the feeling' (*EY*, pp. 357–8). More common, however, especially in Wordsworth, is the sense that the 'incidents' of narrative are extraneous to the poem. This is clear in a letter in which he discusses *Salisbury Plain*:

I am resolved to discard Robert Walford and invent a new story for the woman. The poem is finished all but her tale. Now by way of a pretty moving accident and to bind together in palpable knots the story of the piece I have resolved to make her the widow or sister or daughter of the man whom the poor Tar murdered. So much for the vulgar. Further the Poets invention goeth not. This is by way of giving a physical totality to the piece, which I regard as finish'd minus 24 stanzas, the utmost tether allowed to the poor Lady. (*EY*, pp. 256–7)

Wordsworth suggests that the accidents of 'story' have little essential impact on the poem. Thus a 'narrative' poem, like a 'lyrical ballad', is something of an oxymoron, a self-divided construct in which narrative is added or superimposed on the poetry.

One of the most important ways in which Wordsworth, in particular, attempted to overcome this fracturing of poetry by narrative was through the 'internalization' of narrative: by implicitly distinguishing between internalized and 'external' narrative, Wordsworth is able to distance his own writing from the degraded form of novels and romances. Thus, writing to Coleridge, Wordsworth criticized Charles Lamb for undervaluing 'The White Doe of Rylstone' and for refusing to understand that actions do not have to be depicted 'particularly when the present tendencies of society, good and bad, are observed', when a narrative poet may...

see if there are no victories in the world of spirit, no changes, no commotions, no revolutions there, no fluxes and refluxes of the thoughts which may be made interesting by modest combination with the stiller actions of the bodily frame, or with the gentler movements and milder appearances of society and social intercourse, or the still more mild and gentle solicitations of irrational and inanimate nature. (*MY*, vol. I, pp. 222–3)

Hazlitt was among the first to point out that this internalization is crucial to Wordsworth's narrative strategies: the fact is that his poetry 'is not external, but internal; it does not depend upon tradition, or story, or old song; he furnishes it from his own mind, and is his own subject' (*Works*, vol. v, p. 156).[11] But Hazlitt problematically equates 'internalized' narrative with 'non-narrative'. As Wordsworth's most famous formulation of such internalization suggests, this is not necessarily the case: in the *Lyrical Ballads*, Wordsworth comments that 'the feeling therein developed gives importance to the action and situation and not the action and situation to the feeling' (*LB*, p. 248). This radical reorganization is far from a denial of narrative: rather, it involves a restructuring of the priorities of the mode. Wordsworth's long explanation of the nature of 'The White Doe of Rylstone', part of which has already been quoted, suggests very clearly the problem that he was facing in attempting to negotiate the seemingly incompatible demands of 'feeling' and 'action'. He told Coleridge that the poem 'could not be popular because some of the principal objects and agents, such as the Banner and the Doe, produced their influences and effects not by powers naturally inherent in them, but such as they were endued with by the Imagination of the human minds on whom they operated' and that 'all the action proceeding from the will of the chief agents, was fine-spun and inobtrusive, consonant in this to the principle from which it flowed, and in harmony with the shadowy influence of the Doe, by whom the poem is introduced, and in whom it ends' (*MY*, vol. I, p. 222). In his reply, Coleridge seems to be saying precisely the opposite when he comments that 'if there were any serious defect, it consisted in a disproportion of the Accidents to the spiritual Incidents', and is concerned that Wordsworth 'bring to a finer Balance the *Business* with the *Action* of the Tale' (*CL*, vol. III, pp. 107, 108). Coleridge is concerned, in part at least, with the technical problems of motivation and coherence, the question of 'Francis's motives' and the imbalance in the (quantitative) treatment of Emily – central questions in any consideration of narrative. Clearly, what both Wordsworth and Coleridge are attempting to do is to negotiate a satisfactory compromise in relation to narrative, to find an altered focus of narrative organization: as Karl Kroeber comments, 'The White Doe' marks a 'significant dividing point in the history of Romantic narrative art', between the 'adventurous narratives' of Scott and Byron, and the refusal by, in particular, Wordsworth, Shelley and Keats to exploit narrative in the same way.[12]

In a number of ways, then, the Romantics may be understood as attempting to resist the degrading and 'artificial' nature of narrative while exploiting its seductive powers. The dream-poem is exemplary in this respect. By structuring a poem around a dream, the writer is able to escape the alluring but confining requirements of the temporalities and causalities of plot. This is suggested in Shelley's review of Hogg's *Memoirs of Prince Alexy Haimatoff*: 'The author is proudly negligent of connecting the incidents of his tale. It appears more like the recorded day dream of a poet, not unvisited by the sublimest and most lovely visions, than the tissue of a romance skilfully interwoven for the purpose of maintaining the interest of the reader, and conducting his sympathies by dramatic gradations to the denouement'.[13] The context of this statement is an attack on the reading public, with whom 'Mediocrity alone seems unvaryingly to escape rebuke and obloquy':[14] while demonstrating an acute insight into the techniques of 'narrative seduction', Shelley also makes it clear that such seductive narratorial tactics are in fact degraded. At the same time he suggests that one of the attractions of dream-poems is the fact that a poet can write a long poem without either having to impose an 'artificial' (because externally motivated) plot structure on the poem or having to use one of the standard genres (such as the journey or the *Bildungsroman*) which would avoid the problem of 'invented' plot.

The dream plot, however, in its very formlessness, its lack of sequential coherence is, like the eighteenth-century Great Ode, in danger of approaching the narrative looseness of 'frantic novels' – and may therefore be open to suspicion precisely because of its lack of narrative coherence. If, on the one hand, the Romantics were critical of narrative because of its arbitrary imposition of external order – what Jay Clayton has called 'the otherness of narrative' – on the other hand, they were highly critical of the *lack* of narrative logic in that most successful representative of late-eighteenth-century narrative form, the Gothic novel. As Clayton points out, the Gothic novel included 'Experiments with fragmented narratives, multiply embedded stories, surprising digressions, improbable points of view, the grotesque inversions of decorum'.[15] Although each of the major Romantic poets attempted Gothic narrative at some point in his career, one reason for each poet's comparative lack of success in the genre may have been the overt transgressions of narrative 'probability' which it allowed: despite the Romantics' often overt antagonism towards the constraints and artificialities of narrative form, it is precisely such impositions that their poetry requires.

ROMANTIC AUDIENCES

> Every body who publishes … claims our hearing in the face of the whole world; and if after all this importance he really tells us nothing, it is very natural that he should first be ridiculed and then neglected.[16]

Despite the Romantics' ambivalence towards the 'otherness' of narrative, their reservations concerning the impositions of narrative in no way inhibited their explorations in and exploitations of the mode. The increase in popularity of narrative verse in the first two decades of the nineteenth century may be understood to be part of a larger 'poetry boom',[17] but it is clear that the Romantic poets not only wrote more poetic stories more overtly organized around narrative more powerfully than any other major poets for at least a century – since, perhaps, Dryden's *Fables* – but that they were also consciously and explicitly concerned, in these poems, with the nature of story-telling and of both the poet's and the readers' relationship with the poetic story.[18] If one anxiety concerning the 'otherness' of narrative involves a recognition of the artificiality or externality of narrative events, equally problematic for the Romantic poets is a certain 'otherness' imposed by the necessary narrative engagement with the addressee.[19] Many of the strategies, the contortions or displacements of conventional narrative form in canonical Romantic poems may be understood in terms of attempts to negotiate the necessary, the inescapable function of audience in narrative. If, as I have suggested, there are certain historical determinants of a hiatus between poet and audience in the early nineteenth century, this hiatus may be read in the functional instability of addressee in canonical Romantic poems. In 1802 Wordsworth added a major section to his Preface to the *Lyrical Ballads* which asked a number of famous questions: 'I ask what is meant by the word Poet? What is a Poet? To whom does he address himself? And what is to be expected from him?'. The answer to these questions is even more famous: 'He is a man speaking to men' (*LB*, p. 255). Although Wordsworth discusses in great detail both the identity of the poet and of poetic language, little more is said in answer to the question 'To whom does he address himself?'. The addressee remains undecidable. Thus many of the *Lyrical Ballads*, from 'The Rime of the Ancient Mariner' to 'Simon Lee', from 'Anecdote for Fathers' to 'Tintern Abbey', may be read as narrations of address, narrations which attempt to negotiate a different relationship between text, poet and reader or addressee. What is being put into question in many of these poems is, finally, the very possibility of narrative address.

With echoes of Harold Bloom's 'anxiety of influence' (and W. Jackson Bate's version of this as 'the burden of the past') we might term the concern in Romantic poetry delineated above, an 'anxiety of audience':[20] by contrast with 'influence', which is directed backwards in time towards a written past, towards a poet's precursors, the anxiety of audience is directed towards an unwritten future, towards the history of a poem's reception. What emerges most clearly from any analysis of the Romantics' concern with narrative is both that there is an anxiety over narrative form and that this anxiety – an enabling as well as a disabling anxiety – tends to be resolved in terms of a conceptual redefinition of narrative in terms of *telling* a story rather than, in any simple sense, a 'succession of events'. Indeed, this anxiety may be said to act as the narrative impulsion for a great many Romantic poems: the poems take as their 'point' their anxiety over their audience.[21] Typically, a narrative poem is organized around an attempt to give a certain kind of aesthetic pleasure, but this desire to generate desire is fissured by the very nature of the reading public, which does not or will not read the poems of Wordsworth, Coleridge, Shelley and Keats, and which these poets tend increasingly to think of as degraded and therefore unworthy anyway.

But Romantic narrative is also split by the even more fundamental problem of epistemological authority. Referring to the etymological connection between 'narrative' and 'knowledge', Gerald Prince has asserted that 'the hallmark of narrative is assurance': for narrative to be convincing, the narrator must profess assurance in his own knowledge of his tale.[22] The Romantics' doubt over certain questions – the significance of the events related, their own qualifications for telling the story, the ethical validity of some of their tales, the superior skills of previous poets, their own ability to teach, affect and influence their disparate audiences, the very possibility of the aesthetic coherence of narrative itself – radically undermines their role as story-tellers.[23] But it is in their difficulty over how to tell stories – as if a whole generation of English poets had been affected by the combined forces of an increasing artistic alienation and a late-eighteenth-century ideology of the vatic poet concerned with higher things than story-telling – that the poets begin to produce a renewed mode of story-telling, inherited, in the first place, from non-'literary' modes and genres such as the nursery rhyme, song, ballad, folk-tale, etc. And it is precisely in their ignorance of both what and how to tell that they can create, most profoundly, in a chiastic inversion of the conventional telling of a story, their narrative: the story of telling.

The anxiety of audience leads us to the question of the Romantics' readers: how does the addressee generate, confine, direct, conflict with, and 'inspire' poetry?[24] The Romantics were writing for a readership fissured by social, political and educational differences, and for whom they held differing degrees of affection, respect, distrust and antipathy. It is my contention that their poetry was generated, to a large extent, by such ambivalence. Because of their problems with audience – not only was it, for all but the phenomenally popular poets Byron and Scott, numerically limited and yet culturally diverse, but early nineteenth-century readers could not be trusted to read in the way that the writers wanted – the Romantics tended, especially in their later years, to direct their poetry towards posterity. This means that the audience becomes an abstract, hypothetical entity, a kind of transcendental signifier equivalent to the visionary gleams striven for in many Romantic poems, and equivalent, also, to the ideology, inherited from the eighteenth century, of the transcendent categories of Genius, Inspiration, Originality, Imagination, Fame and Poetry. On the other hand, and, again, precisely because of their problems with a public audience, the Romantics tended to direct their poetry towards a private, personal, even a family audience and defensively in relation to hostile reviewers, uncaring critics, and an ignorant public. This is the background for some of the poetic manoeuvres performed by the Romantic poets. There is a crisis, a hiatus, between at least three different audiences: the 'private' (self, family, friends); the 'public' (potentially friendly, but suspiciously bad readers of novels and verse romance and including the potentially hostile reviewers); and 'posterity' (by whom the true poet will, by definition, be recognized). The problem for the Romantic poet has recently been concisely summarized by Linda Zionkowski with reference to a rather earlier poet, Thomas Gray:

Rather than enhancing communication, the market in texts deprived poets of their authority to interpret experience, for instead of writing to a circle of like-minded friends, they found themselves directing their verse to an unfamiliar public. Gray's uncertainty about addressing his readers and his pessimism about the future of literature signal his disillusion over the loss of an intimate elite community – an idealized union of writers and their audiences that seemed a better alternative to the present literary system.[25]

It was this problem of authority and audience which the Romantics inherited a few decades later and for which the 'Romantic ideology' may be understood to be, in part at least, a response.

If the combined effect of 'the breakdown of the patronage system, the increase in commercial printing, and the growth of a large reading public'[26] resulted in the alienation of writers from their audience in the latter half of the eighteenth century, this does not mean that the reader is excluded from being inscribed within the production of poetry. Indeed, combined with the fact that, very often, the Romantics presented themselves as writing specifically for and towards close friends and family, this alienation from and aesthetico-moral confusion about the 'reading public' simply complicates the problem and increases what Coleridge calls the 'anxiety of authorship' (*BL*, vol. I, p. 233).[27] During the early years of the nineteenth century, the need to 'figure' the reader – to determine as far as possible the addressee – becomes urgent. One aspect of this attempt at redefinition involves the Romantics' dissatisfaction with the 'passive' reader: Coleridge is most explicit on this point in Essay Two of *The Friend* and in his concept of the 'co-operating power' of poetry.[28] Characterizing the Romantic prose writer, John R. Nabholtz speaks about all types of Romantic discourse when he says that the writer 'sought to engage the reader as an active participant, often as the protagonist'.[29]

Indeed, the Romantics were usually very clear about distinguishing both the type of audience and the type of response which their poems required. But it is precisely the attempt to discriminate between addressees which most profoundly problematizes audience. Coleridge, for example, distinguishes between sympathy, pity and admiration in response: 'Sympathy the Poet alone can excite/any Dabbler in stories may excite Pity. – The more I think, the more I am convinced that Admiration is an *essential* element of poetical Delight' (*CN*, 957). Similarly, the rare reader who can respond well to poetry is described and contrasted with other types of readers in Coleridge's well-known delineation of four different types of reader, borrowed, it seems, from Donne's *Biathanatos*: 'Spunges that suck up every thing'; 'Sand Glasses ... whose reading is only a profitless measurement & dozeing away of Time'; 'Straining Bags, who get rid of whatever is good & pure, and retain the Dregs'; and, lastly, the 'Great-Moguls Diamond Sieves ... these are the only good, & I fear the least numerous, who assuredly retain the good, while the superfluous or impure passes away & leaves no trace' (*CN*, 3242). In this sense, it is the ease with which novels may be read, the lack of rigour required, which accounts for some of Coleridge's distrust of them: 'the habit of receiving pleasure without any exertion of thought, by the mere excitement of curiosity and sensibility, may be justly ranked among the worst effects of habitual novel reading'.[30]

One consequence of the predominant sense of either a degraded or a divided reading public was a deferral of reception to the future.[31] T. N. Talfourd, a relatively early admirer and propagandist for Wordsworth, analyses this problem in an essay published in 1815

('An Attempt to Estimate the Poetical Talent of the Present Age'), and suggests, just as Wordsworth himself does in his 'Essay, Supplementary to the Preface' of the same year, that reading can only take place in the future:

The finest poetry is not that which presents every thing in full glare to the mind – but that which by the magic power of its thoughts, awakens within the reader a train of delightful images and half forgotten associations, and rather gives the key to a range of noble sublimities, than fully explores them. In this case, therefore, the success of the poet depends greatly on the susceptibility of the reader to receive lofty impressions, and the richness of his fancy, who is to fill up the outline presented to his mind. The best works are therefore by no means the most likely to be popular, or at least to be most read, until criticism has pointed out to common observance the deep and sequestered springs of inspiration, with which their retired haunts are refreshed, and until time has hallowed what the suffrage of the enlightened has sanctioned.[32]

Talfourd's analysis of reading suggests very clearly the consequence of the kinds of active reader-participation for which Romantic poetry calls: reading must wait for an after time, a time after itself.

If reading is conceived by the Romantics as a problem, at its most extreme this involves a reflexive disintegration of the poetic text itself. Hazlitt, for example, argued that the degraded nature of the reading public had a direct effect on the ability of poets to write poetry. If reading habits are corrupt, these in turn will corrupt the source of their own being, literary texts: 'The public taste hangs like a millstone round the neck of all original genius that does not conform to established and exclusive models. The writer is not only without popular sympathy, but without a rich and varied mass of materials for his mind to work upon and assimilate unconsciously to itself; his attempts at originality are looked upon as affectation, and in the end, degenerate into it from the natural spirit of contradiction, and the constant uneasy sense of disappointment and undeserved ridicule' (*Works*, vol. v, p. 96). And Thomas De Quincey makes the degraded nature of the reading public precisely his argument for the impossibility of great poetry in the early nineteenth century.[33]

Inevitably, perhaps, the increasing hiatus between poet and audience leads to the development of the metaphor of a legal 'contract', a metaphor which begins to provide a crucial articulation of the Romantic conception of the relationship between narrative and audience.[34] Between the convention of the ideal and idealistic

contract which the Romantic poet makes with the muse – Wordsworth's 'I made no vows, but vows / Were then made for me: bond
unknown to me / Was given, that I should be – else sinning greatly
– / A dedicated spirit'[35] – and the pragmatic contract with Mammon which the poet actually makes with his publisher, there is a
contract, both imagined and real, which the Romantic poet makes
with his or her reader, what Coleridge calls the 'previous and well
understood, though tacit, *compact* between the poet and his reader'
(*BL*, vol. II, pp. 65–6). That the contract is intended to be reciprocal
is made clear, rather playfully, by Sir Walter Scott in his Postscript to
Waverley: 'Our journey is now finished, gentle reader; and if your
patience has accompanied me through these sheets, the contract is,
on your part, strictly fulfilled'.[36] Within the context of the radical
absence of the addressee which I have been attempting to establish,
however, the possibility of any such 'contract' becomes inherently
problematic. As David Simpson has commented, it is precisely the
contract between the author and reader that Romantic poetry itself
puts into question: 'Romantic poetry is organised to make us
confront the question of authority, especially as it pertains to the
contract between author and reader'.[37] Indeed, it is the uncertain
status of the contract which may be said to generate such discussions
as, for example, Wordsworth's attempt to explain the precise nature
of the relationship between the poet and the reader in the Preface to
the *Lyrical Ballads*:

It is supposed, that by the act of writing in verse an Author makes a formal
engagement that he will gratify certain known habits of association, that he
not only thus apprizes the Reader that certain classes of ideas and expressions
will be found in his book, but that others will be carefully excluded ... I will
not take upon me to determine the exact import of the promise which by the
act of writing in verse an Author in the present day makes to his Reader; but
I am certain it will appear to many persons that I have not fulfilled the terms
of an engagement thus voluntarily contracted.[38] (*LB*, pp. 243–4)

Wordsworth suggests that writing is a performative which involves
an uncertain promise: the paradox of the pragmatics of writing, for
Wordsworth, is that a promise is both made and unknown. The
hiatus of audience may be understood to undermine the very grounds
of any such contract: the poet promises not simply what he cannot
deliver but, more radically, what he cannot know.

In the absence of any clearly defined relationship between text and
audience, between poet and addressee, Romantic poetry inhabits a

liminal and unstable space in which the 'moral' or 'message' or 'point' of a narrative becomes highly uncertain. Either too obscure or too direct, Romantic narratives were subject to the problem of an irreducible absence of addressee such that there is no possibility of a suitable level of narrative commentary. In a letter to Wordsworth of 1801, for example, Charles Lamb criticizes the poet's tendency in 'The Cumberland Beggar', to make 'the instructions conveyed in it ... too direct and like a lecture: they dont slide into the mind of the reader, while he is imagining no such matter': according to Lamb, 'There is implied an unwritten compact between Author and reader; I will tell you a story, and I suppose you will understand it'.[39] Lamb suggests that Wordsworth breaks this contract by explaining in too much detail, by patronizing and lecturing his reader (the criticism made later by Hazlitt and by Keats in his description of Wordsworth's poetry as having 'a palpable design upon us', *Letters*, vol. I, p. 224). As William Labov has shown, evaluation is an important part of story-telling: related to 'point', the trope tells the listener what to look for, and explains why he should listen to the tale.[40] But, as Lamb comments, and as the Horatian principle that *ars est celare artem* suggests, such overt pointedness as Wordsworth in particular is often accused of, threatens the aesthetic value of poetry. The point was made very clearly by Hugh Murray in 1805: 'the reader might be apt to revolt against [the narrator's] appearing as a dictator in matters of conduct. That instruction is likely to be most effectual which appears to be undesigned, and to flow from the natural impulse of taste and feeling'.[41]

There is a fine balance to be maintained between over-emphasizing the point of a story and so breaking the contract with the reader, and going too far the other way and making the story too mysterious or ambiguous, again breaking the narrative contract. Despite Edmund Burke's valorization of obscurity as a signifier of the sublime, all the major Romantic poets were repeatedly accused of the fault of making their poetry too obscure.[42] Coleridge provided two paradigmatic examples in 'The Ancient Mariner' and 'Christabel': both poems generated a series of distinctly unnerved responses, part of the disturbance in the case of 'Christabel' being due to the incomprehension with which it was read, and the feeling that this was caused simply by a lack of manners, a transgression of co-operative principles on the part of the writer: 'The reader is obliged to guess at the half-developed meaning of the mysterious incidents, and is at last, at the end of the second canto, left in the dark, in the most abrupt and unceremonious manner imaginable' (Reiman, AI, p. 373). An anonymous reviewer of Mary Shelley's *Frankenstein* went so far as to ask '[s]hould not an author, who has a moral end in view, point out rather that application which may be more generally understood? We recommend, however, to our fair readers ... to draw from it that meaning [given in Shelley's preface] which we have cited above' (Reiman, CI, p. 43).

Generally, then, the Romantics might be said to have been caught between the Scylla of lecturing, of pandering to the inept reading skills of a degenerate public, and the Charybdis of obscurity in meaning and consequent obscurity before the public eye. I suggest that this double-bind is of fundamental importance to Romantic poetry and its attempts to negotiate a radical absence of addressee. On the one hand the Romantics increasingly sought redemption in an ideological defence of solipsism, private vocabularies and mythologies, a redescription of audience as posterity, and an idealization of the Artist.[43] On the other hand there is, articulated in Romantic poetics, an intense desire to be read and to be understood, a belief in the revolutionary redemptive powers of literature itself. Romantic figures of reading might be understood as attempts to integrate these conflicting poetic ideologies through the use of more or less trustworthy narrators, embedded narration, *mise en abyme*, narrative parody, and a self-conscious exhibition of narrative anxiety: the anxiety of audience provides important generative energies for Romantic narrative form.

The paradigmatic Romantic trope employed to position the reader, and, in particular (what is for the story-teller, *qua* story-teller, most important) his or her position *vis-à-vis* the poet, is that of *mise en abyme*, or the inclusion of what Gerald Prince has called 'reading interludes'. Indeed, in view of the fact that 'literature' is usually seen as detachable from the context of its production, a context which, in other types of discourse, tends to determine the 'point', it would seem to be essential that a poem includes some kind of code – an implicit contractual definition of the reading situation – in order to attempt to direct the reader's attitude towards the text. This is not to say, of course, that any individual reader will obey these instructions: rather, Prince points out, such codes provide a potential grounding for the (real) reader. As Lucien Dällenbach has commented, 'in resorting to *mise en abyme*, texts manifest their fears about their own readability, either because the need for readability so obsesses them that they forbid the reader to fill in the [hermeneutic] gaps as he wishes, automatically and according to the rhythm of his reading, or because, readability being truly in danger, the reader might risk being unable to fill in the gaps'.[44] And as Ross Chambers explains, in certain texts self-reflexivity is a *situational* self-reflexivity: these texts define themselves as 'literary' and at the same time define, or at least attempt to restrict, the ways in which they are read precisely by means of such embedded representations of reading – the texts are not only self-reflexive in the sense that they comment on themselves, on their own workings, but also in the sense that they self-reflexively comment on, and in so doing to some extent define, the writer-reader interaction, the 'narrative situation'.[45]

In the present study, figures of reading are understood in terms of poetry's future critical reception, such that the criticism of Romantic – specifically Keatsian – poetry may be understood in terms of the paradoxical (re)inscription of posterity into Romantic poetics. To conclude this chapter, I shall briefly attempt to suggest ways in which Wordsworth's 1815 'Essay, Supplementary to the Preface' redefines posterity in terms of the death of the reader – an indefinite deferral which is an exemplary Romantic figure of reading.

ROMANTIC POSTERITY

Wordsworth's theorization of posterity as an audience for his poetry is elaborated most explicitly in the 1815 'Essay, Supplementary to the Preface'. There is a significant development between the 1802 'Preface' to the *Lyrical Ballads* in which the audience is figured as 'men' and the 1815 'Essay', where audience becomes abstract and hypothetical. The bulk of the 'Essay, Supplementary' is concerned with writing a new literary history explicitly on the basis of what would now be termed *Rezeptionsästhetik*. Wordsworth argues that poets popular in their day are unlikely to be valued beyond the time of their own death and that, conversely, those that are undervalued during their lifetime often achieve lasting fame. A number of problems, however, fracture this argument. When Wordsworth has to approach the question of authors who were popular in their own day and are still held in high esteem, his argument tends to falter: discussing Shakespeare, for example, Wordsworth is impelled to make a distinction between dramatic writing and other forms by pointing out that a dramatist 'must adapt himself to the taste of the audience'; he is also forced to admit that he is not 'sufficiently versed in stage antiquities' (*Prose*, p. 394) to judge whether Shakespeare was admired as much as his contemporaries. Similarly, discussing the admiring contemporary reception of James Thomson, Wordsworth claims that 'we must distinguish between wonder and legitimate admiration' (*Prose*, p. 400). These faulterings or fault-lines in the argument indicate the anxiety which impelled Wordsworth's justification of his theorization of the legitimate audience as constituted by posterity.

The 'Essay, Supplementary' articulates a conception of poetry as potentially threatened by readers, by their incorrigible tendency to misread poetry – that is to read it for the wrong reasons, and with the wrong preconceptions – and their inability, ever, to be ready to read. Wordsworth attempts to distinguish between contemporary reading and the reading of posterity. This results in a tension in Wordsworth's argument which inevitably undermines his theory:[46] in showing that only true poets last, he must show that such poets are appreciated in the present day (and not in their own day), but in showing that they are now appreciated, he would have to suggest that there is, in the early nineteenth century, an appropriate audience for poetry – precisely what he is attempting to refute. Wordsworth found two ways round this dilemma: the first is to show that in fact poets are still not properly appreciated or are only appreciated by the few (readers without 'vicious' taste). This argument, however, leads to the unsettling possibility that such an audience as 'original' poetry deserves may never evolve.[47] The second way round the problem is to argue that 'every author, as far as he is great and at the same time *original*, has had the task of *creating* the taste by which he is to be enjoyed' (*Prose*, p. 408) because although '[t]he predecessors of an original Genius of a high order will have smoothed the way for all that he has in common with them ... for what is peculiarly his own, he will be called upon to clear and often to shape his own road' (*Prose*, p. 408). That is, the true poet or genius, despite his place in a tradition (the tradition is almost exclusively male), is always irreducibly different and has to teach readers to read his poetry precisely to the extent that he is original: in fact there is no literary tradition for the poet of genius. Again, the argument suggests a vision of an indefinitely deferred reading because if there is no way for readers to learn from tradition, they may never learn to read properly. Similarly, the proof of the original genius creating the taste by which he is appreciated would be that that taste has been created, an idea which Wordsworth is at pains to deny.

Throughout his brief literary history, Wordsworth has difficulty demonstrating that 'original' poets were both scorned in their day and appreciated later: in almost every case Wordsworth is forced to admit either that the genius in question was appreciated when alive, or that the modern audience is still unable to understand his poetry (or both). Thus, according to Wordsworth, Shakespeare is currently scorned by the French and the Italians and only the Germans 'are approaching towards a knowledge and feeling of what he is' (*Prose*, p. 395). But 'what he is', even in England, is still not understood: Wordsworth quotes the anonymous opinion that Shakespeare constitutes a 'wild irregular genius, in whom great faults are compensated by great beauties' and asks 'How long may it be before this misconception passes away ... ?' (*Prose*, p. 395). Milton presents a similar case: although his poems 'are now much read, and loudly praised', Wordsworth is unable to say whether his poetry is 'at this day justly appreciated' (*Prose*, p. 396). Pope is understood by 'the judicious' to have damaged his poetry by 'undue exertion of those arts' of poetry (*Prose*, p. 398) – a hedging which fails to deal with the question of why, in the early nineteenth century, Pope was still admired and read.[48] Thomson, like Shakespeare and, perhaps, Milton, is only justly admired by a small number of readers: *The Castle of Indolence*, which represents most clearly the 'true characteristics of Thomson's genius as an imaginative poet ... is at this day the delight only of a few!' (*Prose*, pp. 401–2). The case of Collins is apparently clear-cut: he was neglected when alive but is now 'universally known' (*Prose*, p. 402). Wordsworth is silent, however, on the nature of this knowledge and on the question of whether Collins is 'appreciated'. The case of Percy's *Reliques* is also difficult to square with Wordsworth's account because of its early popularity and its contemporary influence, but Wordsworth is able to argue that Dr Johnson's criticism caused it to sink into 'temporary neglect'. In the case of Macpherson, Wordsworth explains both that he is unworthy of his popularity and uninfluential (*Prose*, pp. 404–6). Finally, Wordsworth castigates Johnson's *Lives of the Poets* with the curious notion that because Johnson omits Chaucer, Spenser, Sidney, and Shakespeare, this proves Wordsworth's argument that poets are only recognized in posterity: in fact, however, Johnson's *Lives* is restricted to seventeenth- and eighteenth-century writers, and the fact that Chaucer and the others are *not* recognized in the posterity constructed by Johnson's *Lives* would seem to contradict Wordsworth's argument that great poets will be recognized by posterity. Wordsworth ends with the primary justification for this new literary history, the case of his own poems: his description has been generated by the 'unremitting hostility' (*Prose*, p. 407) which has met his own poems. But instead of now being able to suggest that having redrawn the map of literary history he has opened the way for his own poems to be appreciated by his contemporaries (that he has succeeded in creating the taste by which he may be appreciated), Wordsworth defers this appreciation to the future in the knowledge that 'the products of my industry will endure' (*Prose*, p. 408).

It is clear from the tensions involved in Wordsworth's argument, then, that the structure of posterity is problematic:[49] Wordsworth has comprehensively failed to demonstrate the mechanism of conventional posterity – that poets spurned in their own time eventually gain their proper (that is both 'universal' and discriminating) audience in posterity. This failure to establish his argument leads to Wordsworth's radical and necessary redescription of posterity itself. If the poets of the past cannot be shown to have found or created their audience, this severely undermines Wordsworth's argument, for he is unable to show that the true genius will ever be appreciated. The contemporary, living audience is unable to appreciate the poet, which means that appreciation is deferred to the future, to a time when the contemporary audience will be dead. The future audience will both have learnt to appreciate the now dead author and be free from the vicious indulgences of the living audience – 'the envy and malevolence, and all bad passions which always stand in the way of a work of any merit from a living Poet', as he expresses it in an 1807 letter to Lady Beaumont (*Prose*, p. 316). That this has not actually occurred suggests that it may never occur, that the degradations of contemporary audiences are inherent to readers *per se*. Wordsworth's notion of posterity, then, involves the sense not that any empirical future audience will be 'fit', but that there is a lack or inadequacy in any empirical audience to appreciate poetry, that poetry can only be truly appreciated once its living audience has died: posterity, future generations, only exist as theoretical constructs based on the death of any particular living audience.

In the 1815 Preface, Wordsworth comments that 'Poems ... cannot read themselves' (*Prose*, p. 376). Towards the end of the 'Essay, Supplementary' this perception recurs as Wordsworth comments that poetry can only survive through its readers: ' ... of *good* poetry, the *individual*, as well as the species, survives. And how does it *survive* but through the People? What preserves it but their intellect and their wisdom?' (*Prose*, p. 412). That there is no other way for poetry to survive is the subtext which provides the last turn in the logic of Wordsworth's argument for the infinite deferral of reception, articulated in the distinction between the public and the people: it is for the latter that the poet writes, but Wordsworth's definition of the people makes it clear that they are far from an empirical, living audience:

... but to the People, philosophically characterised, and to the embodied spirit of their knowledge, so far as it exists and moves, at the present, faithfully supported by its two wings, the past and the future, [the poet's] devout respect, his reverence, is due. (*Prose*, p. 413)

Wordsworth's qualifications suggest the possibility that the spirit does not, perhaps, exist 'at the present', that it only exists in the past and the future, that in as much as it is embodied it is embodied in a corpse, and that 'devout respect' and 'reverence' are due to the deceased and not to the living.[50] The final irony occurs in the last sentence of the essay, in which Wordsworth recognizes that the reception of his poetry will always be, like *The Recluse* to which he refers, 'a thing that had never been' (*Prose*, p. 413).

If we are able to discern a pragmatic poetics of audience in Romantic writing, then, it is important to see that such a pragmatics is fractured, irreducibly divided, by the Romantic construction of audience in posterity, as always deferred to the future, the posthumous life of writing. The audience for Romantic poetry is figured, ultimately, in the death of the reader.

CHAPTER 2

Keats's letters

It is the burden of this book to suggest that the problematic nature of the addressee in Romantic poetics constitutes a crucial determining force for the poetry of John Keats. Before discussing ways in which the poetry itself engages with audience, in the present chapter I shall examine ways in which reading, audience, publication and the addressee are figured in Keats's letters. Not only is the problem of audience repeatedly elaborated in the letters but the letters also provide an important contrast, in terms of addressees, with the poems. While the poems are written within a context of radical uncertainty with respect to the addressee, letters generally, and Keats's letters in particular, are directed towards individual, particularized recipients. To say as much, however, is not to ignore ways in which the addressee of a letter is itself uncertain. The most radical form of such doubt is Jacques Derrida's notion that 'it belongs to the structure of the letter to be capable, always, of not arriving'.[1] In this respect, in spite of their differences, both letters and poems may be understood to be determined by the problematics of audience.

In Keats's letters we can observe the poet figuring his addressees – both meeting the projected responses of his readers and attempting to determine those responses. More fundamentally, he attempts, at the same time, to determine the addressees themselves. Despite his frequent 'rhodomontades'[2] on poetry, metaphysics, politics, women, health, Leigh Hunt, and so on, Keats's letters discriminate very carefully between addressees. Tonal discriminations may be discerned between, for example, letters to his sister Fanny (avuncular), to the Reynolds sisters (flirtatious teasing), to J. H. Reynolds (expansive and playful friendship), to his publishers (the self-justification of a misunderstood author), and so on. But in adapting themselves to their addressees, the letters also adapt, or construct, those addressees.[3] If Keats adopts avuncular discursive strategies in

36

writing to his sister, then she is implicitly constructed as to some extent ignorant and naïve; if he flirts with and teases the Reynolds sisters, then their role with respect to Keats is implicitly sexual.

The division in Keats's dual construction of and response to the addressees in his letters becomes clear on a number of occasions on which he disrupts the complacency of writing 'to' someone with the notion of writing 'at' someone. In April 1819, for example, he tries to write a preface for the 1820 volume of poetry 'at' the public – 'I have of late been indulging my spleen by composing a preface *at* them' (*Letters*, vol. II, p. 144). The antipathy that he feels towards the public is evident in the choice and emphasis of 'at', rather than 'for' or 'to': language is a weapon.[4] But he uses the same phrase, to write 'at', in a different sense when writing 'to' his brother George but simultaneously 'at' his sister-in-law Georgiana, in a letter which explicitly engages with the possibility of a self-divided audience and a necessary double writing:

I must take an opportunity here to observe that though I am writing *to* you I am all the while writing *at* your Wife – This explanation will account for my speaking sometimes *hoity-toityishly*. Whereas if you were alone I should sport a little more sober sadness. I am like a squinti[n]g gentleman who saying soft things to one Lady ogles another – or what is as bad in arguing with a person on his left hand appeals with his eyes to one on the right. His Vision is elastic he bends it to a certain object but having a patent sp[r]ing it flies off. Writing has this disadvan[ta]ge of speaking. one cannot write a wink, or a nod, or a grin, or a purse of the Lips, or a *smile* – O law! One can-[not] put ones finger to one's nose, or yerk ye in the ribs, or lay hold of your button in writing – but in all the most lively and titterly parts of my Letter you must not fail to imagine me as the epic poets say – now here, now there, now with one foot pointed at the ceiling, now with another... (*Letters*, vol. II, pp. 204–5[5])

This is double writing which figures its audience as split into two: such a division in the audience is literally divisive for the writer, who must direct his linguistic gaze in two directions at once, and the tensions of such writing are conveyed in the force of the patent spring. At this point, Keats's discourse itself flies off on to the question of the difference between reading and writing and, while arguing parodically for the priority of speech, his description itself demonstrates the advantages of writing. The diacritics of body language are absent in the written word: instead writing has uninterrupted space to digress or dilate, to play with an idea, to construct a series of tropes around a single notion, both to figure the writer's role and at the same time to configure reading. And with this split in addressee and the split in writing which it produces, Keats also (by negation) suggests another important doubling or division in Romantic writing: that between speech and writing.

Writing 'to' or 'at' is extended by the idea of writing 'for'. Again, writing to George and Georgiana, Keats addresses his new sister-in-law:

Ha! my dear Sister George, I wish I knew what humour you were in that I might accomodate myself to any one of your Amiabilities – Shall it be a Sonnet or a Pun or an Acrostic, a Riddle or a Ballad ... [?] (*Letters*, vol. I, p. 303)

A few days later he records almost exactly the same sentiment in a letter to Reynolds: 'I wish I knew always the humour my friends would be in at opening a letter of mine, to suit it to them nearly as possible' (*Letters*, vol. I, p. 324). The comments suggest the impossibility of *knowing* the humour of one's epistolary (let alone poetic) addressee: instead, one must figure the reader, construct a role for audience. Writing 'for', in this sense, is impossible: one can only write 'to' in the hope that the letter will arrive at its destination but in the knowledge that this destination, the addressee, must be constructed by the text itself; or one can write 'at', an aggressive form of defence which suggests the impossibility of arrival ('at' or 'towards' an addressee precludes the arrival suggested by 'to').

The undecidability of epistolary destination is compounded by the irrepressible paronomasia of Keats's letters. This undecidable multiplicity of words and meanings is exploited in a postscript to a punning letter to Marian and Sarah Jeffrey: Keats writes a postscript – both a postscript and a consideration of postscripts, both a script after a script and a commentary on inscription – on the abbreviation for 'postscript':

P. S. has many significations here it signifies Post Script – on the corner of a Handkerchef Polly Saunders – Upon a Garter Pretty Secret – Upon a Band Box Pink Sattin – At the Theatre Princes Side – on a Pulpit Parson's Snuffle and at a Country Ale House Pail Sider. (*Letters*, vol. I, p. 291)

The linguistic *trompe l'oeil* here might be compared to effects exploited in Sterne's *Tristram Shandy*: 'P. S.' both is and is not part of the postscript, it both announces the postscript and constitutes its grammatical subject. The postscript also plays with the conventional pragmatic force of a postscript, which usually provides supplementary information, but here does not supplement the letter in the sense that it constitutes a self-contained meditation on itself. Moreover, by dividing the word into its constitutive parts and capitalizing those parts – 'Post Script' – Keats also manages to pun on 'post' as 'after' and 'post' as 'mail', and in this sense the postscript acknowledges the irreducible temporal delay of (epistolary) writing, writing which 'comes' after itself. And, finally, the postscript recognizes its paradoxical position as both part of the letter and after it – a postscript. What comes *after* the definition of P. S. as 'Post Script', however, is also interesting. The P. S. parodies the sisters' polite modesty and the constrictive semiotics of middle-class codes of behaviour by disrupting the stability of linguistic reference. The postscript suggests ways in which polysemic indeterminacy is, coerced by context, determinable to the extent of becoming banal. But it also points to the way that if language exists within a 'context', this only increases the instability of meaning: the semantic explosion of the signifier is itself predetermined by the epistolary context of flirtation, but this erotic context only adds to the undecidable significance of such a postscript. Thus Keats seems to suggest that writing is inherently a form of postscript, a writing that comes after, determining its context in its reading, a reading which is always already 'figured'. Although Keats is often to be seen distorting the conventions of epistolary correspondence in his letters, nowhere do we have a better sense of such conventions being exploited and disturbed.[6]

The letters, then, present Keats as attempting to figure or to figure out his private epistolary addressees: the explicitly interactive or pragmatic nature of epistolary discourse determines, to some extent, the form of that discourse. The letters allow us to consider Keats's writing within a notion of language as communicative or pragmatic while at the same time acknowledging the problematic disruptions involved in such dialogics. It is important to recognize the difference between the pragmatics of Keats's epistolary writing – writing which is determined by and determines the addressee named at the start of each letter – and poetry which does not (usually) name its addressee, which is written *for* publication (that is, at least, *for* more than one person – named or unnamed) and which, by definition, cannot 'know' its reader. But even in Keats's letters we can discern a problematics of address to which the poetry is more radically subject.

It is difficult to disentangle the question of the relationship between Keats and audience from the mythology of the poet's death. Most notoriously, this death is related to the idea, promulgated not least by Shelley's *Adonais*, that reviews of Keats's poetry actually *caused* his death. The story has the virtue of a certain dramatic pathos and its apparent implausibility – again most neatly summed up in a poem, Byron's idea of the poet 'snuffed out by an article' in *Don Juan* – is reduced by the suggestion that Keats was already suffering from tuberculosis and the reviews simply weakened his will to live. However unlikely the story might be, the significance of this particular figuration of an old myth should not be underestimated in our discussion of the Romantic ideology of poetry and publication. Keats's letters, however, suggest a rather less melodramatic, if equally agonistic and fascinating narrative of poet and audience which I would like to explore.

As I have argued in Chapter 1, above, the reasons for an 'anxiety of audience' are not hard to find in the early nineteenth century, when the poet was caught between the contradictory desire for a personal artistic integrity which is inevitably threatened by the desire for fame, and for appreciation and applause from a wider public – a public whose heterogeneity increased in proportion to its size and in proportion to the increased availability of affordable books and to the spread of literacy.[7] The particularly difficult and paradoxical nature of these contradictory pressures was, at least in part, a product of the recent and sudden increase in the book market, which, while bringing new possibilities for 'success', tended to restrict the terms of such 'success' to the question of the number of books sold.[8] I suggest that the nature of the poetry book market was a particularly acute problem, as well as a particularly powerful energizing force for the poetry of Keats, poetry which at once seeks to express the personal, the private, the 'inward feel', while at the same time attempting to appeal, through this very privacy of experience, to a mass audience.[9] If Keats's letters can be read in terms of the problematics of address, they can also be read, thematically, for evidence of Keats's anxieties with regard to publication. There is evidence in the letters of a dissatisfaction with the kind of reception which Keats received and expected to receive, as well as an increasing impatience with the audience which read (or failed to read) his poems: as with

Wordsworth before him, Keats comes increasingly to appeal to 'posterity' as audience for his poetry. And it is the tensions in Keats's notion of audience and of posterity as expressed in his letters, a nexus of anxieties in his construction of the public, posterity, and fame, which may be understood to produce the richly textured poetry of 1818 and 1819. By briefly surveying the developing conception of audience in Keats's letters, then, we shall engage with a crucial generative force for his most intense poetry.

Keats's first major outburst against 'the public' comes in relation to the writing of the Preface to *Endymion* in April 1818. In a number of texts written in the throes of prefatory writing, Keats expounds the implicit distinction between his readers and the public.[10] A brief summary of the strategies for addressing his audience in the Preface and its drafts will suggest the extent of the difficulties involved from very early on. In the spring of 1818 Keats wrote the first draft of a preface to *Endymion*. The draft preface is revealing of Keats's anxiety of audience. In the third paragraph, Keats recalls the reception of his 1817 *Poems*:

... it was read by some dozen of my friends, who lik'd it; and some dozen whom I was unacquainted with, who did not. Now when a dozen human beings, are at words with another dozen, it becomes a matter of anxiety to side with one's friends; – more especially when excited thereto by a great love of Poetry.

I fought under disadvantages. Before I began I had no inward feel of being able to finish ...[11]

The implicit slippage from a discussion of the reception of the 1817 volume to the composition of *Endymion* suggests that the 'matter of anxiety' is a generating force for the writing of poetry: siding with one's friends here means writing more poetry. Writing poetry becomes fundamentally connected to an anxiety of audience. But this anxiety is itself produced by a splitting or doubling of the poet's audience into, on the one hand, the poet's friends and friendly reception, and on the other hand the anonymous larger audience.

The draft preface goes on, however, to make a somewhat disturbing claim that language itself, the 'Phraseology' of writing, is not necessarily the last word in poetry:

It has been too much the fashion of late to consider men biggotted and addicted to every word that may chance to escape their lips: now I here declare that I have not any particular affection for any particular phrase, word or letter in the whole affair. I have written to please myself and in hopes to please others, and for a love of fame; if I neither please myself, nor others nor get fame, of what consequence is Phraseology?[12]

What emerges is a quite extraordinary and apparently self-defeating poetic manifesto: if the poet has no lasting 'affection' for his 'phraseology' it would seem that poetry is written for the pleasure of the moment, and for the momentary pleasure of its readers. Poetry, according to this analysis, is irreducibly transitory. As the preface progresses, however, its tone and its purport become increasingly unstable, increasingly caught in the circular logics and inextricable rhetorics of self-effacement and modesty: these tropes conflict with the purpose of any preface, which is to advertise and explain the poem to the public. The draft preface attempts to inhabit an impossible space of publication without a public. Similarly, the preface – that which would speak 'for' or before, a pre-speech – itself constitutes a denial of that for which it speaks. This pathological self-division is suggested most clearly, perhaps, by the inclusion of a quotation from John Marston's prefatory 'To My Equal Reader' which introduces his play *The Fawn* ('let it be the Curtesy of my peruser rather to pity my self hindering labours than to malice me'). Marston's early seventeenth-century play concerns a sycophant who exposes the folly of others both by imitating them and by flattering them into even greater folly. To the fawning preface Marston added a 'Prologus' which teases the audience with coy abandon:

> I know there's not one ass in all this presence,
> Not one calumnious rascal, or base villain
> Of emptiest merit, that would tax and slander
> If innocency herself should write, not one we know't.
> O you are all the very breath of Phoebus.
> In your pleas'd gracings all the true life blood
> Of our poor author lives; you are his very graces.
> Now if that any wonder why he's drawn
> To such base soothings, know his play's – *The Fawn*.[13]

Marston cynically exposes the sycophancy which directs the writing of a preface while expressing the suppressed anger of the dramatist caught in this web of deceit: by grafting a line from Marston's preface on to his own, Keats signals a prefatory acknowledgement of authorial deceit and desire.[14]

The draft preface was read by Keats's friend John Hamilton Reynolds. Reynolds apparently had some criticisms and reservations about the proposed preface, for in a subsequent letter to Reynolds, dated 9 April 1818, Keats feels obliged to defend the draft. In this letter Keats distinguishes between 'writing for myself for the mere sake of the Moment's enjoyment', and writing 'to the Public' (*Letters*, vol. i, p. 266), and categorically states that 'I never wrote one single Line of Poetry with the least Shadow of public thought' (*Letters*, vol. i, p. 267). The letter goes on to express a particularly hostile view of 'the Public' in a paranoid vision of readers and, in particular, reviewers, as porcupines:

My glory would be to daunt and dazzle the thousand jabberers about Pictures and Books – I see swarms of Porcupines with their Quills erect like 'lime-twigs set to catch my Winged Book' and I would fright 'em away with a torch ... if there is any fault in the preface it is not affectation: but an undersong of disrespect to the Public. (*Letters*, vol. i, p. 267)

Given the context of the kind of attack, on 'Cockney' poetry generally and on Keats in particular, which the poet was to be subject to in the future from, for example, John Gibson Lockhart, such pride, anger, and obstinacy might appear to be a reasonable response. In fact, however, there is a strange disjunction between the violence of this language on the one hand, and the actual reception that Keats's 1817 volume of poetry had received: in as much as they took any notice, critics were as much favourable towards this volume as critical. It would seem, then, that the richly imaginative anger of the letter may be attributed both to a growing realization of how 'smokeable' *Endymion* might be, how open it might be to criticism and ridicule, and at the same time to a growing understanding of the rift between the *possible* reception of such poetry in the social conditions of 1818 and the reception which Keats and his friends considered due to him. The passage might suggest the way in which Keats was beginning to develop a model of poetic reception as, by definition, inadequate or corrupt.

Despite the defensiveness of this letter to Reynolds on the defensive draft Preface, the very next day Keats wrote a new Preface which was eventually published with *Endymion*. The second Preface presents an extraordinarily self-critical introduction to the poem which virtually amounts to a request to his audience not to read it. Keats 'regrets' making the poem public; he accuses himself of 'great inexperience, immaturity, and every error denoting a feverish attempt, rather than a deed accomplished' and suggests that 'The two first books, and indeed the two last' – which leaves nothing except perhaps the preface itself – 'are not of such completion as to warrant their passing the press'. Keats presents no defence of the poem, only the hope that he may be 'plotting, and fitting myself for verses fit to live' while *Endymion* is 'dying away'. It is not *this* poem that we should read, he suggests, but poems that he will write in the future. If this Preface (or pre-face) is speaking for or before the poem, it is speech which seems to want to silence speech, a preface which attempts to efface the poem. The drama of the Preface to *Endymion*, its draft, and the letter defending the draft, suggest the extraordinarily powerful conflicts within Keats's conception of audience.

Almost a year later, on 18 February 1819, Keats again considers the question of publication. In a letter to his brother and sister-in-law, he declares that he will publish again – despite his contempt for public opinion – for the sake, he says, of his brother and sister. His view of the public has altered somewhat after negative reviews of *Endymion* and a lack of sales:

I have no doubt of success in a course of years if I persevere – but it must be patience – for the Reviews have enervated and made indolent mens minds – few think for themselves – These Reviews too are getting more and more powerful and especially the Quarterly – They are like a superstition which the more it prostrates the Crowd and the longer it continues the more powerful it becomes just in proportion to their increasing weakness – I was in hopes that when people saw, as they must do now, all the trickery and iniquity of these Plagues they would scout them, but no they are like the spectators at the Westminster cock-pit – they like the battle and do not care who wins or who looses ... (*Letters*, vol. II, p. 65)

These opinions are, to an extent, conventional: the reviews were often criticized for the fact that they made reading and thinking for oneself unnecessary. Indeed, the letter may be compared with Wordsworth's exasperated 1815 'Essay, Supplementary to the Preface', in which the older poet engages in a damning analysis of different methods of reading employed by different categories of reader: Keats's letter echoes Wordsworth's essay in both its belief in the degradations of the present age, and in the possibility of a future recognition.[15] Once again, however, Keats, like Wordsworth, is able to defer his hopes for reception to the future, as 'a course of years' suggests.

However, it is clear that Keats is beginning to think of his audience in more analytical terms, attempting to define exactly what they want and in what way he can provide this. In August he writes about 'Isabella', which he finds too 'smokeable', and once again the notion of posterity disturbs the possibility of publication:

There is too much inexperience of li[f]e, and simplicity of knowledge in it – which might do very well after one's death – but not while one is alive. There are very few would look to the reality. I intend to use more finesse with the Public. It is possible to write fine things which cannot be laugh'd at in any way. Isabella is what I should call were I a reviewer 'A weak-sided Poem' with an amusing sober-sadness about it ... it is enough for me. But this will not do to be public. (*Letters*, vol. II, p. 174)

Publication is problematic because of the topical – social and political – derision to which the living writer is subject. By contrast, there is an alteration in the public response to poets after their death (he may be thinking of poets like Chatterton and Kirke White, or, again, of Wordsworth's 1815 'Essay, Supplementary to the Preface'). This perception dovetails with Keats's assertion that he will be 'among the English Poets' *after* his death (*Letters*, vol. I, p. 394). It is also significant that Keats's delineation of the projected response to such a poem is very precise – its 'inexperience of life and simplicity of knowlege' leading to a refusal by readers to 'look to the reality', his intention to 'use more finesse with the Public' in order that his poems will not be 'laugh'd at in any way', and his imagining what a reviewer would say about the poem.

It is important to recognize the intricate dynamics of the relationship between Keats and his (potential or projected) audience. The effect is not simply negative. Indeed, bad reviews did not necessarily mean a negative response, as Keats and his friends understood: commenting on attacks made upon *Endymion* in *Black-wood's* and the *Quarterly*, Keats says:

Even as a Matter of present interest the attempt to crush me in the ⟨Chro⟩ Quarterly has only brought me more into notice and it is a common expression among book men 'I wonder the Quarterly should cut its own throat'. (*Letters*, vol. I, p. 394)

As Richard Woodhouse commented to Keats a few days later, 'God help the Critic [in the *Quarterly*], whoever he be!' (*KC*, vol. I, p. 46). But Woodhouse also made the important point that such a review would only be effective in convincing a certain type of reader about the quality of the poem: it may have the effect of 'scaring from the perusal of the Work some of the "Dandy" readers' who only want to know what is fashionable and prefer to be saved the trouble of deciding what is worthy themselves (*KC*, vol. 1, p. 47). Indeed, in a powerful piece of vituperative rhetoric, Woodhouse claims that the review 'carries in it the sufficing cause of its own destruction' (*KC*, vol. 1, p. 47) because of the way that the '⟨bungling⟩ cobbling, carping, ⟨shallow⟩ decasyllabic, finger-scanning-criticaster' (*KC*, vol. 1, p. 48) employs indiscriminate condemnation, and Woodhouse declares that people will be persuaded to read by the critic's lack of sensitivity.

In fact, Woodhouse appears to have been correct on the subject of the increased sales likely to result from the controversy over the poem, however slight an increase: writing to John Taylor a few days later, J. A. Hessey records:

I have much pleasure in saying that Endymion begins to move at last – 6 Copies have just been ordered by Simpkin & Marshall & one or two have been sold singly in the Shop – there is nothing like making a Stir for it – the papers have said so much about it many persons will doubtless be curious to see what it does contain – & here & there a man of taste may be found to admire its beauties… (*KC*, vol. 1, pp. 52–3)

As Byron's example shows and as Elizabeth Eisenstein has noted, a reputation could be gained by an author 'not by respectability but by a *succès de scandale*; *épater le bourgeois* was also a profitable venture'.[16] Indeed, Keats himself could believe that artistic success was instrinsically related to critical disapproval: 'One of the great reasons that the english have produced the finest writers in the world; is, that the English world has ill-treated them during their lives and foster'd them after their deaths. They have in general been trampled aside into the bye paths of life and seen the festerings of Society' (*Letters*, vol. 11, p. 115). It is, for Keats, the antagonistic relationship between poet and 'Society' which generates English poetry. And anyway, it is only in posterity that English poets will be read.

The tensions involved in negotiating the gap between poetic integrity and poetic popularity, between 'a vulgar popularity and an insubstantial isolation', lead, as many of Keats's comments show, to a slippage between 'the Public' and posterity, a slippage which repeats the movement of Wordsworth's 'Essay, Supplementary to the Preface': in both cases, there is a growing displacement of audience into the future, and a crucial rethinking of the notion of fame.[17] Fame, for Keats, involves both a promotion into the Pantheon – an impossible integration of the living writer into the eternal category of poet in posterity – and also, more troublingly, popularity. These problematic tensions were expressed in Keats's two sonnets 'On Fame', written on 30 April 1819, just before the spring odes. In the first sonnet ('Fame, like a wayward girl, will still be coy'), the ambivalence of the poet towards fame is suggested in the descriptions of fame as 'a wayward girl', 'a gipsey', 'a jilt', 'sister-in-law to jealous Potiphar', and, at the same time, the desire of the poet, nevertheless, for this abstraction. In the second sonnet ('How fever'd is the man who cannot look'), fame is described as a vexation which distorts the processes of nature such that roses, plums, and Naiads defile themselves by narcissistic auto-eroticism: fame is a 'fierce miscreed' with which the poet 'teases' himself.

WRITING FOR A LIVING: JUNE–SEPTEMBER 1819

On 17 June 1819, Keats proposes to make 'one more attempt in the Press' (*Letters*, vol. II, p. 120).[18] This last 'attempt' is impelled by a desire to make money from publication and involves the decision to give up publishing poetry and take up an alternative profession if the attempt should fail. The fact that Keats was still discussing the possibility of financial gain from poetry at this late stage is significant because it is evidence of the fact that despite his antagonism towards 'the Public', and his refusal to write 'for' it, making a living from writing was a constant temptation. Indeed, between June and September 1819, there is a significant alteration in Keats's attitude towards the public, mediated by an impending financial crisis and a consequent alteration in his view of work and of poetry as work. During this period, Keats's letters demonstrate a determination to write for a living, to make money from publication. And, significantly, it was during this period that he wrote and rewrote what may be understood as his most 'public' poetry – 'The Eve of St Agnes', 'Lamia', 'The Fall of Hyperion', *Otho the Great*. Keats's determination to write for money during these months seems to be matched by a poetry determined to engage with its contemporary audience.

I would like to consider the letters of these months in some detail in order to suggest ways in which, at a crucial moment in Keats's writing career – just after the spring odes and just before the *end* of his major writing – the rhetoric of the letters is bound up with questions of the economics of writing and writing as a profession. In the months leading up to the writing of what is usually considered to be Keats's last great poem, 'To Autumn', on 19 September 1819, Keats produced an aesthetics of writing as work which contrasts sharply with letters before May and after September. Before and after these crucial months the letters present a conception of writing as necessarily leisurely and indolent, a conception which resists any connection between writing, work and money. The period between the end of May and the end of September 1819, however, may be read as a 'window' in this predominant attitude. In the letters of this period, there are constant references to the poet's precarious financial position and to two possible solutions to the problem: conventional work or writing for money. Poetry comes to be seen primarily as a means of making money.[19]

On 29 May 1819 Keats made a 'general clearance of all lent Books' and a 'conflagration of all old Letters and Memorandums' (*Letters*, vol. II, pp. 111, 112), in an apparent effort to make a new, diligent, start on poetry – to make poetry work. Writing to Sarah Jeffrey two days later, Keats declared that 'I have the choice as it were of two Poisons … the one is voyaging to and from India for a few years; the other is leading a fevrous life alone with Poetry' (II, 112–13). In a subsequent letter the choice had altered slightly: 'I have my choice of three things – or at least two – South America or Surgeon to an I[n]diaman – which last I think will be my fate' (II, 114): Keats's pragmatism is apparent in the suppression of the third choice – presumably writing. By 9 June, however, he had given up the idea of being a surgeon aboard an 'Indiaman' (II, 116), and writing on 17 June, there is a tone of quiet desperation in his request to B. R. Haydon to repay a loan of £30: 'I was the day before yesterday much in want of Money: but some news I had yesterday has driven me into necessity … My purpose is now to make one more attempt in the Press if that fail, "ye hear no more of me" as Chaucer says – Brown has lent me some money for the present' (II, 120). The 'attempt in the Press' is clearly an attempt to gain financial reward from publication, at the same time as it is a recognition of the financial gamble which this constitutes. On the same day, writing to his sister Fanny, Keats declares that he is going to 'try the Press onece [*sic*] more', a project which Charles Brown seems to have persuaded Keats was a viable proposition: 'I was prepa[r]ing to enqu[i]re for a Situation with an Apothecary, put [*sic*] Mr Brown persuad[e]s me to try the press once more' (II, 121). On 6 July he writes Fanny that he has retired to the Isle of Wight 'to try the fortune of my Pen once more' (II, 124), where the pun implicitly acknowledges the chanciness of financial gain from writing.

The tension between writing poetry for the sake of writing and for the sake of money is never far from the surface in the letters of these months, and is explicitly expressed on 11 July in a letter to J. H. Reynolds (who had, himself, abandoned poetry for the legal profession): speaking of both *Otho the Great* and 'Lamia', Keats defines success in terms of 'the world' when he says that he has 'great hopes of success ... but in Case of failure with the world, I shall find my content' (II, 128). These tensions appear again a few days later when Keats tells Fanny Brawne that 'I have three or four stories half done, but as I cannot write for the mere sake of the press, I am obliged to let them progress or lie still as my fancy chooses' (II, 130). By early August, when his writing is going well, however, he tells Fanny that 'as I am in a train of writing now I fear to disturb it – let it have its course bad or good – in it I shall try my own strength and the public pulse' (II, 137), which suggests a more positive approach to 'the public'. But the 'public pulse' includes 'the drawling of the blue stocking literary world' which he hopes to 'upset' (II, 139), and there is a strong sense that, as he reports to Fanny on 16 August, Keats feels himself to be 'above all matters of interest' (II, 141).

This ambivalence between the possibility of writing for the public and a refusal to countenance such a scheme is explicitly expressed a week later when Keats makes a formal request to John Taylor, his publisher, for a loan which he sees as an advance on *Otho*, 'from which we [Brown and Keats] hope to share moderate Profits' (*Letters*, vol. II, p. 143). Having promised that the play will be popular, however, Keats immediately qualifies this by the assertion that although

I feel every confidence that if I choose I may be a popular writer; that I will never be; but for all that I will get a livelihood I equally dislike the favour of the public with the love of a woman – they are both a cloying treacle to the wings of independence. I shall ever consider them (People) as debtors to me for verses, not myself to them for admiration – which I can do without. I have of late been indulging my spleen by composing a preface *at* them: after all resolving never to write a preface at all. (*Letters*, vol. II, p. 144)

Taylor will comment, Keats predicts, that the letter displays 'pride and egotism', but, he continues,

Just so much as I am hu[m]bled by the genius above my grasp, am I exalted and look with hate and contempt upon the literary world – A Drummer boy who holds out his hand familiarly to a field marshall – that Drummer boy with me is the good word and favour of the public – Who would wish to be among the commonplace crowd of the little-famous – who⟨m⟩ are each individually lost in a throng made up of themselfes? is this worth louting or playing the hypocrite for? To beg suffrages for a seat on the benches of a myriad aristocracy in Letters?... Pardon me for hammering instead of writing. (*Letters*, vol. II, p. 144)

Clearly, Keats's position is difficult, and he deals with it by reversing the relationship of debt, so that 'I shall ever consider them (People) as debtors to me for verses, not myself to them for admiration – which I can do without' suggests both that 'People' cannot do without his verses, and, by implication, that the relationship of debt between poet and publisher may be rather more complex than it seems. Again, the next day (24 August), in a letter to Reynolds, Keats expresses a similar ambivalence when he writes that 'I feel it in my power to become a popular writer – I feel it in my strength to refuse the poisonous suffrage of a public' (II, 146): the syntax of this double-jointed declaration is deeply ambiguous – it is hard to know whether he is independent because he is able to be popular or despite this fact, or if he is able to be popular because of or despite his independence.

Although his financial situation was temporarily relieved by a cheque for £30 from James Hessey in early September, after a period in which (with only slight exaggeration, perhaps) he has been 'in fear of Winchester Jail' (*Letters*, vol. II, p. 154),[20] by 22 September, having decided that money was not to be got for poetry (II, 185–6), Keats is once again writing about the possibility of making a living from periodical writing, specifically with the idea of designing his work for the public. In three letters written on the same day, to Richard Woodhouse, Charles Brown, and C. W. Dilke, he expresses this quite clearly and clear-mindedly: 'I shall enquire of Hazlitt how the figures of the market stand' (II, 174), 'I will write, on the liberal side of the question, for whoever will pay me' (II, 176), 'I shall apply to Hazlitt, who knows the market as well as any one, for something to bring me in a few pounds as soon as possible' (II, 177), 'Yea I will trafic. Any thing but Mortgage my Brain to Blackwood' (II, 178–9). But concomitant with the idea of writing for money is the realization that poetry cannot be written for financial reward: 'I could not raise any sum by the promise of any Poem – no, not by the mortgage of my intellect' (II, 185: see also II, 211). Moreover, beneath these assertions the strain is never very far from the surface, and there is a sense of writing for money as the work of a literary trickster:

> It is fortunate I have not before this been tempted to venture on the common. I should a year or two ago have spoken my mind on every subject with the utmost simplicity. I hope I have learnt a little better and am confident I shall be able to cheat as well as any literary Jew of the Market and shine up an article on any thing without much knowledge of the subject, aye like an orange. (*Letters*, vol. II, p. 179)

Throughout these months there is a developing theorization of poetic writing as literary work, and again and again the word 'diligence' is related to writing poetry, something alien to an earlier conception of poetic creation which had been seen largely as a product of creative indolence. Indeed, in two previous uses of 'diligence' in the context of writing, the word had specifically been related to indolence – 'delicious diligent Indolence' (*Letters*, vol. I, p. 231), and an attempt to relate diligence to a relaxed, indolent sense of luxury (II, 56). The alteration in attitude is announced on 31 May 1819, when Keats declares that 'I would rather conquer my indolence and strain my ne[r]ves at some grand Poem' (II, 113), and then repeated in his declaration two weeks later that he will 'try the press once more ... with all my industry and ability' (II, 121). For the next three months assertions of 'diligence' (together with declarations of hard work and a lack of indolence) recur at frequent intervals in the letters: 'I am at the diligent use of my faculties here' (II, 127); 'You will be glad to hear ... how diligent I have been, & am being' (II, 128); 'I will not make my diligence an excuse for not writing to you sooner' (II, 134); 'I am not idle enough for proper downright love-letters' (II, 136–7); 'Thank God for my diligence! were it not for that I should be miserable' (II, 137); 'Remember I have had no idle leisure to brood over you' (II, 140); 'The more I know what my diligence may in time probably effect; the more does my heart distend with Pride and Obstinacy' (II, 146); 'I have still been hard at work' (II, 148). Moreover, it is clear that such industry is explicitly seen as a financial transaction, a bartering of work for leisure. He addresses the public in the proposed preface to *Endymion*: '"There are so many verses", would I have said to them, "give me so much means to buy pleasure with as a relief to my hours of labour"' (II, 144); and later he declares that 'I will settle myself and fag till I can afford to buy Pleasure – which if [I] never can afford I must go Without' (II, 179).[21] During this period Keats decided that, rather than being in debt to his readers, his readers were in debt to him (see II, 144).

By the end of September, however, an interesting volte-face has taken place with regard to the cash-work nexus of poetry: having decided to 'prose' for the reviews, a split between the two types of writing occurs, and the 'diligence' which Keats has been advertising in relation to his poetry becomes 'idleness'. On 22 September, along with his decision to write for 'whoever will pay me', Keats claims that 'I have never yet exerted myself. I am getting into an idle minded, vicious way of life, almost content to live upon others' (*Letters*, vol. II, p. 176): that this is unjustifiably self-denigratory is evinced both by the letters of June–September 1819 and by the poetic output of those months. But what is interesting is that the anxiety of monetary poetics should finally be decided in these terms: it is a return to an earlier sense of poetry as a product of leisure and of indolence, a return to the conventional early nineteenth-century ideology of poetry as pleasure, and pleasure as synonymous with leisure – antagonistic to work, diligence, and money. The four months between June and September constituted a period in which Keats's letters articulated a particularly pragmatic view of poetry as (potentially) plugged into the economic structure of society, and of the poet as a worker within that structure. The letters of 22 September which both declare Keats's determination to find gainful employment with the periodical press, and assert a view of poetry as leisure/pleasure, were written, significantly, the day after he had given up his last major long poem, 'The Fall of Hyperion': the trivialization of poetry seems to lead directly to its abandonment.

What the letters of these four months show, then, is not only that Keats's financial situation was extremely precarious, and a source of uncertainty and anxiety,[22] nor simply that writing was for this reason as never before in his life inextricably connected with 'the market', but that during these months the question of money, and the related question of popularity had become a major motivating force for the poetry: now more than ever 'writing' had become 'writing for a living'.

KEATS AND READING: THE READER AS LOVER

As critics have recently begun to suggest, the function of the reader is central to Keats's ideas about poetry.[23] In this section I shall discuss ways in which the Keatsian poetics of reading involve a figuration of the reader as lover. Perhaps the most famous statement of Keats's poetics of reading is his early assertion that things take their 'reality' from the 'ardour of the pursuer':

> I am sometimes so very sceptical as to think Poetry itself a mere Jack a lanthern to amuse whoever may chance to be struck with its brilliance – As Tradesmen say every thing is worth what it will fetch, so probably every mental pursuit takes its reality and worth from the ardour of the pursuer – being in itself a nothing – Ethereal thing[s] may at least be thus real, divided under three heads – Things real – things semireal – and no things – Things real – such as existences of Sun Moon & Stars and passages of Shakspeare – Things semireal such as Love, the Clouds &c which require a greeting of the Spirit to make them wholly exist – and Nothings which are made Great and dignified by an ardent pursuit ... (*Letters*, vol. I, pp. 242–3)

The idea of there being 'real' things recurs throughout Keats's letters, and becomes a mark of Keatsian distinction: it is clear that of these three categories, most literature, apart from Shakespeare, is likely to be in the middle, 'things semireal ... which require a greeting of the Spirit'. Reading may be understood as precisely such a 'greeting', reading involves active participation in the making of the text. This reciprocity of reading, the 'greeting' which the reader must perform, is expressed by Keats in a number of ways: in his comments on books and poems he tends to start from where they leave off, developing lines of thought often far from directly related to the works themselves; in his letters he comments on stories he has read, but he also rewrites them for his own personal audience; in his poems he also rewrites stories, alluding or referring to them, embedding them within his own tales, and carrying out a full-scale rewriting of classical mythology in poems like *Endymion* and 'Hyperion', or reworking more recent poets like Boccaccio in 'Isabella' and producing imaginative dilations on popular superstitions like 'The Eve of St Agnes' and 'The Eve of St Mark'.

In particular, this reciprocity works like Pope's idea of 'what oft was *thought* but ne'er so well *exprest*'. Poetry should seem to be part of the reader's unconscious experience before meeting its expression in a book: it 'should strike the Reader as a wording of his own highest

thoughts, and appear almost a Remembrance' (*Letters*, vol. I, p. 238),
or as Keats put it in an equally famous passage that includes his
theory that ideas should be 'proved upon our pulses', 'We read fine
– things but never feel them to thee full until we have gone the same
steps as the Author' (*Letters*, vol. I, p. 279). In both cases – reading as
a remembrance and a proving upon our pulses – the idea is that the
reader's perception must coincide with authorial perception.

In a series of letters to the Reynolds sisters in September of 1817,
Keats produces a complex figuration of reading by the dual strategy
of configuring the sisters and figuring himself as a reader: the letters,
apparently driven by ambivalent sexual desires towards their
recipients, are teasing, suggestive, flirtatious, allusive, punning,
joking, obscure, and prickly.[24] There seems to have been a running
battle between Jane Reynolds and Keats on the question of reading,
so that he resorts, eventually, to writing down 'in black and white
briefly my sentiments thereon' (*Letters*, vol. I, p. 157). His sentiments
are enlightening:

Imprimis – I sincerely believe that Imogen is the finest Creature; and that
I should have been disappointed at hearing you prefer Juliet. Item Yet I feel
such a yearning towards Juliet and that I would rather follow her into
Pandemonium than Imogen into Paradize – heartily wishing myself a
Romeo to be worthy of her and to he[a]r the Devils quote the old Proverb
– 'Birds of a feather flock together' – Amen. (*Letters*, vol. I, pp. 157–8)

This yearning, and the desire to be a 'Romeo', to enter the fictional
space of Shakespeare's play, seems to be characteristic of Keats as a
reader as it is of Keats as a 'cameleon' poet. The passage indicates an
important aspect of Keats's poetics of reading: there is no ontological
separation between 'reality' and 'fiction', between the reader and
the characters in a fictional text: reading, for Keats, involves a
(solecistic) reciprocity of 'fiction' and 'reality'. The passage also
introduces the idea of the Keatsian reader as lover: it is significant
that Keats yearns for Juliet, the archetypal lover, rather than
Imogen, who represents the archetypally chaste heroine. Reading
involves sexual desire rather than admiration or awe: the pleasure of
the text takes priority over the lesson of the text.[25] Indeed, the trope
of the reader as lover recurs in a letter of August 1819 to Benjamin
Bailey:

I am convinced more and more every day that (excepting the human friend
Philosopher) a fine writer is the most genuine Being in the World –

Shakspeare and the paradise Lost every day become greater wonders to me
– I look upon fine Phrases like a Lover ... (*Letters*, vol. II, p. 139)

The duplicity of 'look upon' suggests a strange congruence of looking
at a book full of 'fine Phrases', and having the attitude of a lover
towards them: Keats both stands aside regarding fine phrases in his
capacity as a critic, and takes part in their existence as a lover of
them.

At other times it is clear that reading for Keats represents other
things, and that reading involves doing other things than reading.
Let a man read a page 'of full Poesy or distilled Prose', he says, and
then let him 'wander with it, and muse upon it, and reflect from it,
and bring home to it, and prophesy upon it, and dream upon it'
(*Letters*, vol. I, p. 231). The whole of the three-page letter from which
this comes is a poetic examination of the reading process, which
develops into Keats's most determined statement of the importance
of a reciprocal passivity/activity, a statement which finds its most
evocative allegory in sexual relations: 'The f[l]ower I doubt not
receives a fair guerdon from the Bee – its leaves blush deeper in the
next spring – and who shall say between Man and Woman which is
the most delighted?' (*Letters*, vol. I, p. 232). And, paradoxically, this
consideration of reading is generated by a neglect of reading: 'I have
not read any Books – the Morning said I was right' (*Letters*, vol. I, pp.
232–3).[26]

Keats's sonnet 'This pleasant tale is like a little copse' presents a
paradigmatic instance of the Keatsian conception of reading. This
sonnet is a paean to the grace of the homiletic allegory of the pseudo-
Chaucerian *The Floure and the Leafe*, a poem which was rooted in the
courtly tradition and, according to D. A. Pearsall, was 'intended to
enforce a moral contrast between, on the one hand, idle and frivolous
pleasure, and on the other, chastity, constancy in love, and prowess
in chivalry'.[27] But what is striking about Keats's poem is the way in
which it disregards the ethics of the poem which it is discussing: the
Chaucerian poem opposes chastity, simplicity, dryness, the colour
white, eternity and the leaf, to the sensuality, temporality, moisture
and greenery of the flower. Keats's response is characteristically
sensuous in its adjectives, emphatically embracing the wetness of
'dewy drops', and asserting a quite amoral passivity. In fact, Keats
overturns the ethical point of the medieval poem so that his assertions
of being trapped and of being seduced into passivity conflict with the

ethics of the text he is 'reading'. Most striking, perhaps, is the description of the reader: 'oftentimes he feels the dewy drops / Come cool and suddenly against his face'. It is not the cognitive or ethical content of the poem that is acknowledged, but the feel of the words – those words self-condemned at the end of the original poem as 'rude' and 'boistous' (line 595). At the same time, Keats's poem describes a precise ontology of readerly entrapment in 'The honied lines do freshly interlace, / To keep the reader in so sweet a place'; although there is no reason why the reader should read, the lines of the poem manage to seduce him into reading on.[28] It is precisely this mixture of power and powerlessness, of writing and reading, action and passivity, freedom and restraint, which Keats constantly points to in his configurations of reading.

In one of Keats's most fascinating passages on Shakespeare, we are able to watch him reading, rereading, reacting, and rewriting. Just as lovers have to defend themselves from being overwhelmed by the object of their desires, a reader must invent strategies of defence against books:

One of the three Books I have with me is Shakespear's Poems: I neer found so many beauties in the sonnets – they seem to be full of fine things said unintentionally – in the intensity of working out conceits – Is this to be borne? Hark ye!

> When lofty trees I see barren of leaves
>   erst
> Which ⟨not⟩ from heat did canopy the he⟨a⟩rd,
> And Summer's green all girded up in sheaves,
> Borne on the bier with white and bristly beard.

He has left nothing to say about nothing or any thing: for look at Snails, you know what he says about Snails, you know where he talks about 'cockled snails' – well, in one of these sonnets, he says – the chap slips into – no! I lie! this is in the Venus and Adonis: the Simile brought it to my Mind.

> Audi – As the snail, whose tender horns being hit,
> Shrinks back⟨s⟩ into his shelly cave with pain,
> And there all smothered up in shade doth sit,
> Long after fearing to put forth again:
> So at his bloody view her eyes are fled,
> Into the deep dark Cabins of her head.

He overwhelms a genuine Lover of Poesy with all manner of abuse, talking about

'a poets rage
And stretched metre of an antique song' –

Which by the by will be a capital Motto for my Poem – wont it? – He speaks too of 'Time's antique pen' – and 'aprils first born flowers' – and 'deaths eternal cold' – By the Whim King! I'll give you a Stanza, because it is not material in connection and when I wrote it I wanted you to – give your vote, pro or con. – (*Letters*, vol. I, pp. 188–9)

In this arabesque of quotation and misquotation, Keats brings various strategies into play to avoid being overwhelmed by Shakespeare's fine phrases.[29] The fact that the fine things in the sonnets are said unintentionally increases the status of Keats's finding them almost to that of co-writing – like the art of ('making'/'finding') *objets trouvés* – and there is a striking similarity between Shakespeare's method of saying fine things 'in the intensity of working out conceits' and Keats's slip of attribution: in passing from one text to another (from Sonnet Twelve to *Love's Labour's Lost*, to *Venus and Adonis*, to Sonnet Seventeen, to Sonnet Nineteen ('thine antique pen'), to Sonnet Twenty-One, to Sonnet Thirteen), Keats's reading repeats the serendipity of Shakespeare's writing. Keats's creative reading is subject to a Shakespearean intensity of working out conceits. But Keats's other unintentionally fine things said in the line 'which erst from heat did canopy the herd', are also instructive: replacing the archaic 'erst' with the standard English 'not' signifies precisely that reappropriation of the past which the Shakespearean text desires – the nostalgic remembrance of Shakespeare's sonnet, which would reinscribe the past in the present, is accomplished by Keats's elimination of the diction of the past. The misspelt 'herd'/'heard' also provides an 'unintentional' improvement, by substituting a misheard rhyme ('herd'/'beard'), for an equally dissonant, but visually homologous eye-rhyme ('heard'/'beard') – a 'deconstructive' improvement, because the rhyme is still, specifically, seen and not heard. Keats's instructive improvement produces a figure of reading: Keats figures Shakespeare's text by attempting to generate a full rhyme, but the rhyme will never be heard and produces, in its solecism, only a desire for reading. The only way to deal with Shakespeare's abuse of the reader, it seems, is either to write like this – with Shakespeare – or to rewrite him, which – apart from the misquotations – takes the form of rewriting the passage about snails in a later letter to Haydon as 'that trembling delicate and snail-horn perception of Beauty' (*Letters*, vol. i, p. 265), and of appropriating a line for a 'motto' to his own poem. This is not to be borne then: it must be re-born. It is in this way, perhaps, that Keats is able to say that reading Shakespeare is new each time, 'notwithstanding that we read the same Play forty times' (*Letters*, vol. i, p. 133). The passage suggests, then, how Keats's figures of reading articulate a dynamic reciprocity of reading and writing: Keats's figures of reading are constituted by refigured readings of the Shakespearean text. As Jacques Derrida has said, in a response to the question of why Paul de Man 'always speaks of reading rather than of writing': 'Well, perhaps because the allegory of reading is writing – or the inverse'.[30]

THE MOUTH OF FAME

Reading and writing, in fact, are conflated in one of the major Keatsian tropes, which encompasses both the inspiration of writing, and reading: breathing. In a marginal annotation to his copy of *Troilus and Cressida*, Keats commented that 'One's very breath while leaning over these Pages is held for fear of blowing this line away'.[31] This figure of reading and breathing also occurs in a letter written in February 1818, when Keats gives his 'axioms' of poetry and says that 'Its touches of Beauty should never be half way therby making the reader breathless instead of content' (*Letters*, vol. i, p. 238). And the most explicit figuration of reading as breathing (in) occurs in his 'On First Looking into Chapman's Homer': 'Yet did I never breathe its pure serene / Till I heard Chapman speak out loud and bold'. As Lawrence Lipking suggests, although 'serene' is associated with purity, the phrase 'pure serene' may also be read as an oxymoron since 'serene' also signifies 'a deadly mist supposed to descend after sunset': 'the phrase would then evoke the double nature of Homeric influence – at once benevolent and deadly'.[32] Reading as breathing suggests both life and death. The association of breathing with death, rather than life, occurs elsewhere in Keats's poetry: in 'Ode to a Nightingale' the poet, in the entrancement of aesthetic response, desires Death 'To take into the air my quiet breath; / Now more than ever seems it rich to die'. In 'Lamia' the inevitable phonetic congruence of death with breath is emphasized in the line 'Then Lamia breath'd death breath' (part 2, line 299). In a letter to his publisher John Taylor, Keats warns of the danger of breathing bad air, the importance of air for one's 'hea[l]th temperament and dispositions', and declares that 'leading an inactive life as you did was breathing poison' (*Letters*, vol. II, pp. 156, 155; see vol. II, pp. 155–7). Finally, breathing in Keats is constantly related to the inspiration of hallucination: if, in 'Ode to Psyche', Keats is 'by my own eyes inspired' (line 43), in the induction to 'Lamia' such inspiration is played out literally: Lamia *breathes* on Hermes' eyes so that he might see his 'sweet nymph' (I, 121–5). In this sense, reading and writing, inspiration and expiration, are figured as a form of hallucination, of seeing things.[33]

In May 1817, Keats wrote a letter to Benjamin Robert Haydon from his lodgings in Margate. The letter proposes Shakespeare as Keats's 'Presider' (*Letters*, vol. I, p. 142), and declares that 'Shakespeare is enough for us' (I, 143); it castigates Leigh Hunt for his 'self delusions', which include his ability to 'flatter [himself] into an idea of being a great Poet' (I, 143); comments that 'A Man ought to have the Fame he deserves' (I, 144); and complains about 'Money Troubles' (I, 142). The letter opens with a quotation from the beginning of Shakespeare's *Love's Labour's Lost*, and a comment:

> Let Fame, which all hunt after in their Lives,
> Live register'd upon our brazen tombs,
> And so grace us in the disgrace of death:
> When spite of cormorant devouring time
> The endeavour of this pre⟨a⟩sent breath may buy
> That Honor which shall bate his Scythe's keen edge
> And make us heirs of all eternity.

To think that I have no right to couple myself with you in this speech would be death to me so I have e'en written it – and I pray God that our brazen Tombs be nigh neighbors. It cannot be long first the endeavor of this present breath will soon be over – and yet it is as well to breathe freely during our sojourn – it is as well if you have not been teased with that Money affair – that bill-pestilence. (*Letters*, vol. I, pp. 140–41)

The letter, and the quotation itself, succinctly draw together Keats's concerns with fame, posterity, memory, money, breath and death. Keats folds the proleptic sense of breath 'buying' honour in the future into the present, and in a bathetic literalization of the figurative 'buy', refers to his financial affairs. Nevertheless, the relation between breathing, dying and immortality is established. And Keats, like Shakespeare's addressee in Sonnet Eighty-One ('Or

I shall live your epitaph to make'), 'still shall live – such virtue hath my pen – / Where breath most breathes, even in the mouths of men'. 'What a thing', says Keats, in a letter written on the same day (to the self-deluding Hunt), 'to be in the Mouth of Fame' (*Letters*, vol. I, p. 139).

CHAPTER 3

The early verse and Endymion

The view that Keats's poems are more – or less – than stories, that they differ in some essential way from conventional narrative, and that they demand a vocabulary different from that used to describe stories, has dominated criticism from the earliest reviews. Leigh Hunt, for example, asserts that 'The Eve of St Agnes' is 'rather a picture than a story' (*Heritage*, p. 172), Peter George Patmore suggests of *Endymion* that, 'as a tale, this work is nothing ... it is not a poem, but a dream of poetry' (*Heritage*, p. 137), and, slightly later, W. M. Rossetti comments that 'Keats had very little head for framing a story'.[1] Story as dream, as picture, and later the perception of the importance of images and the poem as a collection of images, are all recurrent themes in critics' denial of the narrative force of Keats's poetry. At the same time, however, the perception that the majority of the major poems consist of or contain clear, strong stories – *Endymion*, 'Isabella', 'The Eve of St Agnes', 'La Belle Dame sans Merci', 'Hyperion', 'The Fall of Hyperion', 'Lamia' – and that even the shorter lyric poems continually refer to, rewrite, embed, and imply narrative, often leads to a recognition of the narrative focus of much of Keats's poetry. In the review in which he refers to 'St Agnes' as a picture, for example, Leigh Hunt implicitly acknowledges the story-based power of Keats's 1820 collection by saying that he will 'abridge into prose the stories which Mr Keats has told in poetry, only making up for it, as we go, by cutting some of the richest passages out of his verse, and fitting them in to our plainer narrative' (*Heritage*, p. 165).

One way of approaching this contradiction is through the very clear denunciation of Keats's narrative abilities which Matthew Arnold provides in his discussion of 'Isabella'. He explains not only his perception of Keats's narrative incompetence, but the reason for that incompetence:

But the action, the story? The action in itself is an excellent one; but so feebly is it conceived by the Poet, so loosely constructed, that the effect produced by it, in and for itself, is absolutely null. Let the reader, after he has finished the poem of Keats, turn to the same story in the *Decameron*: he will then feel how pregnant and interesting the same action has become in the hands of a great artist, who above all things delineates his object; who subordinates expression to that which it is designed to express. (*Heritage*, p. 327)

It is clear that Arnold is pointing to a crucial problem in Keatsian narrative, a problem which critics reflect when they oppose Keats's pictures, dreams, images, or his sensuousness, to narrative: just as Jean Ricardou points to a 'continual belligerence' between description and narration in narrative,[2] what is perceived as 'Keatsian' in Keats's poetry is generated by the problematic relationship between telling and the told, between 'story' and 'discourse'. This belligerence is a product of an almost tactile apprehension of words which Keats articulates, a desire to feel words 'Come cool and suddenly against his face' ('This pleasant tale', line 6). But a concomitant belligerence is the 'anxiety of authorship' (*BL*, vol. I, p. 233) which we observe in Keats's poetry as a self-consciousness about the structure of stories and a consequent withholding, turning, or delaying of narrative. In the criticism of Keats this problematic tends to be read as a denial of narrative in the poetry. We might, however, reread this tension in Keatsian narrative as articulating the pressures and contradictions within narrative itself. The essential point which has been so often missed about Keats is that, as Marilyn Butler says, 'He liked to tell a story'.[3]

THE 1817 VOLUME

Keats's early poems are littered with abandoned tales: tales hardly begun, interrupted, borrowed, echoed, alluded to, and tellings attempted, embedded, and neglected. Indeed, it often seems that, rather than any particular tale to tell, the poetry is impelled by the desire to *be* poetry. The primary intensity of the early poetry is a certain intertextuality.[4] This itself accounts for the remarkable generic range of the early poems, a range and intensity of intertextual reference, allusion, naming and repetition which suggests, most strongly, a nostalgia for narrative. In the early poetry there are imitations of Spenser, Huntian Romance openings, ballads,

eighteenth-century odes, songs, Shakespearian/Wordsworthian sonnets and Thomsonian loco-descriptive poems. Such generic fecundity
is matched by a plenitude of intertextual allusion to story-telling:
Keats's early poems are overwhelmed by references to other poets'
stories and allusions to other people's narratives by reference to
historical, mythological or literary characters. In particular, the list
includes a number of nominal clusters such as Dido and Lear
('Imitation of Spenser', lines 21–2); 'Armida the fair, and Rinaldo
the bold' ('On Receiving a Curious Shell', line 8); Calidore, the Red
Cross Knight, and Leander ('Woman! when I behold thee flippant,
vain', lines 12–13); Belphoebe, Una, Archimago, Titania, and
Urania ('To Charles Cowden Clarke', lines 35, 36, 37, 40, 41);
Psyche, Syrinx, Pan, Narcissus, Echo and Endymion ('I stood tip-
toe', lines 141, 157, 158, 180, 192); Dryope and Diana (*Endymion*,
book 1, lines 495, 512); Ulysses, Cyclops, Juliet, Hero, Imogen and
Pastorella (*Endymion*, book 2, lines 26, 27, 31, 32). The narrative
nostalgia implied by such nominal intertextuality is reinforced by the
repeated assurance that the poet is incapable of telling his own tales
– 'Ah! could I tell ... ' ('Imitation of Spenser', line 19); 'how shall I
/ Revive the dying tones of minstrelsy ... ?' ('Specimen of an
Induction', lines 31–2); 'that I may dare ... / To stammer where old
Chaucer used to sing' (*Endymion*, book 1, lines 133–4); 'Ah, can I tell
/ The enchantment... ' (*Endymion*, book 1, lines 572–3) – a modesty
topos which reinforces the value and emphasizes the inadequacy of
contemporary stories. Narrative is also foregrounded through the
trope of embedded story-telling and reception: there is the refugee
from the urban who, in the country, reads 'a debonair / And gentle
tale of love and languishment' ('To one who has been long in city
pent', lines 7–8); or the idea that 'the bright glance from beauty's
eyelids slanting' generates 'Some tale of love and arms in time of old'
('To My Brother George', lines 15, 18); and there are Endymion's
companions, who 'all out-told / Their fond imaginations' (*Endymion*,
book 1, line 392), while Endymion's spiritual sickness is indicated by
his unwillingness to participate in such an activity. Finally, there are
numerous references to the effects of unspecified tales and stories in
the poems up to and including *Endymion*, for despite the attenuated
narrative energy of these early poems, the poems systematically and
explicitly value stories and story-telling: 'The enchanting tale – the
tale of pleasing woe' ('To Lord Byron', line 14); 'the story divine'
('On Receiving a Curious Shell', line 7); 'I will tell you / Such tales

as needs must with amazement spell you' ('To My Brother George', lines 65–6); 'A lovely tale of human life we'll read' ('Sleep and Poetry', line 110); 'to tell delightful stories... And when a tale is beautifully staid, / We feel the safety of a hawthorn glade' ('I stood tip-toe', lines 124, 129–30); 'This pleasant tale... What mighty power has this gentle story!' ('This pleasant tale is like a little copse', lines 1, 10); 'this sweet tale' ('On *The Story of Rimini*', line 3); 'All lovely tales that we have heard or read' (*Endymion*, book 1, line 22).

The importance of story-telling is further emphasized by the significance attributed to stories, to the extent that life itself is described as 'The reading of an ever-changing tale' in 'Sleep and Poetry' (lines 90–91). Alternatively, reading poetry is, in the hands of great poets – Homer, Ovid, Tasso, Spenser, Shakespeare, Leigh Hunt – a voyeuristic process in which one can watch 'Belphoebe in a brook, / And lovely Una in a leafy nook, / And Archimago leaning o'er his book' ('To Charles Cowden Clarke', lines 35–7), and is, furthermore, a sensuous activity, an activity to be undertaken when in 'voluptuous vein' ('On Receiving a Curious Shell', line 37). Indeed, story-telling involves the sensuous participation of readers in stories: in 'Sleep and Poetry', Keats asks for ten years 'that I may overwhelm / Myself in poesy' –

> First the realm I'll pass
> Of Flora, and old Pan: sleep in the grass,
> Feed upon apples red, and strawberries,
> And choose each pleasure that my fancy sees;
> Catch the white-handed nymphs in shady places,
> To woo sweet kisses from averted faces, –
> Play with their fingers, touch their shoulders white
> Into a pretty shrinking with a bite
> As hard as lips can make it... (lines 101–9)

Reading poetry involves sleeping, eating, seeing, catching, wooing, kissing, playing, touching, biting: reading as polymorphous hallucination. Most succinctly, in his sonnet on 'The Flower and the Leaf', Keats describes poetry as trapping the reader and making him feel 'the dewy drops / Come cool and suddenly against his face' ('This pleasant tale', lines 5–6) – the dewy drops of words being read, which Hazlitt describes as 'holding [the soul] captive in the chains of suspense' (*Works*, vol. v, p. 44).

Despite Keats's narrative nostalgia, however, he has little success in actually writing narrative poems: it is only with 'Isabella' in the spring of 1818 that Keats is able to write the kind of story – in which narrative energy becomes a decisive force – which his early poems desire. The early poems recognize the irresistible force of narrative while at the same time suggesting the irreducible desire by which such narrative is structured. The very failure of narrative in Keats's early poems signals at once the necessity and the impossibility of narrative.[5]

Keats's first attempts at narration are, perhaps, most striking for the fact that he lacks a story: the poems are often overwhelmed – and broken off – by the absence of generative narrative energies.[6] The fact that his early poems are replete with borrowed tales indicates a dilemma which might be defined as a problem of 'tellability': there were numerous tales available for retelling but, without an audience, no *reason* to retell any of them. Apart from *Endymion*, Keats was, in his first years of serious poetry-writing from 1816 to early 1818, without a plot: lacking a story, but with an intense desire to write, Keats ends up writing poems which, as Walter Jackson Bate points out, have 'virtually no other subject than how it feels to lack subjects'.[7] The attenuation of narrative energy in Keats's early verse might be understood as a response to the absence of any public audience: many of the early poems are written directly for or to close friends and relatives, but beyond this their potential readership is vague or non-existent. As such, the story of Keats's poems (in the technical sense of *histoire* or *fabula*) is obsessively focused on the personal: the tale of becoming a poet. The fact that many of Keats's early poems are explicitly addressed to friends and relations, might suggest that his inability to write stories is a product of his intimacy with his 'actual' readers (his friends and family): there is little frictional energy (the product of distrust, antagonism, desire, etc.), and 'tellability' is not a prerequisite for narration.[8] These early poems inhabit a strange position with respect to audience. Like letters – and these poems are often first written either *in* or *as* letters – many of the early poems have explicit and singular addressees. Often it is precisely the relationship between the poet and the named addressee which is the topos of the whole poem: 'To Charles Cowden Clarke', for example, never moves far from the poet's anxieties with regard to Clarke's superior wisdom and reading. And yet there is a fundamental difference between a letter and a poem. The former is, by convention, private, convoluted within an envelope, sent to a specific destination, delivered and written *by hand*, etc. A poem, on the other hand, while it may be determined by a singular destination, is also, almost by definition and increasingly during the early nineteenth century, determined by publication and by public response. However private or personal a poem might be, it is structurally determined by the possibility of publication: whether or not it is published, and whether or not it is written to be published, a poem presupposes the possibility of a reader other than the reader empirically determined by the address which begins a letter. Indeed, this itself might explain the extraordinary contortions of address in poems like 'To Charles Cowden Clarke'. A letter, by contrast, is structurally determined by privacy such that publication involves a kind of scandal. Even letters specifically written for publication are determined by and, indeed, exploit this necessary privacy of the epistolary. Keats's early poems are remarkable, not least, for their inhabitation of this liminal space of poetic privacy.

Keats's first extant attempt at narrative poetry, his 'Imitation of Spenser', contains no hint of a story, apparently proceeding under the misapprehension that Spenser's poetry involved only description. Indeed, there is an implicit assertion that description makes narrative redundant:

> Ah! could I tell the wonders of an isle
> That in that fairest lake had placed been,
> I could e'en Dido of her grief beguile;
> Or rob from aged Lear his bitter teen...   (lines 19–22)

In beguiling Dido and Lear from their sorrows and troubles, Keats is both asserting the seductive emotional force of poetry and asserting the power of description to rewrite narrative: by beguiling these fictitious characters from their grief, Keats would be rewriting the tale of Dido and Aeneas, and *King Lear*. Two years later, nostalgia for Spenserian description has modulated to become the Huntian-chivalric 'Specimen of an Induction to a Poem', beginning with the unpromising assertion that 'Lo! I must tell a tale of Chivalry' and continuing with an explanation for this necessity which is equally discordant and badly rhymed 'For large white plumes are dancing in mine eye'. But this assertion, and the talismanic references to 'Archimago's wand' (line 6), narrative elements such as 'some lady sweet' (line 13) and her 'stout defender' (line 16), a 'good knight' (line 19), a variety of apparatus borrowed from Leigh Hunt and Scott, such as a 'tournament' (line 28), the 'dying tones of minstrelsy' (line 32) and 'gothic arches' (line 33), soon become an anguished assertion of the poet's inability to tell the tale he so much desires: the narrative impetus changes from an introduction to a tale of chivalry to the spectacle of a markedly weak-willed poet attempting to come to terms with the role of story-teller. What Keats wants to tell in this induction is how things look rather than what happens: narrative energy is inhibited by a rage for description and is attenuated to assertions of narrative desire – 'Lo! I must tell a tale of chivalry ... Lo! I must tell a tale of chivalry ... Yet must I tell a tale of chivalry' (lines 1, 11, 45).[9] Indeed, the 'super-abundance of detail' which Hunt criticized in his review of Keats's first volume (*Heritage*, p. 58) was the most pressing problem for the poet as a story-teller.

The chivalric tale itself, a stunted potentiality of a Romance – 'Calidore: A Fragment' – attempts to negotiate the interplay of action and description but ends where the action should begin. There is an urgency of a desire to tell unmatched by an impulse towards any particular tale. Indeed, this collision of desires is signalled by the grammar of the poem, which modulates nervously and unnervingly between the present and past tenses.[10] The changes in 'Calidore' from the present tense (used in lines 1–3, 6–26, 34–52, 58–72, 90–92, 134–46) to the past (all other lines) create a curiously unbalanced sense, a sense that the poem is uncontrolled. This is particularly evident where the modulation occurs within a single sentence, as it does (twice) in the following passage (past-present-past):

> And whether there were tears of languishment,
> Or that the evening dew had pearl'd their tresses,
> He feels a moisture on his cheek, and blesses
> With lips that tremble, and with glistening eye,
> All the soft luxury
> That nestled in his arms.   (lines 88–93)

This instability of temporal focus seems to figure a crucial uncertainty in narrative energy, as if the 'continuous belligerence' engendered by the contradictory requisites of 'narration' and 'description' has been excavated and exposed by an inexperienced narrator and a poet ignorant of the mechanics of narrative discourse.[11] The problem could be described as the poet being seduced into description instead of attempting to seduce his audience: indeed, the dislocations in the *histoire* or *fabula* seem to be the product of a poet overwhelmed by the idea of his tale, instead of attempting to overwhelm the reader. Each scene (the transitions between which display all the narrative neglect of the eighteenth-century ode) is a set-piece cameo designed more for the exploitation of visual, aural, and tactile experience than for the exploration of narrative potential: the central character's delight and enthusiasm for his surroundings seem to preclude both narrative development and any recognition of an audience in his solipsistic *jouissance*.[12]

However, it is not only the belligerence of narration and description which is evident in this ambiguity of tenses: there is also a collision of narrative desires – to tell a tale or to tell one's self. Emile Benveniste has shown that in French the present tenses indicate *discours*, an attention to the speaking/writing situation, a self-reference which inhibits the course of the 'historical' events, while the aorist 'excludes every "autobiographical" linguistic form'.[13] We may discern a similar distinction – if not such a rigid demarcation – in English grammar, and conclude that if one of the things which Keats had to learn was to balance story and discourse, the significance of this instability in narrative tenses is related to his uncertainty over his own attachment to/detachment from his own poetry, the question of 'disinterestedness', of 'negative capability' (*Letters*, vol. II, pp. 79, 129, 279; vol. I, p. 193) – inherited, internalized and transformed from the aesthetics of William Hazlitt. Paul Ricoeur has recently argued that the present tense is 'the basic tense of discourse because it marks the contemporaneousness of what is stated with the "instance of discourse". It is thus bound up with the self-referential character of the instance of discourse'.[14] To use the present tenses for the actions recounted may be understood as an elision of the distinction between teller and tale, or between story and discourse. Moreover, Ricoeur argues that the use of the past tense signifies an urge towards narratorial 'relaxation' and 'uninvolvement' – concepts crucial to the poetry and poetics of the later Keats:

What grammars call the past and the imperfect ... are narrative tenses, not because a narrative basically expresses past events, real or fictive, but because these tenses are oriented toward an attitude of relaxation, of uninvolvement. What is essential is that the narrated world is foreign to the immediate and directly preoccupying surroundings of the speaker and the listener.[15]

The disturbing instability of tenses in Keats's early verse seems to evince an instability of authorial control. It is only, I suggest, when Keats is able to control the effect of story on discourse, as it is only when he learns to balance an apprehension of the inward feel of things with a strategic 'disinterestedness', that he begins to write tales that tell: our investigation of the trajectory of Keatsian narrative form will repeatedly meet this central problem, the relationship between 'inner' and 'outer', 'subjectivity' and 'objectivity', the private and the public, between authorial 'involvement' and poetic control. In his early poetry, the implicit solecism of private and public never becomes a generative force for narrative: secure within its narcissistic privacy, the early poetry is structured by the poetic solecism of hermetic subjectivism. In his later poetry, such solecistic energies will be exploited to write such narratives as 'Isabella' or 'The Eve of St Agnes', poems which work, not least, through their exposure of the hidden or secret or private. In these early poems, though, what is exposed is the desire to write without exposure, to publish without publication.

'I stood tip-toe' marks a distinct stage in Keats's conceptual development of narrative possibilities and may be read as a poem which makes a certain transition towards the narrative force of the 1819 poems. What distinguishes the poem is a new narrative focus on story-telling itself, marked by a sophisticated manipulation of embedded tales. In Keats's later poetry it is precisely such an awareness and exploitation of the complexities of narrative which constitute one of the most compelling aspects of the poetry. In 'I stood tip-toe' the reciprocal power of narrative is explored and exploited within the terms of the narrative logic of the loco-descriptive mode, a mode which constitutively both produces and resists narration.

The loco-descriptive might be defined in terms of an assertion of adequate visuality, of the plenitudinous indifference of 'nature' to narrative. While the mode presupposes a certain minimal narrativity (the movement from one locus to another), in 'I stood tip-toe' the resistance to narrative is rather more forcefully disrupted by the metamorphic potential implicitly embedded within the mythological subtext of natural enumeration. What John Clare objected to in Keats's 'constant alusion or illusion to the grecian mythology' – the 'wearisome' anthropomorphism of the sense that 'behind every rose bush he looks for a Venus & under every laurel a thrumming Apollo' (*Heritage*, pp. 155, 156) – means that as descriptions are constantly invaded and overwhelmed by mythological characters, they are, in various ways, inhabited by stories. Description constantly fractures – from the articulation of an autonomous, self-identical perceptual

I/eye – into the proliferating dispersal constituted by narration. Keats's rage for description which overwhelms narration in earlier poems is, in 'I stood tip-toe', turned into a rage for narration.[16] What starts out for the first 100 lines as eighteenth-century loco-descriptive verse filtered through the diction of Leigh Hunt, modulating to Wordsworthian musings on the mythological origins of art, becomes, at line 141, a catalogue of compressed embedded narrations: in a paradigmatic Keatsian inflection of narrative, the mythico-theoretical ponderings on how it feels to be inspired to tell stories begin to produce stories.[17] The tales of Cupid and Psyche, Syrinx and Pan, Narcissus and Echo, Cynthia and Endymion are all compressed and grafted on to this form.

In Keats's early poems, narration acts as a gravitational pull to the transcendental desires for lyric transcendence: if lyric seems to be valued over any other form of poetry, then the poems within which such judgements are made continually digress from the stated ideal. Keats's other major poetic achievement of 1816 is the most profoundly proleptic of his early poems, 'Sleep and Poetry'. The tensions of narrative are apparent in the narratorial desires, the changes of tense, and the episodic structure of the poem. A brief summary of the little narratives which inhabit and constitute the narration of 'Sleep and Poetry' might suggest ways in which the gravitational pull of narrative produces poetry. At line 96 Keats's major narrative of this poem begins, the proleptic narrative of his potential creative future figured as a series of allegorized actions. The different stages through which the poet must pass are represented as various evolving scenes. Breaking off at line 162, Keats then devotes three verse-paragraphs to the story of the attenuation of poetry from its apotheosis in classical myth, to the insignificance of the Augustan couplet. Having narrated the decline and fall of poetry, Keats is then in a position to claim that there is a renascence in the early nineteenth century, and he can return to his theme of finding metaphors and similes for poetry (lines 235–47) which modulates to an extended allegory beginning at line 248. But with the perception of the contemporary renewal of poetry comes the realization that a poet in 'whining boyhood' (line 273) may be understood to be speaking presumptuously, and the remainder of the poem is taken up with a reconsideration of the poet's relationship with poetry. The significance is clear: from the exploitation of conventional narrative form, in which 'discourse' provides an account of the 'story' (albeit often in the future tense) the emphasis is reversed and the focus is now on the mode of writing rather than on an allegorized vision of the written text. What is most clearly and most urgently missing from 'Sleep and Poetry', is any sense of the narrative situation – the relationship between the three elements of teller-tale-reader – which is such a crucial element in Keats's development as a poet, and in the de-idealization of poetic discourse. The intense luxury of language and perception allows no space for a disruption of narcissistic self-reflection: solecism in 'Sleep and Poetry' – and the whole poem may be understood as a solecism – excludes the public.

Both 'I stood tip-toe' and 'Sleep and Poetry' are instructive, however, in two ways: firstly, the use of embedded tales and embedded tellings provided Keats with a major source of narrative texture in his later poetry, a valuable training in the art of narrative stratification, and in the production of levels to transgress, as well as in a method of manipulating reader response by means of what we might term 'telling interludes' (the hypothetical reader learns how to read poetry empathically by understanding the empathic process of poetic creation). Secondly, Keats's continuing preoccupation with the relationship between the 'real' world and the transcendental/classical/timeless/mythological is emphasized in his failure to tell a story. This failure is generated in some part, at least, by a desire for what we might define as non-narrative form: the choice of sleep as both a substitute for and the inspiration of poetry signals an attempt to escape the restrictions and confinements of linear narrative. In the poetry of sleep, narrative order may be disregarded so that, in the logic of dreams, any set of arbitrarily related 'incidents' tends to be symbolically and therefore causally related simply because they are dreamt within a single dream. By contrast, the double logic of progressive contingency and retroactive necessity is rather more demanding, and dreams therefore tend to be bad models for stories. Indeed, the copulative grammar of 'Sleep and Poetry' simultaneously asserts identity in the two titular categories and distinguishes between them: this is an early example of the generative tensions involved in the desire to escape narrative through sleep – concomitant with the attempt to escape into the lyric mode – in Keats's poetry. But Keats's use of embedded tales signals the need for narrative, for plot, a necessity which becomes rather more urgent in his extended version of the Endymion myth, where sleep and plotting again conflict. The failure may be understood to have been occasioned by the implicit audience for the poems – those friends that surround Keats, sharing his experience of English weather and Hampstead mores.[18] In later poems, the potential antagonism of audience and the ironies, paradoxes and contradictions which this produces, will be one of the most important generative forces in Keats's poetry.

ENDYMION

Roland Barthes has described narrative in terms of an '*espace dilatoire*', a space which involves digression in order to achieve a particular 'end' – as Peter Brooks glosses it, a space 'of retard, postponement, error, and partial revelation ... the place of transformation: where the problems posed to and by initiatory desire are worked out and worked through'.[19] Paradoxically, the dilatory *espacement* of narrative, far from simply constituting a resistance to or interruption of narrative, is the necessary mode of narrative itself: dilation is the paradigmatic organizational structure of narrative. And, as Patricia Parker has suggested, the rhetorical figure of dilation involves the double topic of the present study – narrative and audience – in that it involves both 'speaking at large', and dilatoriness or delay: the 'link between verbal dilation and temporal delay' is that speaking at large leads to delay.[20] If we discuss *Endymion* in terms of the dilatory, the digressive, the delaying, then, we shall also be considering ways in which the poem engages with questions of audience.

The *reductio ad absurdum* of dilation would be a poem such as *Endymion*: an attempt to 'make 4,000 Lines of one bare circumstance and fill them with Poetry'. The dilation necessary for such poetic fulfilment is apparent in the poem's lexical and descriptive abundance, from a poet who tends, anyway, to be 'overlanguaged' (*Heritage*, p. 361). But Keats defended such indecorous expansion, in his well-known letter on *Endymion* and 'invention':

> Besides a long Poem is a test of Invention which I take to be the Polar Star of Poetry, as Fancy is the Sails, and Imagination the Rudder. Did our great Poets ever write short Pieces? I mean in the shape of Tales – This same invention seems i{n}deed of late Years to have been forgotten as a Poetical excellence{.} (*Letters*, vol. I, p. 170)

Indeed, as Keats points out, he is going against the early nineteenth-century grain when he valorizes invention, a category of rhetoric with a distinguished history, but of late reduced under the influence of the imagination (by, for example, both Sir Joshua Reynolds and William Wordsworth[21]). Samuel Johnson's discussion of Pope's 'invention' suggests an interesting connection with dilation: Johnson defines invention as the means by which 'new trains of events are formed, and new scenes of imagery displayed ... and by which extrinsick and adventitious embellishments and illustrations are connected with a known subject'.[22] If we take as the 'known subject' the tale of Endymion's love for Cynthia – so lucidly narrated to his sister by Keats in about 200 words (*Letters*, vol. I, p. 154) – then the 4,000 lines are well described as 'extrinsick and adventitious': dilation.[23] As Keats recognizes in his letter, in the early nineteenth century such dilation was itself a solecism: such writing was open to charges of digression, irrelevance, prolixity, delay, dilatoriness. But as Keats also recognizes, this has not always been the case: the *OED* quotes Dryden as saying that 'The first happiness of the poet's imagination is properly invention, or finding of the thought' (from the Preface to *Annus Mirabilis*), and even more pertinent is an earlier appraisal of invention by George Gascoigne in 1575: 'The first and most necessarie poynt that euer I founde meete to be considered in making of a delectable poeme is this, to grounde it upon some fine inuention. For it is not inough to roll in pleasant woordes'.[24] The distinction between 'roll[ing] in pleasant woordes' and grounding a poem in 'some fine inuention' is crucial to Keats's early poetry – particularly *Endymion*: what propels the poem is the energy generated by the tension between rolling in words and the necessity and impossibility of invention. Invention thus becomes at once digressive, expansive, delaying, dilatory and the source of onward progression, of narrative impulsion.[25] At the same time, the extent of dilation in *Endymion* produces a poem implicitly solecistic, always encroaching on the tedious and overly expansive, a poem which constantly threatens to explode the boundaries of its own narrative.

The senses of dilation which we have delineated, then, the senses of expansion and of delay, are also dissected, and dilated, by the distinction between space and time: this latter distinction (expanding in space, delaying and expanding in time) is crucial for Keats's *Endymion*. What Patricia Parker has described as 'the poem's hidden conflict' is the paradox of 'the tension between the perpetually forward, or displaced, movement of questing and the dilation of the present moment into a totality of presence, an *espacement* which simultaneously embowers'.[26] Keats's *Endymion* is a romance which threatens the scandal of exploded form: it is a *reductio ad absurdum* of the dilation of narrative.

The temporal pole of dilation in *Endymion* is evident in many ways, not least in the delaying tactics employed by Keats himself, who uses the poem to traverse what, in the Preface to the poem, he calls the 'space of life between' a boy and a man,[27] and in the temporal implications of dilating 200 words into 4,000 lines. But there is also a sense in which Keats provides his own metanarrative commentary with the paronomastic elliptical compression of 'space': 'a space of life between' becomes an important metaphor in *Endymion*, where 'space' means 'time' on a number of occasions. In book 2, line 612, 'every minute's space' is so spatialized that the temporality of 'space' seems at once decisive and ineffable:

> Long he dwells
> On this delight; for, every minute's space,
> The streams with changed magic interlace   (2, 611–13)

Space interlaces with time. A similar effect is achieved some 200 lines later, when the intertextual transformations of the tale of Endymion are being described: a poet heard the 'ditty' sung by a lake...

> and in it he did fling
> His weary limbs, bathing an hour's space,
> And after, straight in that inspired place
> He sang the story up into the air,
> Giving it universal freedom.   (2, 835–9)

The espaced time of 'an hour's space' modulates to de-spatialization when the story is freed into the air ('enskied'). During Glaucus's narration of his life history, narrative time is spatialized in his request to 'pass a cruel, cruel space' of time (3, 639) without narrating it. Finally, less than 100 lines later, there is a complete conflation of time and space in the ambiguity of 'space' in Glaucus's prophetic book:

> *all lovers tempest-tost,*
> *And in the savage overwhelming lost,*
> *He shall deposit side by side, until*
> *Time's creeping shall the dreary space fulfil*   (3, 703–6)

In another poem, the sonnet 'To J. R.', Keats most succinctly exposes a yearning for dilation and collapses the distinction between time and space: 'O that a week could be an age', he cries,

> So could we live long life in little space;
> So time itself would be annihilate;

> So a day's journey, in oblivious haze
>   To serve our joys, would lengthen and dilate.[28]

But the temporal/spatial solecism of 'space' is simply the most
economical conflation of the two orders in this poem, the least
dilated:[29] more overt, and with far more dilation and dilatory delay,
are the digressive structure of the poem and the spatial digressions of
Endymion. As Stuart Sperry has said, 'the poem is labyrinthine and
overgrown, a little wilderness amid whose tangles one can wander
happily but at the risk of becoming lost': metaphors of teeming space
borrowed from the poem ('labyrinthine', 'overgrown', 'wilderness',
'tangles', 'wander', 'lost') become inevitable whenever critics
attempt to describe its form.[30] Once again, Keats's letters provide the
key to such wandering dilation:

Do not the Lovers of Poetry like to have a little Region to wander in where
they may pick and choose, and in which the images are so numerous that
many are forgotten and found new in a second Reading: which may be food
for a Week's stroll in the Summer? (*Letters*, vol. 1, p. 170)

The dilatory narrative structure of *Endymion* is in marked contrast to
the urgency with which Keats announces his intentions to write in the
induction to the poem (1, 34–62): the temporal development of
narrative is here contrasted with that of its discursive formation. The
sense of narratorial urgency conflicts with the luxuriance of natural
description in the passage – 'roll[ing] in pleasant woordes' against
'fine inuention': 'I will begin / Now ... / Now' (1, 39–41); 'Many
and many a verse I hope to write, / Before ... ' (1, 49–50); 'and ere
yet ... / ... I must be near the middle of my story. / O may no wintry
season, bare and hoary, / See it half finished' (1, 51–5); 'And now at
once, adventuresome, I send' (1, 58); 'and quickly dress / My
uncertain path with green, that I may speed / Easily onward' (1,
60–62). Such narratorial urgency is unmatched by any urgency on
the level of narrative (the discursive delays of Endymion's journey) in
a tale which dilates and delays, which digresses, repeats, and rolls
around in and with words. The problematics of starting are related to
the implicitly solecistic dilatory structure of the poem: the poem
cannot begin because it doesn't know how to end.

With this dilation into the thematics of delay in mind, we may
survey *Endymion* briefly with the intention of seeing (a) how Keats
effects expansion and delay in his prolix poem, and (b) ways in which
embedded narrations are used to expand the poem on the one hand,

and on the other to attempt to deal with an anxiety of audience by providing both narrative energies and models for readers to follow. Ultimately, if any pleasure is to be had from Keats's poem, it must be taken from the paradox of the dilatory space which, expanding and delaying, digresses towards the end. Our pleasure must be found in the fact that the convolutions of narrative simply represent an extreme mode of plotting: 'Plot', as Peter Brooks puts it, 'is a kind of arabesque or squiggle toward the end'.[31]

One major technique of 'filling' the dilatory space of 4,000 lines of narrative is to graft alien stories on to the frame of the main plot. What we have referred to as narrative nostalgia, the invocation and evocation of mythological, literary, and folk tales which figure in, and to an extent disfigure, the early poems, finds its place in *Endymion*, where, as well as dilation, it provides alternative narrative energies to the brief story of Endymion. The organization of *Endymion* revolves around and evolves through surrogate texts – rather than Susan Wolfson's 'subtext' (Keats's '"feverish attempt" to write "verses fit to live"'[32]) – and surrogate plots – as opposed to the convention of subplots.[33] Although critics have attempted to read a certain thematic coherence into the embedded tales,[34] it seems impossible to integrate them into a reading of the poem as a whole: they resist reduction to what Peter Brooks defines as the classical subplot – 'a different solution to the problems worked through by the main plot' or illustrations of 'the danger of short-circuit'.[35] Therefore, we might term the dilatory delays in the narrative progression of *Endymion* 'surrogate stories', stories which stand in for the main plot by providing narrative energy lacking in the dilated tale of *Endymion* as it wanders from its narrative path.[36] The surrogate stories figure a fissure in the narrative of *Endymion* which is marked by the irreducible tensions between story and discourse, the need to 'fill' 4,000 lines.

It is at the end of the hymn to Pan that the first substantial evidence of surrogacy occurs: the stories which follow seem to be generated by the idea of 'some strange history, potent to send / A young mind from its bodily tenement' (1, 324–5), words which are followed by thirty lines of stories, sending the young poet from his narrative tenement. The catalogic surrogacy of the tales of Hyacinth and Zephyr, Niobe, and the Argonauts, seems to explain, formally, Keats's avid consumption of such story-collections as Ovid's *Metamorphosis*, Dante's *Divine Comedy*, Boccaccio's *Decameron*, Chaucer's

Canterbury Tales, Burton's *Anatomy of Melancholy*, and the classical and mythological dictionaries of Lemprière, Tooke, and Spence (see *KC*, vol. II, p. 148). But these overt allusions to traditional narratives are not the only surrogates: as in earlier poems, in *Endymion* Keats's very descriptivity verges on narrative at all times. The continuous belligerence of narrative and description produces an unstable narrative form: description is continually articulated in terms of allegory, of the narrative implicit in anthropomorphism. For example, the early lines, 'the dew / Had taken fairy phantasies to strew / Daisies upon the sacred sward last eve, / And so the dawned light in pomp receive' (1, 91–4), personify the dew in order to write a fallacious narrative of natural function, an Ovidian metamorphosis of explanation.[37] On the other hand, although the elders, in 'vieing to rehearse / Each one his own anticipated bliss' (1, 372–3) describe non-narrative (because eternal or eternally recurring) actions, each 'bliss' provides a minimal narrative of hypothesis and aspiration. And the competitive action of story-telling provides a model of telling which displays a deep indeterminacy of telling in the line 'Thus all out-told / Their fond imaginations' (1, 392–3): 'out-told' might mean 'told out' – like 'spelt out' – but it also suggests boastful competition as if they are out-telling each other, so that 'fond' employs its full semantic weight, in both 'eager' and 'foolish'. It is not insignificant, then, that Peona takes Endymion away before attempting to exchange stories: reading the episode as an embedded narrative of poetic production, we might read into this drama the anxiety of a young poet whose sense of 'the Public' involves a conception of the corrosive nature of publication and popularity.

The hypotheses which Peona makes about Endymion's melancholy are significantly couched in terms of surrogate stories:

> Hast thou sinn'd in aught
> Offensive to the heavenly powers? Caught
> A Paphian dove upon a message sent?
> Thy deathful bow against some deer-herd bent,
> Sacred to Dian? Haply, thou hast seen
> Her naked limbs among the elders green;
> And that, alas! is death. (1, 508–14)

It is almost as if *Endymion* could be sent along an alternative narrative path, and one way to understand these surrogate tales is within the poem's own rhetoric of wandering and mazes: they are dilatory dead-ends, paths not taken in the search for story. Although

Peona's hypotheses are incorrect, however, they do have the effect of engendering the true story of Endymion's apathy. Peona's stories generate the impulse to narrate, and this is one of the central narratorial urges in *Endymion*: to exchange stories for stories. But before narrating, Endymion makes the curious assertion that it is Peona who is 'pale' and suffering from an 'ailment' (1, 517, 519): he explains this as Peona's reaction to 'the change / Wrought suddenly in me' (1, 520–21) and asks 'What indeed more strange? / Or more complete to overwhelm surmise?' (1, 521 2). Surmise is precisely what Peona's hypothetical stories (surrogate tales to mend her ignorance) have attempted: figured within *Endymion*, surrogate stories are constructed as surmise, but surmise itself as lost within textual mazes and labyrinths – overwhelmed by narrative.

Like the impacted resonances of 'space', this overwhelmed surmise points to another series of paronomastic matrices which structure the poem and figure reading:

> maze – amaze
> wander – wonder
> wilderness – bewilder

These words (and their cognates – mazy, amazement(s), wanderer, wandering(s), wondering, wonderment, wonderful, wondrous, wild(s), wilderness, wildering, wilder'd – as well as other hints, like the conjunction of 'entanglements, enthralments' at 1, 797) provide an undilated, a minimally extended key to the narrative structure of the poem. As this schema makes clear, there is a significant homology between physical wandering or disordered space on the one hand, and imaginative or mental wonder(ing) or confusion on the other. There is, in these words, a meeting of the micro- with the macro-narrative: they express, in small, the narrative macro-structure of *Endymion*. Indeed, these homologies threaten aporia in their extremities of scope. This is most clearly the case when the concepts are deliberately convoluted – for example, when Venus tells Endymion to

> 'still obey the guiding hand that fends
> Thee safely through these wonders for sweet ends'   (2, 574–5)

where 'wonders' are also 'wanders'; or when Endymion declares:

> 'No, never more
> Shall airy voices cheat me to the shore
> Of tangled wonder, breathless and aghast'   (4, 653–5)

where wonder is itself (spatially) tangled; or in a description of Endymion's wandering:

> Verdant cave and cell
> He wander'd through, oft wondering at such swell
> Of sudden exaltation   (2, 678–80)

where the proximity of the two words makes identification inevitable; or when 'amaze' is a substantive, as in:

> Hereat, she vanished from Endymion's gaze,
> Who brooded o'er the water in amaze   (2, 131–2)

so that 'in amaze' is also 'in a maze' (here, again, space signifies, in the paronomastic elision of typographical spacing between 'a' and 'maze'). If Endymion wonders in his wandering, if he is amazed by mazes and bewildered by wilderness, there is an important sense in which reading itself is subject to wondering, amazement, and bewilderment by the confusing and dilated organization of the poem – a sense which Keats emphasizes in writing of readers who can 'wander' through a poem in order to 'pick and choose'.[38] The paronomastic wondering wandering presents a crucial figure of reading in *Endymion*. And this wandering structure, often rightly criticized as unreadable, should be valued for the bemusement which it offers. It is precisely this sense of narrative defamiliarization, the bemused confusion produced by the tangled, dilatory narrative of *Endymion* that marks the poem's generative solecism.

Surrogate stories abound in the complex embeddings, the wandering narrative line of *Endymion*. The paradigmatic surrogate story is that of Glaucus which takes up most of Book Three, a narrative which one critic has called 'pure narrative'.[39] Despite the fact that Glaucus 'had not from mid-life to utmost age / Eas'd in one accent his o'er-burden'd soul, / Even to the trees' (3, 228–30), his autobiography is told with the consummate skill of a practised story-teller. In a sense, we might consider the 'Glaucus episode' as providing a model for story-telling: both the frame narrative (Endymion's meeting with Glaucus) and Glaucus's embedded story benefit from an *histoire* sufficiently expansive for the dilation of *discours* (a *discours* which is 400 lines instead of 4,000). Endymion's enchanted response to the tale presents a figured reading with which to direct our response. Indeed, what looks like a digression problematizes the notion of the relationship between narrative and digression itself: the amount of narrative material impacted within Book Three, its internal consistency of point and continual narrative interest, contrasts with the overtly time-serving nature of *Endymion* as a whole. To the extent that the inset story provides a model of narrative tact and coherence, it might be argued that the relationship of frame to the framed is overturned, and that we see the Endymion story within the terms of the exemplary inset narrative: just as Glaucus is subservient to his prophetic book, *Endymion* is subservient to the narrative standards set by the tale of Glaucus. That Book Four opens with a sceptical critique of story-telling only reinforces the view that the digression of Book Three presents a protocol for narrative form.

It is this which eventually leads to Endymion's own disillusionment with his fantasy life (4, 615ff.). The narrator's boredom or dis-illusionment with his tale is quite explicit: 'so on / I move to the end in lowliness of heart' (4, 28–9). Similarly, in despair, Endymion reduces his tale to a minimum – he will die soon, he says, 'And all my story that much passion slew me' (4, 114). This narrative negation, the sense that stories are worthless, is met, in answer to Endymion, by Phoebe's narrative scepticism, when, parodying his melancholy, she asks

> 'Do the brooks
> Utter a gorgon voice? Does yonder thrush,
> Schooling its half-fleg'd little ones to brush
> About the dewy forest, whisper tales?' (4, 128–31)

So that when Endymion says, at last, 'no more of dreaming' (4, 669), he means, too, and Keats means, 'no more of story-telling'.

Such narrative suspicion is evinced by the renewed conflations of narratorial level in Book Four lines 30–97, where Endymion first sees the Indian maid: not only is the tale told in the present tense, but the narrator actually addresses his hero, Endymion. The anxieties of narration infect the decorum of narrative form. Book Four is, if anything, more wandering, more labyrinthine and dilatory than the previous three, as Keats himself seems to recognize when he breaks off at line 770:

> Endymion! unhappy! it nigh grieves
> Me to behold thee thus in last extreme:
> Ensky'd ere this, but truly that I deem
> Truth the best music in a first-born song.
> Thy lute-voic'd brother will I sing ere long,
> And thou shalt aid – hast thou not aided me?
> Yes, moonlight Emperor! felicity
> Has been thy meed for many thousand years;

> Yet often have I, on the brink of tears,
> Mourn'd as if yet thou wert a forester; –
> Forgetting the old tale.   (4, 770–80)

This is destructive in its unlacing of the formal levels of narrative, and deconstructive in its reversal of the logic of story and discourse: the conflation of Endymion the character within Keats's tale, and Endymion the mythological 'Emperor' distinct from any particular telling, is achieved by the coincidence of address in this verse-paragraph (thee – thy – thou), and disturbs the characterological illusion of narrative. The narrator's grief, which we can share, that Endymion has not yet been 'Ensky'd' leads, it seems, to a frustrated critique of the very foundations of narrative discourse.

When *Endymion* works, I suggest, it does so by employing the narrative energies of supplementary or surrogate tales. And the poem works best when Keats is able to digress from the narratively limited story of Endymion and create other tales. In particular the surrogate tales provide figures of reading which suggest the importance of narrative economy and the self-destructive dilatoriness of *Endymion*'s wandering form. The neglect of narrative form, itself a neglect of or refusal to acknowledge audience, will never again structure Keats's poetry.

CHAPTER 4

'Isabella'

It seems likely that one of the motives for writing 'Isabella' was Keats's desire to make money – that is, to find a public for his poetry. As Herbert Wright has shown, translations and rewritten tales from Boccaccio were particularly popular in the early nineteenth century, and critics often refer to a comment by Hazlitt in his lecture 'On Dryden and Pope' to the effect that such translations 'could not fail to succeed in the present day'.[1] Together with his friend John Hamilton Reynolds, Keats planned to write a series of such translations and publish them as a commercial venture.[2] The tensions and antagonisms that we have seen in Keats's construction of the 'public', however, make any such project problematic. In 'Isabella' Keats's anxiety of audience is suggested most clearly by ways in which space is constructed around inclusion and exclusion, the inside and the outside. The multiple thematics of space in 'Isabella' include, in particular, elaborations of secrecy and publication, of the phenomenon of voice, and of the semiotics of what I shall call 'inner space'.[3]

The thematics of secrecy and of inner and outer space in 'Isabella' can be enumerated as follows: the secrecy of the lovers' affair and their inability to reside in the same house without an expression of passion; the secrecy of the brothers' plotting; their taking of Lorenzo into the woods to kill him and their burying him in the ground; their secrecy as to his fate; Isabella's private vision of Lorenzo's ghost; Isabella's secret journey to disinter Lorenzo and to remove his head from the ground; her reburial of Lorenzo's head in the pot; the excrescence of the head by way of the basil plant; Isabella's secret and inward grief, outwardly expressed in tears; the brothers' exhumation of the head; the brothers' escape (out of the house and out of the poem); the outward expression of Isabella's grief in the public song which circles round and (en)closes the poem. These thematic polarities of secrecy and space are also suggested by the verbal pressure of language in the poem, a poem in which, as John Barnard has commented, the sense of 'claustrophobic physical and mental violence is all'.[4] This is evident in the stanza form itself, which applies inward pressure on the language – an enclosing delimitation of linguistic invention and narrative dilation. In this way, the lax, flowing expansiveness of *Endymion* becomes far more taut – if repetitive – in 'Isabella', where each stanza demands a separate 'theme' and a separate, minimal dilation on that theme.[5]

What is particularly notable is the association of inwardness with secrecy in, for example, the repetition of the word 'close' in stanza eleven: 'All close they met again... All close they met... Close in a bower... Unknown of any, free from whispering tale' (lines 81–6). Secrecy and inwardness are figured as necessary for safety. This suggests that it is the publication of such knowledge which leads to danger. It is, precisely, the poetic telling of love, the possibility of its becoming public knowledge, which threatens it. Such is the anxiety expressed in stanza eleven:

> All close they met again, before the dusk
>   Had taken from the stars its pleasant veil,
> All close they met, all eves, before the dusk
>   Had taken from the stars its pleasant veil,
> Close in a bower of hyacinth and musk,
>   Unknown of any, free from whispering tale.
> Ah! better had it been for ever so,
> Than idle ears should pleasure in their woe.

The lines elaborate a crucial paradox which determines the figure of reading in 'Isabella': the tragedy of 'Isabella' is constructed by the event of narration, that is by reading. The publication of the tragedy is itself implicated as a cause of that tragedy. In a metaleptic reversal of cause and effect, a kind of reader-response *Nachträglichkeit*, the reader is held responsible for the tragedy he or she is reading. There is a pressure on readers to equate their own 'pleasure' with the 'idle ears' of the audience/public and to draw the unstated conclusion that it is through its reception that the tale becomes tragic. In one sense this can be read as a confusion of the 'double logic' of 'retroactive necessity' and 'progressive contingency' – for the reader, a narrative becomes necessary once it has been told – so that the reader's perception of causality itself leads to the events in the narrative. The 'secret' of 'Isabella' seems to be the secret of reading: readers cause the narrative that they read.[6]

The secrecy, closeness and inwardness of the lovers is matched only by the secrecy of the brothers, who are 'self-retired / In hungry pride and gainful cowardice' (lines 129–30), even before they commit a crime:[7]

> As two close Hebrews in that land inspired,
> Paled in and vineyarded from beggar-spies   (lines 131–2)

Under the pressure of thematic inwardness everything becomes inner and inward: 'close … in … *in*spired … Paled   in … vineyarded'. Under the same pressure we acknowledge the inward force of 'inspired' – breathed into – while we also find, inside the word, the homophony of the next line-ending, 'spies': 'inspired' encloses 'spy' and 'spyer' (one who spies), and sounds very much like 'in-spied'. The word is a linguistic double-agent, exposed by its precarious position at the edge of a line, that paradigmatic locus of liminal poetic space. In the next stanza, however, it is the brothers who are spies: 'How was it these same ledger-men could spy / Fair Isabella in her downy nest?' (lines 137–8). The very locutions seem to revolt against the confines of language: it is as if at each mention of 'in' or inward, there is a linguistic bending of grammar. Thus, for example, having 'unconfined' (line 163) their thoughts to each other, the brothers murder Lorenzo: 'There was Lorenzo slain and buried in, / There in that forest did his great love cease' (lines 217–18). The unusual collocation 'buried in', produces a doubling, a tautology, of inwardness. Similarly, after Isabella has dreamt of Lorenzo, she decides to dig him up, a decision which is announced in the rhetoric of space – 'she the inmost of the dream would try' (line 342): despite the conventional nature of a dream being conceived of as 'inside' or of there being an 'inmost dream', the centre or heart of the secret or private dream, Keats privatizes 'inmost' by bending its grammar into a substantive. In the most problematic stanza, the detailed vicarious horror of which leads to narratorial doubt over 'wormy circumstance', we reach the core of the problem:[8] while Isabella digs for Lorenzo's body, 'That old nurse stood beside her wondering, / Until her heart felt pity to the core' (lines 377–8), an inwardness which is repeated five lines later when they reach the body – 'At last they felt the kernel of the grave'. This gruesome pun – the 'core' of the nurse's heart (at line 424, Isabella moistens the potted head 'with tears unto the core') and the 'kernel of the grave' – seems once again to scandalize the semiotics of inwardness. It would seem that the core of the story is a solecism.[9] But if solecism is conceived in terms of the publication of the private or secret, then this 'core' would itself seem to be solecistic in its transgression of the hermetic or enclosed: paradoxically, the core of 'Isabella', its 'inmost', involves a revelation of that which should remain hidden both thematically and aesthetically. Similarly, the final gruesome inward image, before the generalized inwardness of the introjection of mourning in the last stanzas, is that of the head buried in a pot:

> So that the jewel, safely casketed,
> Came forth, and in perfumed leafits spread.   (lines 431–2)

This seems to parody the thematic inwardness of the poem in its idea that by being safely inside one can 'come forth', and it seems to produce a solecism by suggesting that the 'jewel' (Lorenzo's head) can 'come forth' through the basil plant – a somewhat gruesome if not illegitimate metaphorization of organic growth. Susan Wolfson has commented that 'The pot of basil itself images the kind of story Keats's narrator serves up to the reader... The narrator ruthlessly uncovers this hidden source: beneath the "thick, and green, and beautiful" foliage (line 426), we are made aware of another order of greenery... namely, the rotting head of Lorenzo'.[10] The pathology of the hidden centre in 'Isabella' is figured by the pot of basil: inside both the pot of basil and 'The Pot of Basil' is an uncontainable, scandalous, terrifying, and gruesome secret.

A case could be made for a reading of the poem along the lines of these thematic polarities of inner and outer, but the complexities of writing and publication confuse the issues involved: if the plot hinges on burial and exhumation, the confining and unconfining of bodies and secrets, and on the liminal semiotics of tears (an outward expression of inner grief, a physical signifier of an emotional signified), the generative anxieties of writing – a process which involves an expression of inner tension, a publication of the private – are also a part of this complex duality. The thematic representation of the problematic relationship between inner and outer might be read as an articulation of the problematics of writing with respect to the public nature of poetry and the way in which this conflicts with the Romantic ideology, and with Keats's personal ideology, of poetry as 'expressive' of the inward, the personal, the private.

The problematics of inner and outer as articulated by the thematics of space are also figured in the poem as the impossibility of speaking, the interruption of communication and the difficulties of ex-pression. And figured, too, as the problematics of voice. There are a series of disturbing questions which might be raised in relation to 'voice': in speaking, is 'my' voice inside or outside my face (is it 'in' my throat with my larynx, my lips, teeth, tongue, or is it constituted by sound-waves); in listening, are the voices that I hear inside or outside my ears; in reading 'silently', are the voices inside or outside my head (or are they in my throat)?[11] Keats's 'anxiety of audience' may most generally be described in terms of the publication of the private, the scandalous exposure which is the solecism of Romantic poetry. In 'Isabella', this is figured, in a kind of *mise en abyme*, as the way that the narrative is constructed around the problematics of communication.[12] The story of 'Isabella', of Isabella's love for Lorenzo, of Lorenzo's death, and of Isabella's mourning, is structured around telling and not telling, the giving and withholding of information: the narrative 'moves' are defined by and structured around difficulties in communication. Speaking, then, is both a theme and a structuring device in the poem. But speaking is also problematized in the telling of the poem, and the question of voice operates both on the level of the story and on the level of narration: not only the characters but the narrative itself is constantly hindered in its telling. The speech-acts in 'Isabella' may be read both as indices of plot moves and as a mediating function between story and discourse: not only do the embedded tellings act as narrative 'kernels' for this poem but they also define our relationship with the poem.[13] Our discussion of the conflictual energies of inner and outer has suggested how difficult the pressures of ex-pression might be in this poem.

In the early stanzas, Lorenzo is represented as a disembodied voice – speaking or not speaking, attempting to speak and half-speaking:

> And his continual voice was pleasanter
> To her, than noise of trees or hidden rill   (lines 13–14)

Hyperbolic metonymy fills the second stanza of the poem, and Lorenzo is reduced to a noise: although the noise 'was pleasanter / To her', enjambment points up the irony in the noise of 'voice ... / ... noise' which both asserts and refuses identity (with its similarity in rhyming diphthongs and contrast in voiceless and voiced sibilants). At the same time, the rhymes in this stanza produce the comedy of noise and meaning: 'tenderer ... stir ... pleasanter / To her' puts comic pressure on the 'feminine' endings of the comparative adjectives. Foregrounding the noise of Lorenzo's voice emphasizes the (phonetic) signifier which undergoes a strange transference from the 'character' of Lorenzo to the text itself.

Throughout the first eight stanzas of 'Isabella', the question of telling one's love provides both the obstacle and the generative force for the narrative: the paranoia suggested by William Blake's lyric 'Never seek to tell thy love' is explored in the pathological anxieties of the lovers in 'Isabella'. But the desire of the lovers to tell their love is repeatedly displaced and both the events of the narrative and the event of narration repeatedly deferred:

> 'To-morrow will I bow to my delight,
>   To-morrow will I ask my lady's boon'. –
> 'O may I never see another night,
>   Lorenzo, if thy lips breathe not love's tune'. –
> So spake they to their pillows; but, alas,
> Honeyless days and days did he let pass   (lines 27–32)

What is at stake in declaring love might be understood in terms of the implicit interdiction of this telling by Isabella's brothers. But it is important that the threat of family violence from Isabella's jealous, incestuous and pathological brothers, a violence which might be used to explain the interdiction of Isabella's and Lorenzo's love, is suppressed: rather than the brothers' violence, what threatens is precisely the speech-act of 'declaring' one's love. In this way, the social or public interdiction of family refusal is internalized in two ways: for the brothers, interdiction is constituted as a secret and unspeakable refusal, a refusal which can only be enacted in physical violence and never spoken because it originates not in a refusal of Lorenzo's desire, but in an interdiction of their own unspeakable desire for Isabella;[14] for the lovers, at least for a time, the brothers' pathological interdiction is internalized and results in a physical blockage to speech. The mechanism of this interdiction might be understood in psychoanalytical terms as the transference of the silencing produced by incestuous desire from the brothers to the lovers.

Lorenzo's inability to speak is figured as a physical interdiction of speech, a psychosomatic silencing of voice, such that his voice is stifled and the danger of speaking is figured as potentially life-threatening:

So said he one fair morning, and all day
  His heart beat awfully against his side;
And to his heart he inwardly did pray
  For power to speak; but still the ruddy tide
Stifled his voice, and puls'd resolve away –   (lines 41–5)

Lorenzo finally manages to speak, after Isabella's prompting, in stanza eight, and having spoken, 'his erewhile timid lips grew bold, / And poesied with hers in dewy rhyme' (lines 69–70): with the release of the pressure of censorship, poetry is figured as kissing. Critics have often referred to these two lines as exemplary of Keatsian 'vulgarity':[15] the scandal of Isabella's and Lorenzo's kiss is transferred to the scandal of Keats's poetry itself.

The physical (dis-)articulation of Lorenzo's voice returns notably when Lorenzo's ghost appears to Isabella later in the poem. The most embodied voice of Lorenzo, the disembodied voice of Lorenzo's ghost, displays a narratorial control of diction, imagery, rhythm and tone (a control which is significantly lacking in the limp and repetitive love-speech of stanzas eight and nine). The ghostly voice achieves power in its very strangeness and estrangement from humanity:

Strange sound it was, when the pale shadow spake;
  For there was striving, in its piteous tongue,
To speak as when on earth it was awake,
  And Isabella on its music hung:
Languor there was in it, and tremulous shake,
  As in a palsied Druid's harp unstrung;
And through it moan'd a ghostly under-song,
Like hoarse night-gusts sepulchral briars among.   (lines 281–8)

Again, the strangeness of voice invades Keats's own lines, where the syntax makes the stanza irregular and awkward, especially in the strangely inept and powerful last line – 'Like hoarse night-gusts sepulchral briars among' – where the rhyme (with 'song') fits – almost – (unlike, for example, Lorenzo's 'live' / 'shrive' of stanza eight) although at the expense of grammar. But grammaticality would destroy the strangeness of those four apparently incompatible words 'hoarse night-gusts sepulchral briars', their apparent incoherence until 'among', and the tongue-contortions of the line that repeat, in the reading mouth, Lorenzo's difficulties of speaking. The ghostly effect of Lorenzo's voice produces an estranging of language in Keats's poem, such that the ghost of Lorenzo might be said to haunt not only Isabella but also the language of the poem.[16] And the voice of Lorenzo is transferred to the voicing of reading: the reading voice figures as the ghostly repetition of the voice of Lorenzo.

Once we recognize the congruence in texture of Lorenzo's voice and Keats's poem, then we might also recognize the ghostly undersong of the poem, Boccaccio's text. The relationship between Keats's and Boccaccio's texts is figured as a productive resistance to writing: there is a significant homology between Lorenzo's 'crime' of speaking his love and Keats's 'crime' of rewriting Boccaccio, just as there is a homology between the ghost of Lorenzo which haunts Isabella (and the brothers) and the ghost of Boccaccio, the 'vision pale' (line 392) which haunts Keats's poem (and reading). The lost language which Keats mourns, both eulogizing it and elegizing it, is the '*gentleness* of old Romance, / The simple plaining of a minstrel's song' (lines 387–8, my italics), just as Isabella mourns Lorenzo 'whose *gentleness* did well accord / With death, as life' (lines 395–6, my italics). Boccaccio's prose is more 'real' because apparently more direct, simpler, seemingly closer to the source of the story than a modern-day elaboration: because Boccaccio's language is plainer, his story is unencumbered by a sophisticated rhetoric which for the modern poet mediates the tragic tale, and so easily converts pathos into sentimentality.[17] Keats's poem displays this anxiety in the texture of its rhetoric, an anxiety generated by an intertextual double-bind: there is at the same time a desire to make of the poem a 'simple' romance, and a feeling that a new version of Boccaccio's tale is pointless unless 'sweet', and if 'sweet' then some kind of a crime ('There is no other crime, no mad assail / To make old prose in modern rhyme more sweet', lines 155–6, and 'For here, in truth, it doth not well belong / To speak', lines 390–91).[18] But if this figures as an anxiety towards its source-text, it implicitly acknowledges an anxiety of audience: it is precisely by making public such a rewriting that Keats risks a 'crime'. And, as we have seen, the crime is double: not only does the poem commit a crime against the old romance, but it also commits a crime against Isabella and Lorenzo by telling, once again, their tragedy.

A related anxiety of decorum is expressed when Isabella and her nurse reach 'the kernel' of Lorenzo's grave: after what is, for the Romance genre in the early nineteenth century, a shockingly unabashed description of exhumation in which the poem transgresses the line between Romance and the Gothic,[19] the story turns again in the next stanza, and the poet breaks off from his plot, wrenching himself away from a peculiar fascination with, a fixation on, the wormy circumstances of digging up a dead body:

> Ah! wherefore all this wormy circumstance?
>   Why linger at the yawning tomb so long?
> O for the gentleness of old Romance,
>   The simple plaining of a minstrel's song!
> Fair reader, at the old tale take a glance,
>   For here, in truth, it doth not well belong
> To speak: – O turn thee to the very tale,
> And taste the music of that vision pale.   (lines 385–92)

We might see this self-critical stanza as at the same time a reaction against pandering to the vicarious desires of readers of the Gothic, and a reaction on a formal level against the mode of description. It is not just that there is an improper attention to the macabre, to which Keats is objecting, but that he is concerned about what Roland Barthes calls the 'scandal' of detail in narrative: the anxiety evinced here is not just an aesthetic or social anxiety, but also a narrative-structural anxiety about how and how many details may be introduced in a narrative. Of 'irrelevant' details Barthes comments that 'such notations are scandalous (from the point of view of structure), or, what is even more disturbing, they seem to correspond to a kind of narrative *luxury*, lavish to the point of offering many "futile" details and thereby increasing the cost of narrative information'.[20] The 'irrelevant' detail confirms the 'referential illusion' produced by the text, 'l'effet de réel', at the cost of narration. What is interesting about stanza forty-nine is that the narrator seems to be asking about the value of details, and seems to come to the same conclusion as Barthes on their scandalous nature, without concluding that they are necessary for the 'mimetic contract' between the narrator and reader: the poet has been drawn into the 'luxury' of narration without being able to offer himself a justification for such a process in a poem so concerned with the abuse of luxury.[21] Following Barthes's analysis, we might also notice that the luxury of detail suitable for the 'realism' of a nineteenth-century novel may not be suitable for a medieval romance, or a modern verse-copy of such a tale, genres based not on our suspension of disbelief, but on our willingness not to care about our disbelief: once the narrator starts to introduce detailed information about the method of decapitation, etc., then the reader, in turn, might begin to question the probability of such a process. There is, then, both an anxiety over the social decorum of gruesome description, and a formal narratorial anxiety over the question of detail. This double anxiety produces generative energies for much of Keats's poetry: the friction of luxuriant description and ascetic narration.

The anxieties of narrative and audience in 'Isabella' – the haunting of Isabella's voice by Lorenzo, the haunting of the poetic voice by the phantom of Isabella-Lorenzo-Boccaccio, and the relationship between this haunting and the semiotics of (inner) space, and the haunting reading by the ghostly revenant of poetry – are expressed most explicitly in the rhetoric of eyesight in 'Isabella'. It is my contention that the resistance to telling the narrative, the resistance to publication, to reception, is finally encrypted within a series of semantic displacements around eyes and inspiration, and as such around the complex of signifiers related to the work of writing itself. In order to argue this, we might return to stanza seventeen, to the anti-Semitic metaphor for the brothers as 'two close Hebrews in that land inspired', and, in particular, to the word 'inspired' (line 131). Not only does this stanza play with the semiotics of space, but it also generates a series of signifying chains which might be constructed or configured in various ways. For example:

> inspire – in – spy – eye – (I) – see – gaze – look – watch
> inspire [out in] – weep [in out] – mourn – death – tomb – crypt
> inspire – introject – secrete/hide (encrypt) – seek – spy – inspire
> inspire – write – publish – reveal (secrets) – scandal – crime – murder/incest

As these examples make clear, the precise configuration of such chains has an indefinite number of potential permutations. Moreover, each chain might be glossed in various ways. For example, these four chains might be unravelled to some extent in the following ways: inspired, I spy, I see with the eye that is inside me, my private eye, my I, which sees, gazes, looks, watches (you) and watches Isabella (and the others), and is watched, but which also weeps (and in weeping produces an outing of what is inside, an expiration) because it mourns (Lorenzo/Isabella/Boccaccio), but is an eye which inspires my I ('I see, and sing, by my own eyes inspired'[22]), a writing I/eye, a private writing which has or contains a secret, like a crypt or a tomb (like Lorenzo's tombs), or is itself like a crypt or tomb ('each eye's sepulchral cell', line 404[23]), which is itself haunted by the death of the

I/eye, an eye which still weeps beyond its death ('the continual shower / From her dead eyes', lines 452–3), as Isabella's look looks on dead things and is dead ('she look'd on dead and senseless things', line 489), and within these secret inspirations, these semantic spies, I find encrypted the problematics of writing, of publishing what should remain hidden, of publishing secrets, scandals and, finally, the subtextual and never spoken, the unspeakable crime of (murder) incest.

A full analysis of these connections, associations, convolute collocations, allosemes, puns, displacements and veilings and un-veilings would be endless, of course. Nevertheless, there is enough in this list, generated from the intense concentration on the word 'inspired', configured as it is by the semiotics of space and sight, and by the problematics of voice and writing, to see that the question of publication is deeply fraught. In particular, this is suggested by the tensions between inspiration – as an incorporation *through the eye* – on the one hand, and on the other by weeping – as an extrusion or expiration of secret passion (everybody weeps in this poem because everybody has a secret), again, *through the eye*. (Weeping: after re-burying, re-encrypting, the head of Lorenzo beneath a basil plant, Isabella's eyes alter their function, from agents of sight to fountains of nurturing moisture, as the text becomes fixated on tears: 'the smeared loam / With tears... She drench'd away... and still she kiss'd, and wept... and o'er it set / Sweet basil, which her tears kept ever wet... And moisten'd it with tears unto the core. / And so she ever fed it with thin tears... the continual shower / From her dead eyes... weeping through her hair', lines 405–72). And within the undecidable disturbance in the functioning of eyes is inscribed the act of writing, the uncanny production of poetry as both inspiration (seeing things, breathing in, being inspired, writing poetry) and expiration (dying, breathing out, but also weeping, mourning, writing poetry).

Who are the spies in this narrative? As we have seen, the two brothers are protected from spies outside their house, they are 'Paled in and vineyarded from beggar-spies' (line 132), but they also spy, and so are spies of Isabella: 'these same ledger-men could spy / Fair Isabella' (lines 137–8), and stanza eighteen provides a full description of the brothers' visual paranoia. Curiously, though, the brothers' secret scopophilia is repeated by Isabella's lover. Lorenzo is a spy, an obsessive watcher of Isabella, from the very start of the poem:

Lorenzo, 'a young palmer in Love's eye' (line 2) (even Love is scopophilic), can't take his eyes off Isabella – 'He might not in house, field or garden stir, / But her full shape would all his seeing fill' (lines 11–12). Both Lorenzo and the brothers have extraordinarily acute eyesight: all three are spies and have eyes like hawks – Lorenzo 'Her beauty farther than the falcon spies' (line 20), and the brothers are described as 'The hawks of ship-mast forests' (line 133). The desiring eyesight of Lorenzo, then, is also that of the brothers: in both cases, sexual desire (in the brothers' case, displaced into paranoid, pathological possessiveness about their possessions, financial or familial) is figured in terms of sight.

Although Lorenzo's vision doesn't necessarily rely on light-waves or sight-lines, it is nevertheless curiously physical:

> He knew whose gentle hand was at the latch,
> Before the door had given her to his eyes;
> And from her chamber-window he would catch
> Her beauty farther than the falcon spies   (lines 17–20)

Isabella's full shape *fills* Lorenzo's 'seeing', the door *gives* her to his eyes, he *catches* her beauty. And at the same time, Lorenzo's gaze becomes both a trap and a spy: she is given to his gaze, so becomes his (visual) property, he catches her beauty, spies on her, watches her. Lorenzo's obsessive concentration of the eye will be repeated in 'The Eve of St Agnes', where the text concentrates on the activity of looking rather than on the gazing eye itself. In 'St Agnes', sight-lines will be figured as guides to the reader's gaze;[24] in 'Isabella' eyes would seem to problematize the very notion of poetic vision and therefore the notion of writing and publishing.

And the power of eyes, the power of spies, is always apparent. In Lorenzo's declaration of love, he suggests the terror of this pervasive sight in an irreducibly double locution:

> I would not grieve
> Thy hand by unwelcome pressing, would not tear
> Thine eyes by gazing   (lines 61–3)

Does this action of gazing at another's eyes make one afraid, or is it that by gazing at another's eyes one might make those eyes fearful? (Perhaps it is a proleptic fear of what his own eyes give away: it is Lorenzo's eyes, of course, which give away his secret lust to the brothers, who 'find out in Lorenzo's eye / A straying from his toil', lines 139–40). But it is the phantom's uncannily living eyes that keep fear *away* from Isabella when she has her vision of the dead Lorenzo:

> Its eyes, though wild, were still all dewy bright
> With love, and kept all phantom fear aloof
> From the poor girl by magic of their light   (lines 289–91)

Later, though, it is Isabella's eyes that signify, when, after Lorenzo's death, she weeps and 'His image in the dusk she seem'd to see' (line 237). Asking her brothers for their murdered man, she must control her eye:

> Oftentimes
> She ask'd her brothers, with an eye all pale,
> Striving to be itself   (lines 257–9)

The identity of the eye is figured as the identity of the I, the self. But this self of the eye implicitly connects with the eye of the reader.[25] The reader's eyes – those inspired spies of reading – are also figured in the eyes of Isabella: earlier, the tragedy of the love story is produced in part by our sight of too many such stories (line 93), later we are asked to 'glance' at Boccaccio's tale (line 389) and to 'taste the music of that vision pale' (line 392), and now, as Isabella goes to disinter Lorenzo, we are asked, in a final scandalous prosopopoeial turn of reading, to 'See, as they creep along the river side' (line 345).

To summarize the strategies of writing and audience in 'Isabella': there is a double interdiction of love – the interdiction of the brothers against the love of Isabella and Lorenzo, but also the unstated and unspeakable incestuous love of the brothers for Isabella which is itself both interdicted by society and generative of the brothers' interdiction of Lorenzo's love. The interdiction of love leads to Lorenzo's and Isabella's incorporation of this interdiction and their inability to speak their love, leading to a concentration on the problematics of voice and finally on the ghostly voice of Lorenzo, which Isabella has incorporated into her own voice by the end of the poem.[26] This interdiction, both private and social, is, precisely, the inability to speak a private love, to publicize love: in 'Isabella' the expression of love is itself a scandal or solecism.[27] And just as Isabella and Lorenzo incorporate this interdiction into the structure of their love, so Keats's poem similarly incorporates a tension between private and public, producing the crypt of love in 'Isabella': the text's obsession with secrets and crypts itself seems to function as a form of concealment (a concealment which also, of course, necessarily reveals). These secrets produce guilt in the narrator and in the narrative (over the question of rewriting Boccaccio), which is then transferred to the cause of that guilt (publication), and therefore the reader: the narrator's guilt as a reader and murderer of Boccaccio is transferred to the reader as the guilt of the murder of Isabella and Lorenzo but also, presumably, of Keats. The audience must, finally, turn their eyes away and look elsewhere just as they turn their eyes away at the scandalous stanzas describing the disinterment of Lorenzo. The invocations to Melancholy to 'turn thine eyes away' (line 481), with which the poem ends, also suggest that the complicit reader should turn his or her eyes away: just as the Preface to *Endymion* suggests that the poem should not be read, so the implicit dynamics of *Nachträglichkeit* in 'Isabella' suggest that the reader's guilt can only be assuaged by turning away from the poem, by not reading. In this sense, our suggestion that the gruesome secret of 'Isabella' involves incest should be understood as an inherently paradoxical reading to the extent that what is pathological about such secrets and therefore about the poem is their resistance to the revelation of what lies at their 'heart': the claim that this reading has disinterred the unspeakable secret, incest, in 'Isabella' would, strictly speaking, be laughable. Instead, incest should be understood as a metonym for the unspeakable, unpresentable core of 'Isabella', a metonym for what this reading cannot know.[28]

If, as Jack Stillinger suggests, the 'main attitude' of critics towards 'Isabella' is 'puzzlement',[29] then this reception is prefigured or configured by the 'secrets' interred in the text: Stillinger's point is not, of course, that critics don't 'understand' the poem, it is not that they feel that there is a hidden secret which they cannot fathom: rather, they are unable satisfactorily to figure the poem within the terms of their narratives of Keatsian development – primarily a question of genre, or tone, or technique, or aesthetic achievement. I have attempted to suggest ways in which what is 'hidden' in the poem (what can never be seen, or read, or spoken) fractures the surface of the poem – fractures the homogeneity of genre, tone, technique, aesthetic achievement – so that critics' 'puzzlement' is figured by the unspeakable secret(s) interred within the (narrative) structure of the Pot of Basil.

CHAPTER 5

'The Eve of St Agnes'

Throughout Keats's career the oppositions generated by the semiotics of vision (imagining/seeing, blindness/sight, words/images, language/painting) provided crucial organizing principles for his poetry: there is not only a constant self-conscious reference to 'The Poet's eye',[1] to the importance of poetic visions, but also an articulation of visionary seeing that often paradoxically precludes sensory apprehension. Indeed, in some of Keats's most famous, his most achieved poetry, the line of vision is profoundly central to the narrative movement of the poem. Despite recent critical interest in the semiotics of perception in the early nineteenth century and despite critics' recognition of the importance of sensory perception to the form and content of Keats's poetry, little work has been done on the relationship between the visual and the visionary in his poetry on the one hand, and on the other hand on the problematic representation of these visions in descriptive language. 'The Eve of St Agnes', in particular, despite recent work on the poem and 'vision' by Stuart Ende and Leon Waldoff, has been overlooked in this respect.[2]

As a number of critics have noted, 'The Eve of St Agnes' involves a double plot, or, at least, a double plotting:[3] while Porphyro requires a visual embodiment of his desires and a physical consummation of those desires, Madeline requires a vision of her desires and a visionary dream of a consummation. This provides Keats with the narrative friction that generates the poem.[4] But around this friction of plotting may be discerned several other frictions: the friction of gender – male/female desires; the friction of narration – the production and disruption of narrative in description; the friction of the antagonism of the visionary to the visible; the friction between sleeping and waking; the friction of response – the conflict between the desires of the poet and those of his reader; and the (related) friction of the reader's gender – the question of male/female reception. Friction generates heat, just as irritability generates life in the eighteenth- and nineteenth-century discourse of physiology: out of the frictions and irritations of 'St Agnes' Keats produced his most seductive narrative poem. And perhaps the most decisive and influential binary opposition in the twentieth-century criticism of 'The Eve of St Agnes', that between the transcendentalism of Wasserman and the voyeurism of Stillinger, may be understood in terms of description, which, as Michel Beaujour has pointed out, constitutes the contradictory locus of the utopian and the voyeuristic.[5]

The central narrative impulsion that draws together the frictions of Keats's fiction is Porphyro's desire for the vision of Madeline (her sight and the sight of her; Porphyro's visual vision of Madeline and her visionary vision of him; his seeing and her unseeing eyes; he unseen and she seen). Not only does the description of Porphyro watching Madeline undress in stanzas twenty-four to twenty-six provide one of the narrative cruxes of the poem,[6] but it also provides the most explicit – the most visible – figure of reading. Not only is reading figured in the vision of Madeline, but it is at this point of seeing, more than at any other point in the poem, that the questions of the gender of the reader, his/her (dis)taste, ethical judgement, vision and desire are most clearly posed. Madeline's undressing impels a series of questions, such as what a female reader is to make of Porphyro's pleasure; whether the poem should be read as a vulgar adolescent fantasy of voyeurism; the intentions (honourable or otherwise) of Porphyro; the extent to which readers (male here, presumably) are implicated in an unreflexive ocular violence towards Madeline;[7] the extent to which the poet can make the reader 'see'; and the question of the congruence of Porphyro's desire with that of the (again, male?) reader. Moreover, the fact that narration is generated by desire in Porphyro, the narrator, and ultimately the reader for this anti-narratorial (or descriptive) epiphany of watching Madeline, means that the mechanics of narrative form may be most clearly interrogated at this climactic moment. The fact that the poetry constantly refers to, entices, and describes visual perception, suggests that the internal duality of the visionary/visible is doubled in the relationship of the reader with the poem. In 'St Agnes', reading is figured in ocular fixation.

In 'The Eve of St Agnes' the narrative is impelled by vision: looking both organizes the plot and figures the reading. At the same time, looking produces a resistance to narration as the characters and narrator attempt to fix the look and halt the narrative. It is, above all, the narrative friction of the double plot in 'St Agnes' – Madeline's plot to 'see' her lover and Porphyro's plot to see his – that produces the narrative friction generative of the complex of narrative relationships – narrator to reader, narrator to narrative, reader to text. Before discussing the implications of textual looking for the narrative form of 'St Agnes', then, I want briefly to delineate the thematic sight lines in the poem, a poem which figures looking in extraordinary profusion, in order to establish the coherence and complexity of the text's engagement with the rhetoric of the visible.

While Porphyro is intent on seeing, Madeline is continually presented as unseeing.[8] Part of this blindness is a requirement of tradition, the convention that in order to have a 'vision of delight' virgins must 'Nor look behind, nor sideways, but require / Of heaven with upward eyes for all that they desire' (lines 53–4). The upward eyes are not looking at all – they 'require' rather than look – for heaven is to be apprehended through vision and not through eyesight. Another aspect of Madeline's blindness is her refusal to see what she does not want to: as she waits to leave the party she 'heed[s] not at all' the other guests (line 59) and refuses to see the 'amorous cavalier[s]' (line 60). Similarly, her 'regardless eyes' (line 64) refuse to see because it is a visionary vision which she requires, and Keats makes no bones about her blindness to 'reality': she is 'Hoodwink'd with faery fancy' (line 70). What Madeline 'sees' are 'visions wide' (line 202) or waking dreams:

> Pensive awhile she dreams awake, and sees,
> In fancy, fair St. Agnes in her bed,
> But dares not look behind, or all the charm is fled.
>
> (lines 232–4)

The distinction between looking in reality and looking 'in fancy' is clearly marked by what Jack Stillinger calls Madeline's 'stuporous insensibility'.[9] In her bed, she is 'Flown', 'haven'd', 'Clasp'd', and, finally, 'Blinded' (lines 239–42): all these participles point to a protective withdrawal from the world of sensation. Indeed, such is Madeline's protective enchantment that Porphyro's problem of converting the magical fantasy of her desire into desire for himself is expressed in terms of the enchantment of Madeline's eyes in stanza thirty-two: 'It seem'd he never, never could redeem / From such a stedfast spell his lady's eyes' (lines 286–7). Porphyro's problem does not immediately dissolve when she wakes: her very soul seems to be expressed in the state of her eyes, which in the immediate moment of (half-)waking are 'blue affrayed' (line 296). Ultimately, her refusal to see threatens to destroy Porphyro's plan: 'Her eyes were open, but she still beheld, / Now wide awake, the vision of her sleep' (lines 298–9). And it is, in particular, the visible change wrought in Porphyro as she wakes, that disturbs her: she complains of his visual difference from her (visionary) dream of him, '"How chang'd thou art! how pallid, chill, and drear!"' (line 311).

Porphyro, by contrast, is intent on seeing. His plan is simple: to see Madeline. In his first appearance on the scene he 'implores / All saints to give him sight of Madeline' so that he might 'gaze and worship all unseen' (lines 77–80). That he must be 'unseen' is also vital to his plot – 'All eyes be muffled, or a hundred swords / Will storm his heart' (lines 83–4) – vital because in remaining unseen he will continue to be the 'mover' of the action: it will be his plot.[10] Throughout the poem there is danger from unfriendly eyes: Porphyro must be led 'in close secrecy' (line 163); Angela's eyes are 'aghast / From fright of dim espial' (lines 184–5); Porphyro is obliged to tell Madeline that they can escape because 'There are no ears to hear, or eyes to see' (line 348); in her paranoia, Madeline perceives 'dragons all around, / At glaring watch' (lines 353–4); and the final eye is that of the bloodhound, who might block the lovers' way but whose 'sagacious eye an inmate owns' (line 366). Despite the fact that Porphyro promises not to harm Madeline by his gaze, not to 'look with ruffian passion in her face' (line 149), looking in 'St Agnes' is represented as potentially violent: sight constitutes power – the power of seeing and of not being seen.

Porphyro's plan, which is a plot of looking, stops, significantly, at the look: Porphyro will be hidden

> in a closet, of such privacy
> That he might see her beauty unespied,
> And win perhaps that night a peerless bride,
> While legion'd fairies pac'd the coverlet,
> And pale enchantment held her sleepy-eyed. (lines 165–9)

His seeing and her unseeing come together in this stanza, and Porphyro's desires are expressed in what Stuart Ende calls a 'jarring pun' on 'peerless':[11] she is peerless because she does not peer.

Porphyro's sight of Madeline, the generating force of *his* plot, at least, if not of the whole poem, is marked lexically by a change from the vocabulary of looking/seeing to that of gazing: 'Now prepare, / Young Porphyro, for gazing on that bed' says the narrator in stanza twenty-two, and six stanzas later this is what Porphyro is still doing: 'Stol'n to this paradise, and so entranced, / Porphyro gazed upon her empty dress' (lines 244–5). There is a danger that, through enchantment, Porphyro will become like Madeline – unseeing. Here, his look is displaced metonymically to her dress, just as hers has been displaced to the ladies' trains, the ceiling, etc. To gaze is to look fixedly or intently, and it also involves bewilderment, astonishment, curiosity: the control and power Porphyro's seeing gives him threaten to be disrupted by this fixed gaze as the narrative force of the poem threatens to come to an abrupt halt. But Porphyro pulls himself out of this gaze and, true to his promise not to employ 'ruffian passion', ''tween the curtains peep[s]' (line 252) at Madeline.

Porphyro's next problem, after he has laid out the feast, is to retrieve Madeline's look for himself: although he asks her to 'Open thine eyes' (line 278), the problem is not so easy to overcome: 'It seem'd he never, never could redeem / From such a stedfast spell his lady's eyes' (lines 286–7). As she eventually wakes and refuses to see her flesh-and-blood lover, Porphyro approaches petrification – 'Upon his knees he sank, pale as smooth-sculptured stone' (line 297) – like the staring statues that surround the poem and that surround the actors in the poem.[12] But Madeline, too, is caught in the fixation of the gaze:

> While still her gaze on Porphyro would keep;
> Who knelt, with joined hands and piteous eye,
> Fearing to move or speak, she look'd so dreamingly.
>
> (lines 304–6)

The interchange of gazes is complex and enthralling: the rhetoric of gazing gets caught up in its own conflations of syntax. Her gaze is on his eye which is on her look: but her 'look' suggests both her active gaze and the look of her – an ambivalence that threatens the enthralment of ocular fixation. These enfolded looks end the drama of vision as it concerns Madeline and Porphyro in this poem – although the narratorial drama of vision continues to the end of the poem – as Madeline breaks through fixation with her first words.

The significance of this brief delineation of sight-lines in 'The Eve of St Agnes' is not primarily thematic: what is important is the way that this internal tale of seeing infects and affects both the narratorial strategies and the reader's relation with the tale. The characters' looks provide potential models, embedded within the text, of the reader's gaze. If the point of Porphyro's plot is to gaze, then the point of Keats's poem is to gaze at this gaze. Indeed, the rhetoric of response which the poem has elicited is overwhelmingly couched in terms of *looking* at the poem: early in the history of the poem's reception, critics translated its rhetoric of the visual into their own. Charles Lamb, quoting stanzas twenty-four to twenty-seven, tautologically compared the description of Madeline undressing to what it describes: 'like the radiance, which comes from those old windows upon the limbs and garments of the damsel, is the almost Chaucer-like painting, with which the poet illumes every subject he touches' (*Heritage*, p. 157). Similarly, Leigh Hunt, describing the poem as 'rather a picture than a story' (*Heritage*, p. 172), registered a similar reception for the scene: the 'rich religion of this picture' (*Heritage*, p. 278) 'falls at once gorgeously and delicately upon us, like the colours of the painted glass' (*Heritage*, p. 173). The light that falls on Madeline also falls, metonymically, on the atmosphere of the whole poem, according to one anonymous reviewer – 'A soft religious light is shed over the whole story' (*Heritage*, p. 218) – or, as George Gilfillan stated later in the nineteenth century, 'Its every line wears *couleur de rose*' (*Heritage*, p. 305). Hazlitt, too, felt affected by the colouring of the window:

The beautiful and tender images there conjured up, 'come like shadows – so depart'. The 'tiger-moth's wings', which he has spread over his rich poetic blazonry, just flit across my fancy; the gorgeous twilight window which he has painted over again in his verse, to me 'blushes' almost in vain 'with blood of queens and kings'. (*Heritage*, p. 247)

In the middle of the nineteenth century Alexander Smith repeated this emphasis when he said that the poem 'is rich in colour as the stained windows of a Gothic cathedral, and every verse bursts into picturesque and graceful fancies... [It is] a perfect chrysolite – a precious gem of art' (*Heritage*, p. 367). A related tradition is that of comparing the poem to a picture, as in, for example, John Scott's comment that in watching Porphyro watching Madeline, 'we know not whether most to admire the magical delicacy of the hazardous picture, or its consummate, irresistible attraction' (*Heritage*, p. 224).[13]

This repeated insistence by critics on the importance of the visual, and their repeated internalization and reinscription of stanzas twenty-four and twenty-five within their own critical rhetoric, marks almost a fixation in the critical response to the poem – an inability to wrench the critical gaze away from the surface imagery, the light cast by the intensely evocative imagery and diction, and to look towards other aspects of the poem.[14]

It seems, then, that in 'The Eve of St Agnes', narrative has been subsumed under the rule of the descriptive, a displaced linguistic representation of the visual: everything in the plot points towards and implies the look, hence description and narration are appropriated towards this end. The *point* of the narrative is the descriptive.[15] It seems, further, that the position of the reader or critic in relation to the poem is inevitably a double of Porphyro's position in relation to Madeline, and this duplicity is redoubled in the text's doubling of the reader's (speculative and specular) relationship with Porphyro: Porphyro watches Madeline, the text watches Porphyro (and Madeline), and the reader watches the text. But this vertiginous series of embedded looks is disrupted by the reader's ability to 'gaze' directly at Madeline, while at the same time the vicissitudes of the visual/visionary delineated throughout the poem are also short-circuited by the occlusion of language: as I shall attempt to show, the reader's ability to 'see' the events of the narrative is precluded by the rich intensity of poetic language. However hard the poet tries, he cannot make the reader see anything: 'The Eve of St Agnes' asserts the priority of the imaginative over the visual, of the word over the (visual) image.[16]

The tropes of seeming and seeing are introduced in the framing narrative of the Beadsman's passage through the castle, as the visual is imbued with projected emotion: 'his frosted breath, / Like pious incense from a censer old, / Seem'd taking flight for heaven, without a death' (lines 6–8).[17] The underlying and unstated rhetorical figure in these lines is a visual image and this produces the question of who sees, who imagines:[18] more than descriptions in these early stanzas, 'seem' presupposes a consciousness which imagines, but it also presupposes a logically prior act of seeing. The repetition of 'seem' in stanza two ('seem to freeze'), emphasizes the same procedure in the opening line, 'Ah, bitter chill it was!', which, through the exclamatory mode, asserts the sensuous apprehension of a narrator (and, by implication, of a reader). Such 'narratorial' perception is based on the following paradoxical logic: narrative seeing leads to narrative imagining (the imaginary is generated by the germ of the visual), but narrative 'seeing' is a trope which is logically subsequent to narrative imagining. This paradox is crucial to the descriptive and generates the seductively textured feel of the poem: the more the language approaches precise specification of concrete detail, the further it moves from verisimilitude.

Keats's Gothic descriptions in the poem similarly oscillate between the fantastic, almost, at times, the phantasmagoric or hallucinatory, on the one hand, and the 'realistic', the 'simply' descriptive on the other: indeed, it is when description is most concentrated that the fantastical is most strongly apparent (a paradox evident in the etymology of fantasy, from the Greek φαντασία, 'appearance'). Thus, in stanza four, what is motivated as description owes its force and peculiarity to the disturbing anthropomorphic grotesquerie of the building:

> Soon, up aloft,
> The silver, snarling trumpets 'gan to chide:
> The level chambers, ready with their pride,
> Were glowing to receive a thousand guests:
> The carved angels, ever eager-eyed,
> Star'd ...
>
> (lines 30–35)

'Snarling', 'chide', 'pride', 'glowing', 'eager-eyed', 'Star'd': anthropomorphism constitutes the major trope of the stanza. As such, the 'carved angels' proleptically parody Porphyro (whose religious rhetoric makes him something angelic) and his gaze, or Madeline (the 'missioned spirit' and 'splendid angel') and hers. But the parody involves a petrification of the viewers which exaggerates the characters' potential fixation later in the poem: the gaze is petrified in stone.

In the early stanzas, narrative is overwhelmingly subsumed under the visual and under the descriptive possibilities of scenic plotting. But the teleological inspiration of the poem's looking and description in these stanzas – as if Keats is preparing readers to look, setting their visual nerves on edge with suspense – is the scene of Porphyro's voyeurism in stanzas twenty-four to twenty-eight. Here the conditions for sight are particularly carefully prepared. Indeed, Keats is so intent on preparing for the look that he almost short-circuits the narrative and the vision at the start of the scene: 'Out went the taper as she hurried in; / Its little smoke, in pallid moonshine, died' (lines

199–200). Both by the proleptic analogue of sexual fulfilment and by the narrative occlusion of the visual (or the conditions necessary for the visual), the lines threaten to end the poem without reaching the desired end. Indeed, the casement of stanza twenty-four is not only an example of poetic serendipity but also a product of *narrative* necessity: the stanza most often quoted as an example of Keats's mastery of the visual/descriptive is motivated, paradoxically, by narrative. Having extinguished the taper in stanza twenty-three, Keats has to provide an alternative source of light for his narrative to continue.

Stanzas twenty-four to twenty-six, which provide the motivating force for both Keats's and Porphyro's plots, and which generate a poetry of the visual, demonstrate, in the texture of their language, the paradox of the language of description:[19] the more descriptive language becomes, the less visual are the descriptions, the less coherent and probable are the possibilities for readers to generate a 'visual' scene in the 'mind's eye'. Descriptive writing operates on different levels from the visual: repetition, antithesis, paronomasia, metaphor, onomatopoeia, the foregrounding of diction, verbal ambiguity, etc., produce a verbal rather than a visual enticement to the reader. Indeed, rather than 'description' we might better use the term 'inscription', where the negative force of the prefix suggests a denial of the possibility of linguistic representation and at the same time a self-contained or even self-convoluted sense of the play of signifiers in the act of 'scripting'. 'Inscription' is felicitous, too, in its geometric sense of one figure delineated within the boundaries of another – Keats's highly geometric descriptions are traced within the geometry of stanzaic form. Rather than suggesting a transference from the referent to the signified, Keatsian inscription emphasizes the priority of the signifier.[20]

A second problem introduced by the descriptive is that of motivation: although one might want to argue that the descriptivity – or inscriptivity – of the poem is motivated by the character of Porphyro (he is a voyeur, therefore the attempt to reproduce sight linguistically in description is both necessary and apposite), it could equally be argued that the character of the voyeur is motivated by Keats's desire to describe.[21] Similarly, although stanza twenty-four is motivated by the narrative necessity for light on the scene, and justified in its baroque elaboration by the Gothic setting, we could equally argue that the extinguishing of the candle in line 199 and the decorous half-light of the scene is generated by the virtuosity of the poet.

But, as I have said, one might want to question the nature of the 'description' in stanzas twenty-four to twenty-six: what seems to be produced above all is the self-reflexivity of language. Philippe Hamon has pointed out that description is 'the lexicographical consciousness of fiction', and that to describe 'is almost always to actualize a latent lexical paradigm based on an underlying system of referential knowledge about the world'. Hamon goes on to comment fruitfully on the dynamics of this process: 'The elements of a descriptive system are organized globally as a *permanent equivalence* between a lexical *expansion* and a lexical *condensation* into a term... A description organizes the persistence in memory of a single sign by means of a plurality of different signs'.[22] The 'single sign' in stanza twenty-four, which includes 'the most celebrated visual imagery in the whole poem'[23] – although seemingly 'casement' – is 'emblazonings':

> A casement high and triple-arch'd there was,
> All garlanded with carven imag'ries
> Of fruits, and flowers, and bunches of knot-grass,
> And diamonded with panes of quaint device,
> Innumerable of stains and splendid dyes,
> As are the tiger-moth's deep-damask'd wings;
> And in the midst, 'mong thousand heraldries,
> And twilight saints, and dim emblazonings,
> A shielded scutcheon blush'd with blood of queens and kings.
>
> (lines 208–16)

'Emblazonings' lights up the poem with heraldic devices: the stanza is a blazon that marks the heraldic heritage of the poem, the provenance of its lexicon and the authority of its imagery. The stanza emblazons its filial descent from the blazonry of old romance.[24]

Hamon points out that the 'extension' of the description 'is related to the *available* vocabulary of the author, not to the degree of complexity of the reality itself',[25] but another constraint upon the descriptivity in 'The Eve of St Agnes' is the space of the stanza: the Spenserian stanza form accounts, to a large extent, for the economy and precision of Keatsian blazonry in this poem, and contrasts markedly with his earlier description-induced poetry (of which *Endymion* is paradigmatic), which knows no bounds. The Spenserian stanza form, which Byron said was 'perhaps too slow and dignified for narrative'[26] provides a precise delineation of dilatory space for

Keatsian narration. For Keats, this enforced lingering provides a framework within which the blazonry operates, like the frames provided by the shield or *cartouche* that, while allowing play within the limits of the frame, strictly delimits the blazon to the space of that frame. Keats's drafts show that stanzas twenty-four and twenty-five were first conflated, after which the two distinct images (the casement and the effect of the light on Madeline) were separated into their discrete stanzaic frames: the stanza form provides a necessary frame for the limits of locution, but the rich wordiness of description constantly threatens to break through the artificially imposed limits.[27] Similarly, the larger frame device of Angela and the Beadsman marks the limits of the narrative and simultaneously incorporates the symbolic oppositions of youth/age, warmth/coldness, life/death, etc: the frame here marks the narrative of Madeline and Porphyro as only one episode in a larger tale while simultaneously providing a boundary for the reader's interest.

Stanza twenty-four provides the reader with a verbal analogue of the visual by the elaborate way in which its language imitates the baroque elaborations of visual detail in the casement. At the same time, the stanza remarks upon its own ocular limits by simultaneously representing a visual image and occluding the visual in the foregrounding of poetic diction: readers can never 'see'. Michael Riffaterre has claimed that the 'primary purpose' of description 'is not to offer a representation, but to dictate an interpretation':[28] Keats's descriptions dictate the reader's ideological position in relation to poetry, to looking and to sexuality. One major function of description in 'The Eve of St Agnes' is to seduce the reader into an acceptance of a potentially scandalous ethos: while it is possible to read it as a narrative of voyeurism and even rape, the critical tradition and, presumably, most readers, tend to read the poem as an extravagantly luxurious romance in which the only scandal is the sheer plenitude of language.[29] Thus, what description calls attention to most of all is its own rich, textured and lexically profuse form, in particular the 'quaint device' of heraldic vocabulary and, like 'La Belle Dame' later, the impacted semantic resonances of descriptive diction. But this also means that another major function of the descriptions is to ensure that such an acceptance is problematic: by undermining the possibility of verisimilitude the descriptions (threaten to) deny the reader an unproblematic or unselfconscious role. The gorgeousness of description not only enhances the reader's pleasure but also estranges him or her from an unmediated experience of the visual: the very virtuosity makes us wary, its very profusion alienates.

The specificity of detail in stanza twenty-four has led Robert Gittings to claim that the window is a simulacrum of windows in Stansted Chapel: nevertheless, it is a pictured window that he 'sees'.[30] Like the picture of somebody reading before an ambiguously painted window described in a letter by Keats to his sister,[31] the casement in stanza twenty-four is undecidably 'real' and seductively 'realistic', oscillating between the texture and the transparence of language, a 'charm'd magic casement'. Rather than allowing our vision out, however, the next two stanzas show that the casement in 'St Agnes' is designed to let warm light in: indeed, the emblazonings of the casement stanza become subject to the necessities of narrative as we move from stanza twenty-four to stanza twenty-five. Throughout the poem, motivation alternates between narration and description. As we move into stanza twenty-five, and read 'warm gules', 'Rose-bloom', 'soft amethyst', 'a glory', it becomes clear that stanza twenty-four is narratively dispensable except for its provision of colouring to the next stanza. The extinguishing of the candle in stanza twenty-three is narratively motivated by the need for decorum; stanza twenty-four is motivated both by narrative and by descriptive necessity; stanzas twenty-five to twenty-six assert the necessity of stanza twenty-four on the plane of narrative, but seek to deny its force on the level of description (the descriptive impulsion and indeed the central *blazon* for the poem, is not the window but Madeline's body).

The third stanza of the scene – the undressing – is what Porphyro has been waiting for, but the vision is non-visual: Christopher Ricks has pointed out that in this description 'the gratifications of the enkindled ear... outdo those of the gazing eye',[32] but this elides the full variety and fecundity of sensory stimulation involved:

> Of all its wreathed pearls her hair she frees;
> Unclasps her warmed jewels one by one;
> Loosens her fragrant bodice; by degrees
> Her rich attire creeps rustling to her knees (lines 227–30)

The pleasures of Porphyro are of an entirely different order to the pleasures of the reader. The latter are created in various ways. Firstly there is the syntax: repetition (of verb – 'frees... Unclasps... Loosens'

– and of noun-phrase – 'wreathed pearls ... warmed jewels') and the interruptions of the semi-colons parody both the repetitive action of undressing and – like a striptease – the impatience of the spectator. But the syntax is more complex than this suggests: there is the holding back, the delaying of tension in syntactic inversion – 'Of all its wreathed pearls her hair she frees' – so that the (notorious) tension-releasing sensation in the lines conflicts with the pressure of delay.[33] A variation on this strategy is the mimetic undressing of enjambment in 'by degrees / Her rich attire creeps' – a lingering of the line on 'degrees' before it creeps down to the next. And for the 'enkindled ear' there is the mimetic rustling in the sound of 'creeps rustling'. Moreover, although Porphyro is watching, the 'enkindled' senses are other than sight: there is touch in freeing and unclasping and loosening, there is the warmth of 'warmed', there is the sound of rustling, there is the smell of the fragrant bodice. Although readers are figured, with Porphyro, as voyeurs in this erotic display, the words provide an opaque screen, a teasing veil over the spectacle of Madeline's body: the picture is painted in non-visual colours.

Similarly, in stanza thirty, the second descriptive climax and the proleptic substitute for sexual union in stanza thirty-six, the visual is subsumed under the aural/oral in the description of food. Leigh Hunt commented that the words 'make us read the line delicately, and at the tip-end, as it were, of one's tongue' (*Heritage*, p. 280): the interplay of vowels – both the sound and the very movements of tongue, lips, mouth and larynx necessary to speak the stanza – provide mimetic reassurance of luxuriant riches.[34] But, again, such mimesis tends to eradicate the descriptive, which is based on the distinction between signifier and signified: once the two have collapsed into each other, description is annulled. The meal is almost unimaginable in its profuse richness, and the exotic diction of its presentation in the poem – like the heraldic vocabulary of stanza twenty-four – marks it as semantically improbable: its significance is expressed in the mimetic effect.

The final descriptive climax of the poem occurs in stanza thirty-six, which is also the most overt narrative and sexual climax (although stanzas twenty-four and thirty also provide potential/displaced/ alternative climaxes: the poem is, in a sense, tri-centred):

> Beyond a mortal man impassion'd far
> At these voluptuous accents, he arose,
> Ethereal, flush'd, and like a throbbing star

Seen mid the sapphire heaven's deep repose;
Into her dream he melted, as the rose
Blendeth its odour with the violet, –
Solution sweet.   (lines 316–22)

As Earl Wasserman has shown so influentially, the stanza provides a
climax of super-sensory apprehension: the whole gist of the imagery
is towards the non-visual, the extra-sensory, the transcendent.[35] But
here again description is strongly asserted and at the same time
strongly questioned, in the phallic imagery of 'he arose, / Ethereal,
flush'd, and like a throbbing star / Seen mid the sapphire heaven's
deep repose'. Visual description is produced by the vehicle of the
metaphor, which is specifically ocular (in the right atmospheric
conditions a twinkling star may, literally, be seen to throb, and
'sapphire heaven's deep repose' is quite coherent as a description of
the sky), but there are a number of problems: firstly, a throb is far
more tactile than visual, and the word finds easier collocations in the
vocabulary of sexual excitement than twinkling stars; secondly, as a
metaphor, and combined with the following lines, the image is
scandalously suggestive in its sexual vision; lastly, 'seen' presupposes
a spectator, which introduces the question of the identity of the
perceiver and immediately disrupts the eminent visuality of the
image:[36] it is not seen, only said.

Porphyro's romance pledge of love and protection two stanzas
later, is curiously couched in terms resonant of stanza twenty-four:
'Say, may I be for aye thy vassal blest? / Thy beauty's shield, heart-
shap'd and vermeil dyed?' (lines 335–6). To the extent that the
central narrative impulsion of 'The Eve of St Agnes' is constituted by
Madeline's body, the poem is structured around the form of the
Renaissance blazon: in these lines, however, Porphyro wants to make
himself a spectacle, Madeline's own personal and human blazon. This
helps us to understand the connection, on one level, between stanzas
twenty-four and thirty-six: some of the emblazonings of stanza
twenty-four are echoed in stanza thirty-six by various forms of
repetition, metonymy, dilation, condensation, or substitution:

Stanza 24	*Stanza* 36
in the midst	seen mid
deep-damask'd	deep repose
A casement high	window-panes
diamonded	sapphire

twilight saints	Etherial ... heaven's
blush'd	flush'd
blood	throbbing

And 'Full on this casement shone the wintry moon' of stanza twenty-five becomes, in stanza thirty-six, 'St. Agnes' moon hath set', while the 'splendid dyes' of stanza twenty-four becomes Porphyro's wish to be 'vermeil dyed' in stanza thirty-eight. Moreover, this allows us to understand the significance of a whole cluster of colour-words that stud the poem and have the cumulative effect of tainting, staining, colouring and blending with the lines 'Into her dream he melted, as the rose / Blendeth its odour with the violet, – / Solution sweet' (lines 320–22). In 'The Eve of St Agnes' there is a repeated description of Madeline as 'pure', 'white', 'untainted', and a repeated sense of the tainting of this purity by colour: indeed, the sense of colour in this poem is more of colouring than of colour – 'Flushing his brow' (line 137), 'Made purple riot' (line 138), 'stains and splendid dyes' (line 212), 'deep-damask'd' (line 213), 'blush'd with blood' (line 216), 'threw warm gules' (line 218), 'Rose-bloom fell' (line 220), 'flush'd' (line 318).[37] Sensory blending, together with the heraldic tainting of a modern poem is expressed in the image of odourful blending (rose and violet are both colours, of course, as well as being flowers) and we have a solution to the narrative thrust of the poem. Madeline has been described as 'free from mortal taint' in line 225: one effect of the gorgeous descriptivity of the poem is the tainting of Madeline's purity, the successful consummation of Porphyro's purple plan to emblazon himself *on* Madeline.

In analysing the poem in terms of visual perception, it is clear that we have – along with most readings of the poem – implicitly read Madeline as a surrogate for the poem itself: we 'look' at her as we 'look' at the text. But we also look at Porphyro, and his desire to emblazon himself has implications for the text itself: 'The Eve of St Agnes' is a blazon that guarantees Keats's poetic credentials, that identifies him as a descendant of poets. That Keats required such a blazon is evident from our knowledge of his anxiety of audience and of the comments on and revisions to 'The Eve of St Agnes' recorded by Richard Woodhouse. In particular, Keats's comments – when riled by Woodhouse's prudish objections to the explicit sexuality of the poem – that he wanted to 'fling [the reader] off at last' and that he did not write for 'ladies' suggest a virulently antagonistic attitude towards his readers (see *KC*, vol. i, pp. 91–2). But this antagonism is counterpointed by the immense seductiveness of the poem – its explicit engagement with readers' desires. In 'The Eve of St Agnes' Keatsian rhetoric is caught up in the contradictions of poetic seduction: not only does Keats want to seduce his readers but he also desires an audience sufficiently detached to appreciate his technical mastery. Although this is expressed most explicitly in Keats's wish 'to fling the reader off at last', it is everywhere apparent in the nuances and matrices of visuality in 'St Agnes'. While both Porphyro and Madeline provide models for the reader's vision, and while the poem provides ample opportunity for readers' imaginative envisioning, the ambiguities and tensions involved in both cases generate their own, internal, flinging off. Thus if we simply accept the ideological implications of a man covertly watching a young woman undressing, entering her bed, and making love to her, and of a poet writing poems about such an imagined experience, then the poem manages to lose much of its point: it is essential that the actions displayed be at least partially shocking for the conflated nuances of tone, colouring, reference, intertextuality, and emotion, to be activated.

Richard Woodhouse, one of Keats's closest, most sympathetic readers, provides a fascinating early reaction to 'St Agnes' in his comments on how a decorous reader might 'look' at the poem:

You know if a thing has a decent side, I generally look no further – As the Poem was orig[y] written, *we* innocent ones (ladies & myself) might very well have supposed that Porphyro, when acquainted with Madeline's love for him, & when 'he arose, Etherial flush[d]' &c.&c (turn to it) set himself at once to persuade her to go off with him, & succeeded & went over the 'Dartmoor black' (now changed for some other place) to be married, in right honest chaste & sober wise. But, as it is now altered, as soon as M. has confessed her love, P. ⟨instead⟩ winds by degrees his arm round her, presses breast to breast, and acts all the acts of a bonâ fide husband, while she fancies she is only playing the part of a Wife in a dream. This alteration is of about 3 stanzas; and tho' there are no improper expressions but all is left to inference, and tho' profanely speaking, the Interest on the reader's imagination is greatly heightened, yet I do apprehend it will render the poem unfit for ladies, & indeed scarcely to be mentioned to them among the 'things that are'. (*KC*, vol. i, p. 92)

The idea of 'looking' at a poem, and the idea that one can 'overlook' the in-decent aspects of a 'decent' poem, or that one can avert one's gaze, is highly significant in terms of our analysis of 'vision' in 'The Eve of St Agnes'. There is an uncomfortable duplicity in the phrase

'I generally look no further', which includes the sense that by 'look[ing] no further' the reader neglects to read: from this it follows that to be read – to be read properly, fully, with attention – the poet is forced to make the poem *in*-decent. To a certain extent this is precisely what Woodhouse is saying: if it appears to be 'decent' then he will overlook any indecencies, he will gloss over what Jean Hagstrum has termed 'the blazing sensuality-become-sexuality of the poem';[38] but in the revised version of the poem Woodhouse finds such a reading strategy impossible. Although the question of whether the revisions make the sexuality of 'St Agnes' more explicit is debatable (indeed, Woodhouse's reading seems to be highly questionable), if we assume this to be the case then we might imagine that Keats's revisions were aimed precisely at this effect – to stop readers neglecting to read.

What both Michael Ragussis and John Barnard have described as Woodhouse's double reading is precisely what is provided for by this poem, a duplicity of the reader's gaze which responds to the 'hazardous magic' of the poem.[39] 'The Eve of St Agnes' is the poem which engages most directly and at the same time most successfully of all Keats's long poems with the desires and anxieties of its audience such that in succumbing to its magic the reader realizes its hazards, in responding to its hazards the reader experiences its magic. The audience is caught, fixated, in the figured gaze: the hallucination of reading in 'St Agnes' is figured in the hazardous magic of the gaze.

CHAPTER 6

'La Belle Dame sans Merci'

'It would be difficult', Earl R. Wasserman begins his chapter on 'La Belle Dame sans Merci', 'in any reading of Keats' ballad not to be enthralled by the haunting power of its rhythm, by its delicate intermingling of the fragile and grotesque, the tender and the weird, and by the perfect economy with which these effects are achieved'.[1] As critics have often pointed out, such enthralment is generated by an intensity of suggestion combined with a vagueness of narrative information: Stuart Sperry has commented that 'La Belle Dame' is 'the most condensed and suggestive' poem Keats ever wrote and that the narrative is characterized by 'brevity and sparseness' while it 'owes much of its power both to an extraordinary clarity and to a suggestiveness of detail'.[2] The reader is enthralled by the combination of an overabundance of semantic and an attenuation of narrative information. This duality might be compared to what Coleridge terms 'pedantry'. Attempting to defend himself against such a charge in *Biographia Literaria*, Coleridge defines two aspects of 'pedantry':

If I am not misinformed, pedantry consists in the use of words unsuitable to the time, place, and company. The language of the market would be in the schools as *pedantic*, though it might not be reprobated by that name, as the language of the schools in the market. The mere man of the world, who insists that no other terms but such as occur in common conversation should be employed in a scientific disquisition, and with no greater precision, is as truly a *pedant* as the man of letters, who either over-rating the acquirements of his auditors, or misled by his own familiarity with technical or scholastic terms, converses at the wine-table with his mind fixed on his musæum or laboratory; even though the latter pedant instead of desiring his wife to *make the tea*, should bid her add to the quant. suff. of thea sinensis the oxyd of hydrogen saturated with caloric. (*BL*, vol. I, p. 170)

The language of the 'man of the world', which is insufficiently precise and therefore ambiguous in the context of a scientific paper, might be characterized as 'rarefaction'; the language of the 'man of letters', who misjudges the situation by employing unsuitably detailed and scientific language in a domestic situation might be characterized as 'impaction'.[3] Coleridge is describing a certain dysfunction of language: we could say that the necessary though not sufficient condition in a definition of poetry would involve a similar recognition of such a dysfunction. In terms of the ideational or 'thetic', at least, the literary might be described as that which blocks or suspends 'meaning', a certain dysfunction in communicative transmission.[4] The solecism of 'La Belle Dame sans Merci' is that of dysfunctional language: the text figures its audience by enthralling its readers within an indeterminate profusion and diffusion of information. Employing a dual strategy of close attention to the resonances of lexis and a limning of narrative attenuation, the present chapter attempts to figure the reader as enthralled by the double logic of impaction and rarefaction – reading as suspended within the indefinite space between desire and repletion.

In 'La Belle Dame sans Merci' the effect achieved by the *story* might be described as rarefaction: although little narrative information is given, a lot seems to be happening including seduction, enthralment, bewitchment, echoes of the Fall, Gothic vision, dream, dream within a dream, a conflation of the narrator with his subject, the exploitation of mythological/Romance convention, and so on. The poem presents a minimally developed *histoire* within which narrative information is highly distended. On the other hand, lexically the poem is highly impacted. In particular, the poem produces a remarkable intensity of verbal resonance: most notably, the diction used is replete with etymological connotation (connotation, particularly, of Middle English and Gothic, with an underlying tension between these – essentially Anglo-Saxon – features and the French language and Romance conventions).

Lexically, then, the poem is highly wrought, introducing an overload of information within the frame of a spare narrative: most generally this impaction is achieved by a contrast between lexically 'innocent' words and words that draw attention to themselves by their apparent incongruity or to which attention is drawn by the narrator:

> And sure in language strange she said –
> I love thee true.[5]

David Simpson has drawn attention to the ambiguity of 'sure', stating that it can be read either as quizzical ('surely she said') or assertive ('I am sure she said'):[6] both of these senses require a filling in of syntactic ellipsis. But a third sense requires no such gap filling:

> And sure in language strange...

she is sure (of herself, at least), and she is sure because she is 'in', is using 'language strange'. As we have seen, the telling of love is a problematic speech-act: the difficulties of telling love are exemplified, for example, by Lorenzo's difficulties in telling his love in 'Isabella', by the assertion in the closely related 'dream' sonnet of 'La Belle Dame', 'As Hermes once took to his feathers light', that 'lovers need not tell / Their sorrows' (lines 11–12), and by other difficult tellings, like Blake's 'Never seek to tell thy love', a poem which plays on the conventional trope that to tell one's love is, mysteriously, to lose it (see Chapter 4, above). With these examples, we hardly need to ask why La Belle Dame needs to speak in language strange – and why, in language strange, she can be sure when telling her love. It is only by speaking in strange language that she can dare to tell her love.[7] Embedded within the telling of 'La Belle Dame sans Merci' is a telling by La Belle Dame which is both successful and assured: if the poem is to be assured (both self-confident and confident of its own meaning), then by implication it too needs to employ language strange.[8]

If Keats estranged his language by means of diction, then, to be sure, this was not without implication. In the context of the second decade of the nineteenth century, the stakes were particularly high with regard to diction, not least because of the way that Wordsworth's Preface to the *Lyrical Ballads* had focused on the importance for modern poetry of 'ordinary' language. Keats himself had already been criticized publicly for his lexical solecisms. No doubt partly in reaction to such responses, later in 1819 he developed a theory of 'chaste' diction (the valorization of words with Anglo-Saxon rather than French or Latin derivations).[9] Keats's theory of English diction is explicitly expressed in his letters. 'Chaste' is associated with the 'purity' of Chatterton in a letter that announces the composition of 'To Autumn' in response to the chaste weather: 'I always somehow associate Chatterton with autumn. He is the purest writer in the English Language. He has no French idiom, or particles like Chaucer⟨s⟩ – 'tis genuine English Idiom in English words...

English ought to be kept up' (*Letters*, vol. II, p. 167). By this definition, even Milton and Chaucer are corrupt and therefore open to criticism:

I shall never become attach'd to a foreign idiom so as to put it into my writings. The Paradise lost though so fine in itself is a curruption [*sic*] of our Language ... A northern dialect accommodating itself to greek and latin inversions and intonations. The purest english I think – or what ought to be the purest – is Chatterton's – The Language had existed long enough to be entirely uncorrupted of Chaucer's gallicisms and still the old words are used – Chatterton's language is entirely northern ... (*Letters*, vol. II, p. 212)

Earlier, it was specifically the French and the French language that Keats distrusted as is evinced by a Francophobic passage in a letter of September 1817, where, writing to his sister Fanny, he warns her against French language and literature:

While I was speaking about france it occured to me to speak a few Words on their Language – it is perhaps the poorest one ever spoken since the jabbering in the Tower of Ba{bel} and when you come to know that the real use and greatness of a Tongue is to be referred to its Literature – you will be astonished to find how very inferior it is to our native Speech ... (*Letters*, vol. I, p. 155)

To a certain extent, Keats's ambivalence towards the 'language strange' of 'La Belle Dame sans Merci' is an ambivalence which is displayed in the alterations which the poem received before its first publication. Although it is difficult to agree with François Matthey that in the *Indicator* (where the poem was first published) the poem is 'less medievalistic',[10] or with Simpson, who – rather overstating the case – claims that the later version is pared down to its essential constituents,[11] without doubt a certain lexical anxiety is involved as to the precise balance of archaisms and poeticisms. Keats is concerned with language, with English and French and the interplay of Middle English, Spenserian archaisms, and modern English.

The first and perhaps most intriguing of these changes occurs in the title itself. Much has been made recently – notably by David Simpson and Theresa M. Kelley – of the alteration from 'Merci' in the manuscript version to 'Mercy' in the *Indicator* text: both critics emphasize the importance of this change and, at the same time, mistake its import. Simpson notes that in Old French both spellings were acceptable 'as the scribe of the "*Indicator*" version may be surreptitiously recognising in his apparent slip of the pen'.[12] In fact, however, both Alain Chartier, whom Keats may have read, and the pseudo-Chaucerian English translation of Chartier's poem by Richard Ros, use 'mercy': in this respect, the *Indicator*'s 'Mercy', rather than a 'slip', is a correction, an authentification of the title's archaic identity. Even more unlikely is Kelley's description of the *Indicator*'s 'Mercy' as 'English'.[13] If 'Mercy' were 'English', it would have to be read as an English word in a French title. What may be considered to be 'English', in fact, is the use of 'merci': the word is marked as French to the English reader by its spelling, whereas 'mercy' threatens confusion because of its currency in modern English by contrast with its archaism in French. The mistake that Kelley makes over the English/French nature of 'mercy' is a mistake that any English-speaking reader might be expected to make both in the late twentieth and in the early nineteenth centuries: although to a French audience the spelling of 'mercy' would signal an archaic, Old French text or referent, it would be rather more unusual for an English reader to pick up this very specific index of historical location. Rather than being less French, the *Indicator*'s 'mercy' is *more* French (in the sense that the English-speaking reader is potentially confused by it), and whether it was Hunt or Keats who changed the word, it seems highly unlikely that the change was unintentional. This despite the fact that the 'correction' actually makes misreading more likely. What this apparently trivial question of the poem's title suggests is that there is something inherently problematic about using 'foreign' language in an English poem and that the problematics of the poem's diction figure the poem's reading. Such usage creates a problem that is compounded by the foregrounding of other lexical elements in the poem that together concentrate the reader's mind on the contrast between 'ordinary' early nineteenth-century usage on the one hand and, on the other hand, on the poeticisms, archaisms, Gallicisms, and neologisms that rupture this surface homogeneity.[14] The lexical impaction produced by such textured semantics contrasts strikingly with the attenuation of narrative information. Indeed, our concentration on lexical phenomena is by no means unwarranted: the lexical foregrounding forces us into such an investigation, and the rarefied atmosphere of the narrative unfolding leaves us no option, no other grip on the tale.

The problematic lexical content encountered here is by no means unproblematic for Keats himself, who demonstrates a certain lexical anxiety, evinced most overtly by some of the other alterations that occur between manuscript and publication. The most notorious of these is in line one, from the manuscript's 'knight at arms' to the *Indicator*'s 'wretched wight': while both phrases are thoroughly conventional and thus involve an impaction generated by lexical connotation, the effect of each is different. 'Wretched wight' seems to be an explicit reference to Spenser, who uses the collocation eight times in the *Faerie Queen* alone: consciously archaic, sentimental, and poetic (poetic both because of the alliteration and because the usual context for 'wight' is poetry), the phrase involves an extreme specificity of intertextuality. If anything, 'knight at arms' involves an even higher degree of impaction, connoting a whole mythopoetic tradition based on the chivalric ethos. Not only do both phrases involve large amounts of generic presupposition, they also involve a conscious distancing of the text from the modern reader. But it is not only the 'wretched wight'/'knight at arms' that achieves this effect; other elements in the first line are also archaic/poetic. There are the conventional vocative exclamations of the opening 'O' and 'Ah'; the archaic/poetic 'thee'; and the significantly unusual question, 'what can ail thee', rather than 'what ails thee'. Already with this question the narrator is suggesting an undecidability of narration. Not only does he not know, he hints that the ailment is unknowable.[15] In line two, 'palely', a slightly awkward adverbial formation (an awkwardness reflected in the word itself which, alternatively, is spelt 'paly'), foregrounds the texture of the word or emphasizes Jakobson's 'poetic function', so that the triple repetition of 'pale' in stanza ten echoes this initial reference. With 'wretched wight' we might be tempted to discern a pun on 'white', so distancing the word and the audience from Romance convention.[16]

The 'answering' or 'explanatory' lines of the second half of the stanza[17] continue the limpid simplicity of syntax and rhythm, and the abstraction and emptiness of narrative tone, while increasing the impacted lexical connotations: for example, the introduction of the lake in the context of a 'Belle Dame' suggesting (illicit) sexual relations;[18] the implicit double-dying of 'withered sedge' and the absence of bird-song (a deathliness emphasized, perhaps, by the abruptly interrupted last line); and the implication that the knight's condition is represented by his surroundings, the conventional images of winter attenuation.

This overloading of lexical connotation in the first stanza is balanced by what might be characterized as the narrative elements: these include, most notably, the lack of narrative context (who is the knight/wight?; where is he?; what is the relationship between him and his surroundings?; who is speaking and why?) which is exaggerated by the abruptness of the *medias res* beginning. Moreover, narrative voice – the question of who is speaking – is highly ambiguous, and lines three and four can act either as the knight/wight's answer or as a narratorial explanation: the absence of any speech marks would seem to suggest that the lines are, in fact, the narrator's explanation of the question, his clarification of narrative motivation (because of the scenic devastation, the knight's 'loitering' is curious and needs to be explained).

The significant lexical developments in stanza two involve 'haggard' and 'woe-begone':

> O what can ail thee, knight at arms,
>   So haggard and so woe-begone?
> The squirrel's granary is full,
>   And the harvest's done.

The use of the obsolete/archaic diction in stanza one, which has already sensitized the reader to etymologies, reminds us of the origins of 'haggard', which includes not only the sense of 'wild' and 'untamed', but also 'witch' and suggests that we disinter the 'hag' within the adjective almost as if the word is a past participle, the result of a passive formation implying that the 'Belle Dame' has used a hag's witchery on the knight. Again, the archaic 'woe-begone' foregrounds the signifier both as a conventional description of a love-stricken youth and as an archaism revitalized in modern usage. It is almost as if these words that come to us from the past in this modernization of the ballad tradition parallel the death-in-life of the knight. In both cases, a 'greeting of the spirit' is necessary for such revitalization. In the case of 'haggard', an awareness of literary context and etymology is required. In the case of 'woe-begone' our apprehension of the word's modern connotations ('unhappy', 'woeful', and so forth) is invigorated and enlightened by our knowledge that the word means literally 'affected by an environment of woe' (*OED*). On one level, an immediate connection can be made between what we have characterized as lexical impaction and narrative rarefaction: what the questioning and answering has implied – that the environment has something to do with the knight's condition – is confirmed by our technical knowledge of the etymological origins of 'woe-begone'. Dr Johnson's rather less precise definition of the word also helps to define the knight's situation and connect it with the narrative itself: 'lost in woe; distracted in woe; overwhelmed with sorrow', the knight is lost, distracted, overwhelmed.[19] But these three adjectives also precisely describe the predicament of the narrator and readers: they are lost in a world that they do not understand and that is strange; they are distracted, as we shall see, by the knight's answer; they are overwhelmed by the pathos of the tale, and unable to assert their own narratorial and readerly authority at the end of the knight's tale.

The sedge and the birds of stanza one and the squirrel and harvest of stanza two are suggestive in their figurative connotations, but the figurative status of stanza three is rather more problematic. As Miriam Allott points out, 'the lily and the rose as emblems of physical beauty are literary commonplaces',[20] but the extreme literalness of 'I see a lily on thy brow ... And on thy cheek a fading rose' calls for an unusually direct response from the reader, who must resist the referential visuality of the stanza in order to 'see' more clearly.[21]

> I see a lily on thy brow
>   With anguish moist and fever dew,
> And on thy cheeks a fading rose
>   Fast withereth too.

The suspension of the sensory in figurative reading is emphasized in the syntactical displacement of the second line of the stanza. We want to read 'dew' as an adjective because of the syntactic parallel of 'anguish moist' with 'fever dew':[22] in fact the line should be read as an inversion of 'moist with anguish and fever dew', where 'fever dew' is a metaphor for sweat caused by illness. In this stanza the solecisms of syntax and metaphor alert us, as do the lexical foregroundings in other stanzas, to the materiality and strangeness, the hallucination, of poetic language, and to the multiple instabilities produced within the impacted texture of the verse. But at the same time they warn us, as do the pedantic precision of 'kisses four' and the neologistic back-formation of 'gloams', that 'language strange' balances on the edge of grammatical incoherence and social impropriety, of scandal or solecism.

As Simpson has pointed out, there is a potential refusal to distinguish between speakers as we pass from stanza three to stanza four, a refusal which is apparently emphasized by syntactical repetition: 'I see a lily', 'I met a lady'.[23] Rather than the epistemological self-doubt that Simpson discerns, we might read this disturbing elision as another instance of narrative rarefaction: the effect of what Karl Kroeber defines as the 'symbolic' style of story-telling. In the rarefied atmosphere of symbolic narration the narrative logics of causality, motivation, and temporality may largely be ignored.[24] Similarly, in the transition between stanzas three and four we meet an *histoire* too fragile, too minimal, to express the detailed inflections required for the differentiation of 'voice' (the question of whether the words in stanza four are those of the narrator or of the knight). On one level this simply involves a neglect of speech marks, but the uncertainty also marks a disruption of subjectivity as the cadences of the narrator's voice merge into those of the knight: if the knight is forlorn and loitering due to some mysteriously tragic faery meeting, then the narrator is suffering the same fate, the knight's posthumous life is the posthumous life of writing. This is borne out by an uncanny similarity in the narrator's and the knight's mode of visual perception: the narrator's complex and detailed metaphorical description in stanza three is continued in stanza four, where

> Her hair was long, her foot was light,
> And her eyes were wild.

All the adjectives seem to demand some kind of figurative reading: the utter simplicity of 'long' and 'light' – their very literalness – seems to demand that we do with these details what we do with 'wild': that is, read them with a double attention. But 'wild' is of a different order: not only does the word suggest the modern sense of undomesticated, savage and turbulent, but it also has other connotations (employed by Keats elsewhere) of strangeness and the imaginary, even, perhaps, of sexual licentiousness. In line thirteen, Keats had first written 'wilds' instead of 'meads', and 'wild' is repeated again in stanza seven ('honey wild') and, most significantly, in stanza eight ('her wild wild eyes'). It is in this latter repetition that the strange wildness of the eyes or the strangeness of the wild eyes becomes apparent. The doubling of the adjective at this point involves a mathematical precision (one wild for each eye?) matched only by the self-consciously pedantic 'kisses four', which is a further mathematical progression: a doubling of the double 'wild', as if such mathematical logic, such precise duplicity could work a spell on, instead of being spellbound by, the wild eyes.

In *Endymion*, that wild and wildering wilderness of a poem, the

lovers, whom Endymion rescues from suspended animation in Book
Three, revel in their freedom:

> Then dance, and song,
> And garlanding grew wild; and pleasure reign'd.
> In harmless tendril they each other chain'd,
> And strove who should be smother'd deepest in
> Fresh crush of leaves.   (lines 933–7)

This peculiarly (early-)Keatsian method of love-making, where
sensuality is sublimed into art (dance and song and garlanding) and
the sensuousness of covering each other with plants (garlanding and
chaining and smothering), is one of Keats's finest pleasures and is
intensified, as this pleasure often is in his poetry, by the sensuousness
of onomatopoeia in 'Fresh crush of leaves' and by the teasing
pleasure of oxymoron in 'garlanding grew wild' ('grew' asserts the
vegetable nature of the garlands which are, however, *manufactured*
leaves and flowers and so do not grow wild but must be tamed). But
this is to misread the uninhibited exuberance of the lovers' actions, a
wildness not reflected in the simulacrum of this love-making ritual
when it reappears in 'La Belle Dame sans Merci':

> I made a garland for her head,
> And bracelets too, and fragrant zone;

a chastity of diction and action which is contrasted with the Belle
Dame's response:

> She look'd at me as she did love,
> And made sweet moan.

The sensuality of her reply seems to confirm our suspicions about the
Lady of the Lake and the sexual licentiousness implied by her 'wild'
eyes. We note the contrasting chastity-sensuality of the knight's and
the lady's actions here and also recognize the symbolic effect of the
garland bracelet and fragrant zone, all of which not only dress and
decorate the Belle Dame, but also surround, enclose, or protect. The
Belle Dame, by contrast, is passive. The narrative threads, the hints
which we have discerned behind the teasingly simple, pellucid
narrative texture of the poem, now seem to be more consciously
organizing themselves by means of contrast, of binary opposition,
into something comprehensible, something graspable not only as plot
(already we have a clear indication that the poem is following a fairly
conventional trajectory in this respect) but as an organizing,

controlling *discours* through which to read the underlying story events.

In stanza six we begin to believe that we are really getting somewhere:

> I set her on my pacing steed,
>   And nothing else saw all day long,
> For sidelong would she bend, and sing
>   A fairy's song.

In setting the lady on his 'pacing steed', the knight is both referring to a set of conventions of which we are already aware (the chivalric code of the rescuing knight) and implying that both he and the plot are moving. While exaggerated, his intense concentration ('And nothing else saw all day long') will at least reassure us that he is intent on his purpose. Again, having already understood the narrative context of faery and mysterious song, we can pass over the apparently distracted and certainly tangential singing of the lady: by contrast with previous stanzas, only 'sidelong' gives pause for thought, reminding us of those wild eyes because this is a look as much as a gesture.

However, our hopes for narrative development are dashed with the next stanza, where, without explanation, the ritual giving continues although the lady is now assertively sensual:

> She found me roots of relish sweet,
>   And honey wild, and manna dew,
> And sure in language strange she said –
>   I love thee true.

The wild food introduces, or reinforces, the sense of 'uncultivated' wildness and the wilderness (which is where the biblical 'manna' leads us). Not only is the narrative interrupted here but the lexical impaction returns, particularly in 'manna dew': the end-stopped 'dew' repeats the un-syntactical 'dew' of line ten, forcing us to draw a parallel between

> With anguish moist and fever dew

and

> And honey wild, and manna dew

so that bodily secretions are translated into the secretions of insects (honey) and of the heavens (manna). This mysterious and mysteriously wild meal (a dangerously wild meal, which is prefigured both by one version of *Thomas the Rhymer*[25] and by the biblical Fall) increases both the temperature in the pleasure thermometer and the ratio of lexical impaction to narrative progress, so that the least strange thing about this stanza is the (uncertainly translated) language strange of 'I love thee true'.

It has been clear from the start that the knight is enthralled by and lost in the land of faery, and the teasingly metaphorical 'fairy's child', which could simply be an exaggeration of her beauty, now becomes, literally, a faery:

> She took me to her elfin grot,
> And there she wept, and sigh'd full sore,
> And there I shut her wild wild eyes
> With kisses four.

With his extreme narrative tact, his refined sense of the mechanics of story-telling, Keats is able to explode the distinction between the precision of realist description and the highly metaphorical and allegorical mode of Spenserian Romance. This conflation is evident in two ways: first, in the contrast between faery-Romance diction ('elfin grot', 'sigh'd full sore', 'wild wild eyes') and the prosaic literalness of the actions ('took', 'wept', 'sigh'd', 'shut'); secondly, in the distinction between the arbitrary motivation of the actions – why does she take him?; why does she sigh and weep?; why does he kiss her eyes?; and why four kisses? – and the syntactical simplicity of the stanza, which gives the illusion of narrative necessity. Keats's alterations in this stanza show how much the effect had to be worked at, but every line except the first was significantly altered in the *Indicator* version in order, it seems, to temper the strange incoherence of motivation:

> She took me to her elfin grot,
> And there she gaz'd and sighed deep,
> And there I shut her wild sad eyes
> So kiss'd to sleep.

Gazing and sighing is more acceptable – less risky – than weeping and sighing; 'wild sad' reduces the potential tautological solecism of 'wild wild', exchanges mystery for emotional banality in the explanatory 'sad', and suppresses the sexual connotation of 'wild'; 'So kiss'd to sleep' again reduces the risk of unmotivated precision. The fine balance between impaction and rarefaction and between realism and metaphor achieved in the manuscript version of the poem is lost with these alterations.

As a result of the high degree of ellipsis which inhabits the narrative of this poem, each stanza seems to generate a world of its own, a different scene with new implications, connotations, and narrative conventions. Thus, although the tender pathos of stanza eight continues in the first line of stanza nine, there is also a disjunction – not only stanzaic, but also logical, tonal, and atmospheric – between the two stanzas:

> And there she lulled me asleep,
>   And there I dream'd – Ah! woe betide!
> The latest dream I ever dream'd
>   On the cold hill's side.

Logically it seems incoherent to move from the knight kissing the lady's eyes to the lady lulling the knight to sleep, and this incoherence is only emphasized by the syntactical repetition of 'And there ... And there'. In reducing this logical disjunction with 'we slumbered on the moss', the *Indicator* version anxiously misses the point. It is not the logic of the *histoire* that we, readers, are after by now, but the enticing logic of *discours*,[26] and this logic involves and has involved binary opposition, the contrastive reciprocity of giving: lulled asleep by the dream of poetry, we dream not of narrative causality – an external, retrospectively imposed production of meaning or *Nachträglichkeit* – but of inner and, if necessary, alogical meaning.

In breaking the frame of his narration in an exclamation of emotive evaluation,

> – Ah! woe betide!

the knight proleptically displays the tautological structure of his 'explanatory' story: like the echoes and repetitions which abound and rebound throughout the poem, both strengthening and disrupting the narration, 'woe betide' echoes the original question of why the knight is 'woe-begone'. If we take 'Ah! woe betide' as a privileged commentary on the story, then the answer to the question of why the knight is 'woe-begone' is 'Ah! woe betide', and betide means not only 'happen', but also 'circumscribed, beset, begone' (*OED*).

Like the threefold and tautological repetition of 'dream' in stanza nine, the repeated 'pale' of stanza ten stops narrative in its tracks and, like the mathematical kisses, strikes us with its very lack of motivation. Within the depths of this doubly embedded story, narrative motivation is completely lost, and now, at the crucial narrative point, the classical moment of *anagnorisis*, rarefaction is almost complete while the impacted lexis offered by earlier stanzas has been exchanged for repetition to the extent that the congruity of names seems to suggest not only that La Belle Dame sans Merci has the knight in thrall, but that 'La Belle Dame sans Merci' has the reader in thrall. Enthralled by the lack of narrative information and the excess of implication, readers tend to submit to the bondage of enthralment, to agree that they are in the poem's thrall.

Stanza eleven at least admits to the Gothic horror of the vision, admits that the spectres are in the tradition of allegorical prophecy, but relents little to our desire for clarification. It simply opens up vast new areas of narrative possibility and mortal fear:

> I saw their starv'd lips in the gloam
> With horrid warning gaped wide,
> And I awoke and found me here
> On the cold hill's side.

The shock of waking from a nightmare as the horror becomes unbearable is akin to the experience of waking from a poem as the narrative possibilities become too awesome.

The last stanza of the poem produces the comedy of a narrator complacently convinced that he has explained,

> And this is why I sojourn here,

– an anaphoric complacency unmerited by his performance.[27] But, of course, we know why he sojourns here and know that the reader sojourns here in the same woebegone way and for the same tautological reasons: the narrator's acceptance that what the knight has said is sufficient is signalled by his silence and by the implied merging of narrator and knight in the knight's repetition of the first stanza. Our compliance with such duplicitous collusion is assumed by Keats as he dares the reader to complain – to notice, even – that the strictly octosyllabic metre of the first three lines in each stanza is disrupted in the nine syllables of the poem's penultimate line. And, like the knight, who thinks that he controls, seduces, enthralls the lady 'with kisses four', the reader tends to remain unaware, consciously, of the mathematical precision of the 'kisses four', which he receives in enigmatic syllables from the poet:

> And no birds sing.

Only a pedant would count syllables or kisses in the passion of enthralment and abandonment, only a reader who applies inappropriate codes to a text that enthralls the imagination. In Keats's only recorded comment on the poem, he remarked on the pedantry of 'kisses four':

> Why four kisses – you will say – why four because I wish to restrain the headlong impetuosity of my Muse – she would have fain said 'score' without hurting the rhyme – but we must temper the Imagination as the Critics say with Judgment. I was obliged to choose an even number that both eyes might have fair play: and to speak truly I think two a piece quite sufficient – Suppose I had said seven; there would have been three and a half a piece – a very awkward affair – and well got out of on my side. (*Letters*, vol. II, p. 97)

As Keats acknowledges, the precision of 'kisses four' is pedantic in the context of a poem, and the figured reader is, therefore, likely to worry about their numerical significance on the principle that everything in a poem is significant, particularly those things which seem unpoetical. Keats's ironic pedantry in this letter demonstrates his acute manipulation of what Coleridge defines as 'pedantry'. Reading is figured and prefigured in 'La Belle Dame sans Merci' within the texture of the disparity, the solecism, between narrative and lexis: the reader is figured as enthralled, and the poem as a mechanism of enthralment.

CHAPTER 7

The spring odes

The odes written in the spring of 1819 – 'Ode to Psyche', 'Ode to a Nightingale', 'Ode on a Grecian Urn', 'Ode on Melancholy', 'Ode on Indolence' – construct a voice of intense subjectivity and produce the illusion or hallucination of 'overhearing' a poet speaking to himself, of reading a text which, in the sublime moment of inscription, seeks to efface, to annihilate its reader. While 'La Belle Dame sans Merci' figures reading as enthralment, the spring odes figure reading as a necessary and impossible absence.[1] At the same time, however, it is precisely through their intense 'subjectivity', their negation of audience, that the odes engage with questions of the poetics of reception. Indeed, as Helen Vendler has suggested, the odes are explicitly concerned to explore the aesthetics of reception through the figure of the receptive narrator.[2] Moreover, the lyrical temporality of Keats's odes is constantly invaded by and engaged in narrative: if, as I have argued, audience is always already figured by narrative, then the intrusion of the 'otherness' of narrative into the self-identical lyric form of the ode necessarily produces an audience-effect.

From the perspective of the present study, concerned as it is with the reciprocal concepts of narrative form and audience, there tend to be two ways in which critics frame the lyric.[3] In the first place, it is defined by contrast with narrative: in the words of a standard handbook on literature, the lyric is 'any fairly short, non-narrative poem presenting a single speaker who expresses a state of mind or a process of thought and feeling'.[4] This is related to the idea that the lyric is 'timeless', while narrative is based on a temporally determined sequence of events. In her study of Emily Dickinson and the lyric, Sharon Cameron puts this point forcefully when she argues that a certain atemporality constitutes the lyric's 'generating impulse':

I have suggested that the contradiction between social and personal time is the lyric's generating impulse, for the lyric both rejects the limitation of social and objective time, those strictures that drive hard lines between past, present, and future, and must make use of them ... the poem is a sequence that conceals its progressions, or synthesizes them so that it appears a completion no process could have prepared for.[5]

While it avoids the trap of calling the lyric 'timeless', Cameron's formulation suggests that one pole of the Romantic lyric's energies involves the desire to 'escape' temporality and thereby to escape narrative. Indeed, in his concise handbook on the subject, David Lindley has suggested both that it is this sense of the 'timeless' that was central to the Romantic concept of lyric, and that this definition originates with the Romantics.[6] One very common way of formulating this sense of the lyric in the late eighteenth and early nineteenth centuries involved an extrapolation from the idea of the 'sudden and bold transitions'[7] encountered in the ode, transitions which resist narrative causality in order to express poetic rapture.

Secondly, and as a corollary to this sense of timelessness, the lyric is conceived in terms of the subjectivity of the poetic speaker, as an articulation of a certain voice or a certain voicing.[8] In the introduction to her typological study of the 'Greater Lyric' of the eighteenth century, Anne Williams discusses various theoretical conceptions of the lyric and defines the 'organising consciousness' of the lyric as 'a kind of *logos* within the poem, a centripetal force which subordinates argument, narrative, or even other consciousness to itself'.[9] The lyric may be seen as a seemingly paradoxical 'representation of an act of self-expression', and Williams quotes Northrop Frye's view that 'the drama is marked by the concealment of the author from his audience' while the 'concealment of the poet's audience from the poet, is presented in the lyric'.[10] Once again it is possible to read a major Keatsian form (the ode) in terms of the solecism of the private made public, of the revelation of that which should remain hidden. But just as 'timelessness' is an ideal of the lyric, the lyric speaker's self-identical consciousness is the state for which the lyric strives rather than that which it achieves: if the poet 'conceals' audience from himself, then the act of concealment is, at the same time, necessarily an acknowledgement. What is, perhaps, most striking about the Romantic ode is the energy expended in repressing audience, energy which only, finally, marks the place of that audience. Keats's odes are not only deeply implicated in these conventions, but also help to define them. In this chapter I shall briefly survey the 'spring odes' in order to suggest ways in which the antithetical forces of both narrative and an aesthetics of reception inhabit and fracture the poems – poems which, as Jay Clayton has remarked, 'always seem about to burst into narrative'[11] – before discussing in more detail Keats's most sustained and elaborate engagement with the question of the lyric audience, 'Ode on a Grecian Urn'.

'Ode to Psyche' is based on a narrative which, in Hunt's *Examiner*, was referred to as 'the loveliest story of antiquity'.[12] The opening line, however, attempts to negate narration in the timelessness of the vocative 'O' and the apostrophic anthropomorphism of address:

> O Goddess! hear these tuneless numbers, wrung
>   By sweet enforcement and remembrance dear,
> And pardon that thy secrets should be sung
>   Even into thine own soft-conched ear ...

The governing figure of the opening lines and of the poem generally is the convolute: the speaker sings the narrative of Psyche to Psyche; Psyche's 'secrets' are sung into her own ear; the lover Psyche is also the speaker's own mind (hence the 'fane' built in some 'untrodden region of my mind'), and so on. If the governing figure is the convolute, it is no surprise that the governing metaphors are those of anatomical convolutes, the ear and the cerebrum. Finally, convolution is suggested by the rhetorical figures of paradox ('tuneless numbers') and paronomasia ('hear' – here – ear). The word 'wrung', with its senses ringing in the ears of a ringing in the ears and of a twisting or convolute (w)ringing of words, most strongly suggests ways in which reception is convoluted: 'tuneless numbers' are both sung and heard and at the same time not sung and not heard into and in the soft-conched ear of an audience consisting of both the self-convoluted inspiration of the poet and the public that reads and hears this poem. That is, the poem is 'heard' both by itself (and therefore not heard) and by an audience that reads the poem and 'hears' it differently (how does one 'hear' a poem on a page?).[13] The poem, like all written poems, both is and is not heard, and, as such, both is and is not a poem. That the mythological narrative becomes internalized within and *as* the poet's consciousness so that 'thine own soft-conched ear' is the poet's own ear, means that communication is short-circuited; that the poem is sung into an ear, and that it is a poem – expressed (written) and published – means that it demands a response from an other. But, at the same time, the other is simply another Psyche, or mind, a Psyche constructed for the uncanny moment of reading by the poem.

Helen Vendler has argued that the speaker in 'Ode to a Nightingale' is figured as 'pure ear, pure audience', that the poem is 'remarkable by the fineness and profundity of Keats's meditation on listening'. Vendler also suggests that the aesthetic object, the bird's song, is 'a voice of pure self-expression' and 'an effortless, purely spontaneous, and socially indifferent art' which is imitated by the poet himself.[14] This description of the voices of the poem brings out the contradictory pressures in 'Ode to a Nightingale' between a meditation on reception and the object of this reception, which resists the very possibility of such reception. Ultimately, in Vendler's analysis, it is the negation of audience which the poem both represents and produces: 'Art utters itself unconscious of any audience, pouring its soul abroad in pure self-expressiveness. Though its audience may be consoled by it, it is indifferent to that audience'.[15] But Vendler's insight into the aesthetic mode of the poem – an elaboration of the responsiveness of audience – conflicts with this formulation. Thus, in spite of itself, Vendler's analysis reveals the paradox of aesthetic reception as expressed in 'Ode to a Nightingale': lyric poetry both demands and precludes adequate response. It is stanza six which most explicitly and most profoundly engages with this tension. And it is this stanza which most explicitly elaborates an aesthetics of response in terms of the subject's self-transcendence, or death:

> Darkling I listen; and, for many a time
> I have been half in love with easeful Death,
> Call'd him soft names in many a mused rhyme,
> To take into the air my quiet breath;
> Now more than ever seems it rich to die,
> To cease upon the midnight with no pain,
>   While thou art pouring forth thy soul abroad
>   In such an ecstasy!
> Still wouldst thou sing, and I have ears in vain –
>   To thy high requiem become a sod.

Just as 'Ode to Psyche' reverses inspiration by figuring poetic making as a breathing into, so in this poem's central figure of reception, the speaker breathes in creative response. Here, though, the line 'To take into the air my quiet breath' conflates breathing and dying and reveals the necessary engagement in death of breathing out, expiration. And the repetition of the figure of expiration in the bird's song – 'While thou art pouring forth thy soul abroad' – suggests that singing and dying are the same: the act of creation is a figure for the posthumous life of writing. But the deathliness of singing is also the deathliness of creative response. The dying song of the bird produces a mimetic response in the listener. In this arch-Romantic figuration of response, to be an addressee is to die in a mimetic act of expiration.

But if narrative generally requires an unresolved tension in order to 'move', and if Keats's poems, above all, both produce and require what I have characterized as an anxiety of audience – a desire and antagonism towards audience – to generate narrative, we might read the poem (and this stanza in particular) in terms of a desire to escape such tension. Leon Waldoff has described the Keatsian desire for death here and elsewhere as 'not a simple wish to die, to cease to exist, but a metaphor for a state of mind in which all anxieties, all tensions, would be dissolved in a moment of luxurious sensation'.[16] With our understanding of the instabilities and tensions necessary for narrative, we might read this desire in 'Ode to a Nightingale' as also a desire to end narrative, to write 'pure lyric'. But from the perspective of the polarities of lyric and narrative form, the poem is deeply compromised: the intensely subjective experience of a present-tense narration is framed by a doubly recursive movement back to the past tense at the beginning and the ending of the ode (the past subjunctive of 'as though of hemlock I had drunk', and the past tense of 'Was it a vision, or a waking dream?'), and is, at a crucial moment, in stanza seven, invaded by 'surrogate' tales of emperors and clowns, Ruth, and Romance. The narrative turns and counter-turns of this poem preclude the temporal self-identity of lyric and produce the responsive desire for death or, precisely, desire.[17]

By contrast, 'Ode on Melancholy' successfully fends off resurgent stories by a concentration on an accumulative rhetoric and a focus on a single emotional state.[18] Rather than stories, the poem involves an intensive investigation of the aesthetics of visual reception. It is explicitly stanza two which introduces the concept of receptive aesthetics in its description of an intense homoeopathic struggle with melancholy: sorrow can be 'glutted' on the vision of a 'morning rose' or a 'rainbow of the salt sand-wave', on 'globed peonies' or 'peerless eyes'. Rather differently, the poem engages with reception in its trope of address: unlike 'Ode to a Nightingale' and 'Ode to Psyche', 'Ode on Melancholy', rather than addressing a mythological or aesthetic object, addresses its reader. This combination of receptive effects has a strange *dénouement* when, at the end of the poem, the very possibility of reading is itself put into question:

> Ay, in the very temple of Delight
> Veil'd Melancholy has her sovran shrine,
>   Though seen of none save him whose strenuous tongue
> Can burst Joy's grape against his palate fine;
> His soul shall taste the sadness of her might,
>   And be among her cloudy trophies hung.

Within the context of an aesthetics of reception provided by a concentration on the visual and an apostrophic address to the reader, these lines may be understood to figure reading itself. The 'strenuous tongue' would, in this sense, belong to the reader and to 'burst Joy's grape against [one's] palate fine' would be a description of the pleasures of the text as the reader articulates (silently or not) the words of 'Ode on Melancholy'.[19] In this sense, the poem repeats the representation of the posthumous life of reading of 'Ode to a Nightingale'.

Tilottama Rajan has recently suggested that 'as a purely subjective form' the lyric is 'marked by the exclusion of the other' and by an attempt to 'mute the gaps between signifier and signified by conferring on the words the illusory unity of a single voice' – in contrast to the dramatized gap in narrative 'between what is told and the telling of it'.[20] This gap is most fully explored in Keats's most overtly narrative ode, 'Ode on Indolence'. In this poem, the narrative of the urn which is no narrative (each time the speaker looks he finds the same figures) is substituted for the story of the poet's receptivity towards the visual. The first line of 'Ode on Indolence' introduces a paradoxical objectification of lyric consciousness in the passive mode – 'One morn before me were three figures seen' – so that the seeing 'eye' is apparently differentiated from the speaking 'I', an implicit antagonism of the homologous 'I'/'eye' which so strongly marks 'Ode to Psyche' ('or did I see...with awaken'd eyes?', 'tender eye-dawn', 'I see, and sing, by my own eyes inspired'). This antagonism provides the plot of aesthetic reception in 'Ode on Indolence' and interrogates the gap between seeing art and the phenomenological 'knowledge' of the art object which such seeing seems to offer. And such a 'gap' seems to be a product of the narrative form of the ode, a form which constantly struggles against temporality and against the work which time demands, and which struggles to capture the indolent eternal moment of aesthetic receptivity.

If this brief survey suggests the constant resurgence of narrativity in the lyric ode and emphasizes the ways in which reading is repeatedly, even obsessively, figured in the spring odes, we can plot such concerns in more detail in 'Ode on a Grecian Urn'. In particular, I shall examine the generative forces of narrative double logic within the lyric form and the ways in which, within the paradigmatic poem of nineteenth-century Romantic aesthetics, reading is figured and reception prefigured.

'Ode on a Grecian Urn' ends in an irreducibly undecidable affirmation:

> 'Beauty is truth, truth beauty', – that is all
> Ye know on earth, and all ye need to know.

The response which this ending has generated is a series of questions such as 'who is speaking?'; 'what does he mean?'; 'to what is he referring?': an endless series of questions, of responses, which both spread from this poetic centre in endless multiplication and, at the same time, repeat the interrogative mode of the figured reading of 'Ode on a Grecian Urn'. Thus a poem about a poet responding to an iconographical tradition both generates and foreshadows a fertile and illustrious tradition of criticism responding to a lyric poem: just as the 'poet' misreads the storied urn as non-narrative, while at the same time searching for a hidden narrative behind the figures, so critics tend to read the poem as the expression of a yearning for timelessness while asking questions about how the relationship between poet and urn develops. What is important and compelling in this poem is not so much what happens on the urn or in the poem, but the way that a response to an artwork both figures and prefigures its own critical response: the critical response to the ode is figured in 'Ode on a Grecian Urn'.[21]

It is not, then, by chance that the most common response to Keats's poem on an urn is a series of questions which repeat the narrator's questions to the urn. Jack Stillinger's 'Who says what to whom at the end of "Ode on a Grecian Urn"?'[22] is only the most explicit of the critics' questions. By asking this question – and Keats's typographical ambiguity fends off any certainty here[23] – we are simply entering the undecidable circle of fictional 'truth' which the poem explores. 'Who says what to whom?' is asking the same sort of question and setting up the same sort of real world/fictional ratio which the questions within the poem – 'who are these coming to the altar?' (etc.) – produce. In both cases, the questions seem to mark the following assumptions:

(a) that the relationship between the reader/viewer and the work of art is fixed: the artwork is silent, enigmatic, frustrating (/teasing);
(b) that what is being expressed is a signifier/signified duality, in which the signifier is revealed and the signified obscure (but ultimately available/verifiable);
(c) that there is a story on/in the artwork, and, following on from this,
(d) that stories are understood in terms of binary oppositions (present – past; discourse – story; signifier – signified).

There are, with regard to these propositions, two questions which should be answered: (1) what is the relationship between propositions a, b, c and d, and the poem, and (2) to what extent are the propositions a, b, c and d, themselves valid? Although we ask them endlessly, we should not, as I say, be tempted to think that we can answer Stillinger's (and most commentators') question because such a question involves a particular aesthetic response which is already figured in the poem: any 'answer' which we give will have been prefigured on the urn. In order 'properly' to read this poem, one would simply have to ask different kinds of questions.

The fact that Keats's ode is often read as exemplary of the ekphrastic genre may be explained, then, by its dynamic intersection of a (mimetic) response to an artwork within the poem with the result of this figured reception – the production (partly by mimesis) of our response to the text as a work of art.[24] As Ross Chambers has argued, the post-Enlightenment writer, in his anxiety of audience, is impelled to insert embedded descriptions of the reader's response into his text (in order to be read right).[25] Keats's poem may be understood to develop this anxiety *ad absurdum*, so that the embedded reflexive episode, an example of what Gerald Prince calls a 'reading interlude', overflows, and, in itself, becomes the poem.[26]

According to Gerald Prince, one way in which a text attempts to stabilize the varying responses which it generates is by performing 'some of the reading operations that a given reader may perform'. Specifically, it 'answers questions pertaining to the nature, the meaning, the role, the appropriateness of its constituent parts'. But in a footnote Prince points out that 'sometimes it even asks those questions' and quotes, as an example, Marcel's reaction, in 'Du Côté de Chez Swann', to tasting the *madeleine* dipped in tea: 'Whence could it have come to me, this all pervading joy?...Whence did it come? What did it signify? How could I seize upon and define it?'[27] The narrative questions which Marcel asks of the (non-narrative) sensation of tasting are similar to those asked by the speaker in the 'Ode on a Grecian Urn' of the urn: and in each case they direct the questions of the reader. The answers to Marcel's questions are elaborated in the twelve volumes of Proust's novel and Keats's questions are explored in the fifty lines of his poem. Elsewhere, however, Proust has eloquently elaborated the dynamic mechanism, the inevitably paradoxical logic of reading which informs the matrix of knowledge and desire in a text such as 'Ode on a Grecian Urn':

And there, indeed, is one of the great and marvelous characters of beautiful books (and one which will make us understand the rôle, at once essential and limited, that reading can play in our spiritual life) which for the author could be called 'Conclusions' and for the reader 'Incitements'. We feel quite truly that our wisdom begins where that of the author ends, and we would like to have him give us answers, while all he can do is give us desires ... if we put to [writers] questions they cannot answer, we also ask from them answers that would not instruct us. For it is an effect of the love which poets awake in us to make us attach a literal importance to things which for them are only significant of personal emotions. In each picture they show us, they seem to give us but a light glimpse of a marvelous site, different from the rest of the world, and to whose heart we would wish they might make us penetrate.[28]

The conflation of knowledge and desire defines memory for Marcel, and art for the speaker of the 'Ode on a Grecian Urn'. The inciting nature of the 'Urn' poem's final couplet is the enticement generated in the poem's readers by the conclusive nature of the lines, a finality emphasized by other forms of rhetorical closure – parallelism, chiasm, aphorism, paradox, enigma, and apparently meaningful hints about the nature of life and art.[29] It is *because* of this finality – rather than in spite of it – that so many critics have responded so quizzically to the last couplet: it is the urn's silence that teases us into and out of thought.

The obscurity of the urn's message is also an obscurity engendered by the poem itself: in the opening lines we may notice the pun(?) on 'still', the oxymoronic sexuality ('unravished bride'), the contradictory(?) personifications ('bride of quietness' but 'foster-child of silence and slow time'), and, most tellingly, the slippage between history and fiction ('Sylvan historian...flowery tale...legend', where even if the historian is emphatically 'sylvan', the word still carries a semantic weight of history as opposed to 'tale' or, different again, 'legend'). It is this tantalizing obscurity, an enticement offering no conclusion which makes the poem balance on the edge of meaning and meanings, as the figures on the urn balance on the edge of ecstasy, and as the urn balances on the edge of narrative. Just as our allegorization of such obscurity makes the obscure signify, the narrator's own questions to the urn give us the beginnings of a story. It may be difficult to think of these questions as directed at the reader rather than – as the illusion represents it – towards the urn, but this is, of course, the case: we are not reading the words of a man speaking to an urn but those of a poet addressing his audience. The questions are rhetorical, both because they have no answers and because it is not the answers that are important but rather the effect of the questions. Although scholars have endlessly searched museums and books in order to find the 'original' urn, in fact all we need is here, the 'words on the page'. The questions themselves tell a story in which the scene is set, in Tempe or Vale of Arcady, wherein some figures, humans and/or gods, are acting out the timeless ritual of seduction in the impassioned temporal moment of wild ecstasy. Only the penultimate question of stanza one interrupts the flow of narrative from scene-setting to consummation, but 'what pipes or timbrels?' also articulates, in small, an essential narrative element – suspense: as in all good narratives, the suspense, what Hazlitt called 'the pinch of the interest' (*Works*, vol. v, p. 10), comes just at the right moment, and also implicitly refers to the main plot (music as both an expression of and substitute for or deferral of love-making). In the micro-narrative of lines 5–10, Keats prefigures the narrative movement of the next two stanzas, and, to a certain extent, the larger narrative movement of the whole poem (an attempt to capture the virgin meaning of the urn, ending in the poised ecstasy of aphorism).

Stanza two throws us back into the extradiegetic position of the first lines (where the poet is standing outside the story in order to make general comments), and this is signalled by a return to, and reiteration of, 'sweet', marked by the paradoxical claim that 'Heard melodies are sweet, but those unheard / Are sweeter'. Even without the implicit contradiction of this claim in the next two lines, where 'heard' melodies play against 'unheard' in the homophony 'ear / endeared' which might be picked up by the sensuous ear, and where the putative rhyme-word 'unhear'd' only 'rhymes' visually[30] – even without these hints, we might notice that 'sweetness' is, if anything, sensuous, and cannot be abstracted away as if it were something like beauty or truth, both of which benefit from a transcendentalizing aesthetic. The sestet in stanza two plays with the notions of what we might call lyric and narrative time schemes (where lyric time is 'timeless', and narrative 'temporal') as the quatrain has played with the concepts of sensuous and non-sensuous (transcendental) sensation. As the story develops at the end of stanza two, the recursive forces of 'lyric' timelessness begin to disrupt narrative:

> Bold lover, never, never canst thou kiss,
> Though winning near the goal –

The syntax of the first of these lines, a syntax which will be developed and exaggerated in the next stanza, turns on an attempt to stall the narrative flow by repetition, while the second line reasserts contingency, playing against the timelessness of 'never, never' the temporality of the present participle 'winning': this teasing conflation of the temporal and the timeless is fully explored in stanza three.

The stanza central to the poem is a stanza which articulates the solecism of scandal: the stanza is scandalous in its major trope (multiple repetition), in its theme (hedonism), in its syntax (an accretion of parallel clauses), and in its diction (the repeated, vacuous, 'happy' and 'for ever'). In this stanza the poem almost breaks in the middle, the language descends almost to incoherence as the tension between 'narrative' and 'lyric' time, between the temporality of language, of poetry, and the timelessness of 'Art' threatens to pull the poem apart.[31] What happens in this stanza is, amongst other things, a culmination of Keats's concern over narrative in his poetry, a breaking of the notion that poetry can exist without narrative and without audience and, at the same time, a breaking of the notion that a narrative can survive on the rarefied oxygen of consummated love. Once desire has been fulfilled there is no tale to tell: just as 'Isabella' had to find a new narrative imbalance at stanza nine when love is declared, and just as 'The Eve of St Agnes' had to change from a love-consummation plot to an escape plot at stanza thirty-six, the 'Ode on a Grecian Urn' almost breaks under the weight of the attempt to express intensity without plot, to represent progress without time.

The problem of the relationship between words and visual objects which organizes 'Ode on a Grecian Urn' may be illuminated by a brief consideration of an essay by Keats's friend, the painter Benjamin Robert Haydon, published in *Annals of the Fine Arts* in 1820. In this essay, Haydon points to the fundamental difference in the languages of poetry and painting and summarizes the prevailing view, since Locke, of the arbitrary nature of words:

> Of course, the languages are different in their essence; the language of poets, with reference to visible objects, is an artificial assemblage of words, agreed on by the respective nation to which each poet belongs, to mean the things to which they are applied, although they have very few natural claims to such associations, and although the neighbouring nations to which they might be read would be perfectly ignorant of their reference; while our language is the imitation of the things themselves, and the most imperfect representation of the thing intended is at once comprehended ... [32]

Keats's attempt to pin down 'happy' in the central lines of the 'Urn' is an attempt to batter the arbitrariness of language into submission, to create happiness from the physical texture of 'happy': the same kind of thing was attempted by Coleridge when he tried to pin down the essence of happiness by studying the different linguistic formations of the experience in 'Joy', 'Bliss', 'Gladness', 'Pleasure', and 'Happiness', or by Keats himself when he asks 'Wherein lies happiness?' and answers it with his 'pleasure thermometer'.[33] But, as Coleridge points out in his notebooks, the semantics and etymology of 'happiness' inextricably connect it with chance, with 'hap': happiness is only happy by chance. In Keats's poem our recognition of this secondary signification is engendered precisely by the attempt to fix the signified to the signifier because the repetition foregrounds the acoustic phenomenon of 'hap' while slighting or endangering meaning.[34] But referring to etymologies or 'secondary significations' of words is itself a process subject to the question of the duality of the contingent and the necessary: is the etymology necessarily present in the word? And do we notice, for example, that such collocations as 'happy chance' are, in one sense, tautologies – and if so, is it possible to ignore the chanciness of 'happy'?

In his attempt to pin down 'happy', to make of it an absolute value, then, Keats has infected his language with chance, or has pointed up the chanciness of language. Arresting the narrative movement in the repetitions of the third stanza, and thereby attempting to de-temporalize his verse, to lyricize it, he has re-inscribed contingency within the very temple of the absolute: narrative, in the sense of the contingent temporal connections between events (connections which it is the prerogative of the narrator arbitrarily to define) returns within the silence of repetition and within the history of words. In turning the urn, and turning his poem to a new subject, to what has been read as a sub-plot or extension of the story at stanza four, Keats exemplifies his role as creator of the arbitrary connections between events in the narrative.[35] Stanza four has been criticized because of its lack of connection with the first stanzas as if, in running out of ideas, Keats had been constrained to invent a new subject. But the 'arbitrary' nature of the intervention of sacrifice into a poem describing a representation of unconsummated passion, simply highlights the 'arbitrary' nature of narrative itself.

The turn at the beginning of stanza four, a turn achieved, it seems, by a literal turning of the urn, brings renewed questions, renewed narrative interest, renewed enticement as compared to the conclusions of stanza three. We have seen, however, that the conclusions of stanza three are shot through by chance, and so, conversely, the enticements of stanza four are shot through by the conclusion of death: the questions which open the stanza, those open-ended, enticingly rhetorical structures, provide their own answer to the question which they ask about significance. The significance of the people coming to the altar is that they are coming to the altar, and so on. Inscribed within the arbitrary, open nature of this stanza is the fixed and closed recognition of death, conclusion. As Keats goes beyond the pleasure principle, a principle which seems to offer absolute value but apparently relies on chance, as he goes beyond this principle, he finds, like Freud later, the drive towards death.[36] Once again, the figure of reading modulates towards a figure of the death of the reader.

Reading might be said to be figured in 'Ode on a Grecian Urn' in a series of 'binary oppositions':

lyric:narrative :: timeless:temporal :: necessary:contingent

It is the latter ratio which is, perhaps, the most interesting: the characteristic nature of narrative, its contrast with 'lyric time' and with the visual arts, is that it is able to establish causal connections where the 'timeless' arts must be silent. Although we are aware that any fictional 'causal' connection is arbitrarily imposed by the writer, is contingent, within the terms of the narrative it seems to be necessary. This is why the turn at the end of stanza three is disconcerting – it is difficult to understand the narrative logic which can make the connection (seem) necessary – and why so many critics write stories for Keats to explain the thematic connections between bold lovers and sacrificial heifers. This double logic of narrative (the ontological contingency and narrative necessity of stories) also, however, accounts for the reader's double experience of narrative, a description of which is embedded within 'Ode on a Grecian Urn' at stanza four. Our recognition of the uncanny power of this stanza is, at least in part, a response to its paradoxical configuration of necessity and contingency. In this stanza, as the narrator's voice oscillates between questioning and asserting, between being led and leading, the reader's position *vis-à-vis* narrative oscillates between control and submission to authority. The allegory of stanza four represents the reader's ambivalent position. The 'heifer lowing at the skies' is, in all probability, a direct reference to a scene from the Elgin Marbles where a heifer, being led to its death appears to be 'lowing at the skies':[37] the poet who wrote this description is a reader of the antique plastic arts. This ambivalence of questioning/asserting, reading/writing, has a structural analogue in the previous stanza, where the relative spatial positioning of actors on the urn and viewers of the urn is described:

> For ever warm and still to be enjoy'd,
>   For ever panting, and for ever young;
> All breathing human passion far above,
>   That leaves a heart high-sorrowful and cloy'd,
>   A burning forehead, and a parching tongue.

There is a crucial indeterminacy in the relative spatial positions of immortal and human beings. The gods, the heavens, the transcendental, the timeless, the immortal, are usually figured as transcendentally 'above' the human, mortal, passionate. Here, however, the human is (arguably) 'above' the timeless realm of art:[38] this ambivalence in what is, after all, one of Keats's most characteristic schemas[39] affects the way that we read the fourth stanza. The uncertainty in the first stanza over 'of deities or mortals, or of both' and 'what men or gods are these?' is a confusion which is repeated schematically in stanzas three and four. Moreover, structurally there is an interesting homology between necessity in gods and the poet (and poetic authority) on the one hand, and contingency in 'men' and the reader on the other: this would account for the ambivalence in the poem as a whole, and particularly in stanza four, over whose tale it is. As with the questions in stanza one, the questions in stanza four represent both a 'reader' (asking for information) and a 'writer' (giving information). But in terms of the poet's reading of the urn, there is a similar ambivalence or inversion: the heifer which is being led to the altar is a visual double of the urn itself: 'What leaf-fring'd legend haunts about thy shape' becomes 'And all her silken flanks with garlands drest'. This coincidence in visual detail makes of the urn a sacrificial victim and the poet a 'mysterious priest': instead of the urn leading the eye of the narrator, the narrator is leading the urn, both by turning it (he makes his own story because either side could be viewed first or the urn not turned at all) and by interpreting it. The viewer's usurpation of narrative control is confirmed by the hypothesis which is made in the last three lines:

> And, little town, thy streets for evermore
> Will silent be; and not a soul to tell
> Why thou art desolate, can e'er return.

The narrator, in the role of reader, is drawing inferences from the objects which he sees and making of these objects both allegory and meaning (in the extrapolations of 'evermore', 'silent', 'desolate' and in the invention of a story for the town). Although he asserts that 'there is not a soul to tell / Why thou art so desolate', in these lines he is both telling us why (the town is, like the urn, silent for evermore because it is a work of art) and making other, similar and similarly telling inferences about the art object.[40]

Having both deconstructed the urn's logic and demystified its tale, the poem proceeds, at stanza five to demonstrate more clearly its delusive nature: the romantically mythical place-names of the scenes on the urn ('Tempe' and 'dales of Arcady') modulate to the factual

'Attic' of the urn's origins; the carefully poised figures become artificially posed, an attitude, with a disconcerting pun as if to trivialize the object; the potentially prurient pun on 'brede' (/breed) increases our scepticism about the narrator's control of his materials; and in transferring the lovers' excitement to the urn in the ambiguity of who or what is 'overwrought', and how, Keats suggests a reflexive scepticism towards artwork. Not only are the puns and ambiguities potentially 'crass',[41] but they also alert us to the arbitrary nature of language once again, its ability to discover unwarranted connections: even if we refuse to recognize these puns and, with John Bayley, call them 'coincidences', we must still be aware of the coincidence – the unmotivated chanciness – of their concurrence.[42] We are 'teased out of thought' because, as Proust suggests, the artwork offers no conclusions, only enticements. But the enticement in the work of art is, as 'Ode on a Grecian Urn' so clearly recognizes, the conclusive nature of the object. Like eternity, in which, as Coleridge said, 'there is no Fortune, no contingency' (*CN*, 3558), the urn entices us with its conclusions. It is an illusion or fantasy or hallucination because, like the speaking voice in poetry, it seems to speak to us, to offer dialogue with the viewer/reader: it is a delusive looking glass through which we pass to find only the reflection of our own desires. It plays tricks, like 'Ode on a Grecian Urn', by proffering us the vision of meaning but refusing, when we take up the offer, to be drawn: 'Cold Pastoral!'[43]

The story of 'Ode on a Grecian Urn' is the story not only of desire and seduction, but also of the desire and seduction of the reader: our apprehension of Keats's poem is prefigured word for word by the narrator's apprehension of the urn: the story – history, tale, legend – involves the necessary connection not between events within the story but between the poem and its audience. It is not only the lovers who are ever more about to achieve consummation; the lover of poetry is suspended in the timeless moment of apprehension, ever more about to understand.

CHAPTER 8

The 'Hyperion' poems

FAILURE

'Hyperion' opens with a catalogue of negations – death, silence, stillness – a catatonic opening to a poem which cannot move and which elaborates the epic negation of Romantic writing, that is the negation, embedded within the modern verse-epic, of the possibility of audience:[1] 'No stir of air ... Not so much life ... not one light seed ... the dead leaf fell ... A stream went voiceless by, still deadened more ... No further ... nerveless, listless, dead / Unsceptred ... realmless eyes were closed' (Book 1, lines 7–19).

There are numerous possible referents for such inaugural negation. In this chapter I shall, however, confine my discussion to just one possibility: I shall follow through the logic of the proposition that the negations which open 'Hyperion' are related to Keats's earlier romance-epic, *Endymion* and, in particular, to the public responses to that earlier poem. The trope of negation which figures the opening to 'Hyperion' will be read as a negation of *Endymion* and, in turn, be read as a response to the critical reception of that poem. Without denying the multiple origins and resonances of 'Hyperion', I shall read it in terms of writing which inhabits the complex space formed by *Endymion*, that poem's critical reception, and the projected reaction of the same audience to another epic.

A crucial 'intertext' for 'Hyperion', then, was Keats's own *Endymion*. Indeed, the conditions of publication for 'Hyperion' themselves announced the relationship between *Endymion*, 'Hyperion', and Keats's audience as once again a poem was presented to the public with a gesture of a denial of audience: Keats's publishers added a notorious 'Advertisement' to the 1820 volume stating not only that 'Hyperion' was printed 'contrary to the wish of the author', but also that the fragmentary nature of the poem was due to the reviews of *Endymion*: 'The poem was intended to have been of equal length with *Endymion*, but the reception given to that work discouraged the author from proceeding'. In fact, of course, the statement is highly dubious: in the first place, Keats is known to have written in the margin of one copy of his 1820 *Poems* next to the Advertisement 'This is a lie'; and secondly, as critics have pointed out, Keats *started* writing 'Hyperion' after the reviews of *Endymion* had appeared, a fact which makes the chronology of the publishers' assertion incoherent.[2] Nevertheless, the Advertisement does indicate a very important source of authorial anxiety which informs the narrative shape of 'Hyperion' and of its rewriting, 'The Fall of Hyperion': rather than preventing Keats from continuing with 'Hyperion' as the publishers' Advertisement stated, the reviews might be said to have provided an important generating force for the writing of 'Hyperion' in the first place.

It is, therefore, worth considering the precise nature of the criticisms of *Endymion*. These criticisms may be schematically enumerated as follows: derivative language and style (especially from Leigh Hunt); irregular versification; 'vicious' diction (neologisms, invented participles, compound epithets, 'cockney' slang); misuse of classical mythology; obscurity/meaninglessness; overuse of 'conceits'; immorality/obscenity; (social/literary) vulgarity; prurience; radical/Jacobinical politics; rambling narrative form.[3] 'Hyperion' can be read, in part, as a reaction to these criticisms: the way in which the poem seeks to assert *Paradise Lost* as its linguistic model implicitly acknowledges the force of (some of) the criticisms by attempting to adopt a more respectable model of poetic decorum than, for example, Leigh Hunt's *The Story of Rimini*. Similarly, the potential for charges of political or ethical subversion in 'Hyperion' is limited not only by a focus on epic rather than libidinal and even incestuous themes, but also by a certain repression of 'sensuous' language and a reduced concentration on sensuous perception. Moreover, there is a significant alteration in narrative form, towards a far simpler, more direct, and less wandering narration.[4] All of these may be seen in terms of acquiescence to criticism (sympathetic or not) to *Endymion*. On the other hand, in once again taking classical mythology as his subject, Keats is defiantly asserting both his right and his ability to rewrite the classics against the sarcastic irony of reviewers who mocked both his education and his class position in this respect. Similarly, the politics of 'Hyperion', which may be read as at least 'liberal' or 'progressive' (if not exactly revolutionary), also stand in defiance of the tone of the critical reviews.[5] Simply by writing a plot of revolution, simply by asking political questions about the nature and effect of revolution, Keats might be seen to be reacting against the kinds of political limitations which certain reviewers of *Endymion* (and the attacks on the 'Cockney School') attempted to impose. Thus, to read 'Hyperion' as a 'reaction' to the more hostile reviews of *Endymion*, is to recognize the tensions within such a reaction, to recognize the contradictions and duplicities within the relationship between a poem and its empirically determined audience.[6]

The silence, the stillness, the lack of speech and inability to speak which structures the opening lines of 'Hyperion', then, might be read as a negation of the fecund wordiness of *Endymion* – the fault of a poet who was, in J. R. Lowell's term, 'overlanguaged' (*Heritage*, p. 361) – a poem which was governed by the intricate arabesque of (micro-) narrative line, and the abundance of embedded narratives.[7] The silencing figured in the opening to 'Hyperion' – represented by the Naiad who '' 'mid her reeds / Press'd her cold finger closer to her lips' (Book 1, lines 13–14)[8] – also involves a repression of narrative form, a silencing, at least, of the extrinsic, decorative, surrogate encrustations of narrative in *Endymion*. Numerous critics have pointed out that Keats seems to have achieved what he said he would in 'Hyperion', that is a poem written 'in more naked and grecian manner', a poem in which 'the march of passion and endeavour will be undeviating' (*Letters*, vol. 1, p. 207). In fact, however, although this seems to be an adequate description of the projected narrative, the extant fragment is characterized most generally by a stunted narrative form, by narrative potential. Most commonly, critics liken the narrative form of 'Hyperion' to a series of *tableaux*, or to the *disjecta membra* which it presents.[9] This impossible narrative trajectory or the impossibility of narrative trajectory itself, is asserted in Saturn's first speech with his agonized claim that 'it must – it must / Be of ripe progress – Saturn must be King' (1, 124–5), and his dilation on this sense of obligatory narrative progression:

> 'Yes, there must be a golden victory;
> There must be Gods thrown down, and trumpets blown
> Of triumph calm, and hymns of festival
> Upon the gold clouds metropolitan,
> Voices of soft proclaim, and silver stir
> Of strings in hollow shells; and there shall be

> Beautiful things made new, for the surprise
> Of the sky-children; I will give command:
> Thea! Thea! Thea! where is Saturn?'   (1, 126–34)

The sense that these potential narratives will remain potential is given by the 'command' which appears as a question, 'where is Saturn?' Similarly, the first description of 'Hyperion' is marked by a comparable force of negation:

> Not at dog's howl, or gloom-bird's hated screech,
> Or the familiar visiting of one
> Upon the first toll of his passing-bell,
> Or prophesyings of the midnight lamp;
> But horrors, portion'd to a giant nerve,
> Oft made Hyperion ache.   (1, 171–6)

It has become increasingly clear, as we have progressed in this study, that such a negation of narrative, or, at least, a problematizing of narrative form, is entirely characteristic of Keats's poetry: there is the interrupted/embedded/nominal narration of the early poetry, the dilated surrogate narration of *Endymion*, the encrypted narration of 'Isabella', the descriptive narration of 'The Eve of St Agnes', the lexicalized narration of 'La Belle Dame sans Merci', and the lyricized narration of the odes. Indeed, it is precisely the resistance to stories in the traditional sense which provides the generative anxiety for Keatsian narrative – an anxiety over tellability which includes both the ontological possibility of their being told and the pragmatic possibility of their gaining an audience.

With this in mind, we might suggest that the narrative trope most characteristic of 'Hyperion' is that which Gerald Prince has defined as the 'disnarrated'. Prince explains the 'disnarrated' as 'all the events that *do not* happen but, nonetheless, are referred to (in a negative or hypothetical mode) by the narrative text'. Prince makes the important distinction between the 'disnarrated', on the one hand, and on the other hand narrative ellipsis, in which events are left untold 'because of some narrative call for rhythm, characterization, suspense, surprise, and so on'.[10] Furthermore, Prince also emphasizes the significance of the disnarrated to the pragmatics of narration. Through the inclusion of the 'disnarrated', the poet can assert the tellability of his story by comparing it favourably with other possible/potential tales: if the disnarrated includes narratives which do not deserve to be told or cannot be told, the narration which *is* told is, by implication, tellable. Bearing in mind that one of the most virulent attacks on *Endymion*, that by John Wilson Croker in the *Quarterly Review*, opens with an assertion that the reviewer was unable to read beyond the first book of the poem (*Heritage*, pp. 110–11), the question of tellability, of enticing or seducing the reader into reading on, might be understood to have been a crucial consideration in 'Hyperion'.

We might elaborate Prince's concept of the 'disnarrated' in terms of its being constituted by two related formal strategies: negation and alterity. The disnarrated produces negation by referring to what is not or cannot be narrated. At the same time, by asserting an alternative to its own narrative this negation produces what we might term 'alterity' or the 'other' of narrative.[11] A narrative is then defined in terms of narratives which are not itself. A few examples of strategies of alterity and negation in 'Hyperion' will give some indication of the extent to which the poem is structured around the 'disnarrated', and the extent to which it is produced by this (de-)construction – by the failure of 'Hyperion'.

In the first of the poem's overtly self-reflexive statements of poetic incompetence, when the narrator attempts to repeat or express Thea's speech, we find a narratorial sense of an alternative discourse:

> Some mourning words, which in our feeble tongue
> Would come in these like accents; O how frail
> To that large utterance of the early Gods!　　　(1, 49–51)

On one level this is a further assertion of the silence of the written text: the pathos of writing is suggested by the negative force of 'tongue … accents … utterance' and by the previous line's foregrounding of the materiality of voice, 'solemn tenour and deep organ tone'.[12] On another level, however, Keats is providing an example of the doubling of the disnarrated: 'Hyperion' is structured as an other of narrative. Similarly, the very syntax of Saturn's speech, his assertion of power and of narrative possibility, are expressed in terms of negation:

> 'But cannot I create?
> Cannot I form? Cannot I fashion forth
> Another world, another universe,
> To overbear and crumble this to nought?
> Where is another Chaos? Where?'　　　(1, 141–5)

Here the repeated negative 'cannot' works against the interrogative mode almost as if the phrase 'cannot I … ' was semantically identical with 'I cannot'. Saturn's sense of his own impotence conflicts with his understanding of 'another universe': thematically, the 'disnarrated' is represented by the fallen Titans' sense of their failure. Moreover, this pressure of negation deep within the language affects the narrative ordering of plot and subplot: moving from Saturn to the other Titans, Keats reproduces the alterity of Saturn's speech so as to assert the congruence of narrative worlds:

> Meanwhile in other realms big tears were shed,
> More sorrow like to this, and such like woe,
> Too huge for mortal tongue or pen of scribe (1, 158–60)

Negation and alterity are explicitly expressed in what might otherwise have been a conventional modulation from one scene to another; but here the lexicon of alterity – 'other ... like ... such like ... too huge ... or' – alerts us to the fact that in this articulation of poetic inadequacy a more crucial sense of potential narrative failure is indicated.

Paradoxically, perhaps, when the modulation is achieved, we find a disconcerting familiarity in the predicament of Hyperion, as if the alternative narrative line, which promised to rescue the threatened silence of the narration of the fallen Titans, is simply a repetition of the first, providing no possibility of development. The descriptions of Saturn and Hyperion overlap in their stillness: 'Blazing Hyperion on his orbed fire / Still sat, still snuff'd the incense' (1, 166–7). The adverbial 'still' of a continuing action also involves adjectival motionlessness and silence: indeed, there is a chiastic reciprocity of grammar and meaning in the two senses, because although the word works grammatically as an adverb denoting continuation, this presupposes a former reference which is unavailable to the reader – an anterior disnarrated – so that the sense of stillness or silence is produced through narrative absence. The phrases also point to another kind of 'disnarrated' in their syntactic echoing of Miltonic inversion. Indeed, this sense of an anterior disnarrated repeatedly disrupts reading with an overwhelming sense of an alternative narrative lying deep within the uncluttered syntax of the verse. Similarly, at 1, 175–6, 'But horrors, portion'd to a giant nerve, / Oft made Hyperion ache', 'oft' asserts an iteration not prepared for by the sense we have that the passage is describing a unique event – a single instance of Hyperion's pain. In a similar narrative transition at 1, 186–7, 'Also, when he would taste the spicy wreaths / Of incense', there appears to be a narrative non-sequitur: 'also' seems to have no referent. Once again at line 190, the opening 'And so...', which is equally illogical, indicates the difficulties involved in proceeding with a narrative so fixedly organized around alterity and negation. These local failures of narrative form, all of them failures of narrative transition (on the level of *discours*), seem to be symptoms of an underlying problem with the narrative form of 'Hyperion', and seem to predict – even to predicate – the 'failure' and abandonment of the poem: if these structural features – the internal mechanisms of narrative – alert the reader to narrative incompetence or solecism, then the superstructure of narrative telling seems unlikely to succeed.

Within the parameters of the present study, the failure of 'Hyperion' may be read in a number of different ways: the stilling of narrative may be understood to be generated by the fear or anxiety that there will be no audience for this poem and a consequent paralysis of narrative; it may be read in terms of a crucial and irreducible disjunction between the language of men and the language of gods by which the epic mode articulates the language of gods and in so doing excludes itself from audience (see 1, 49; 2, 101; 2, 120); it may be read in terms of the mode of reading configured by the poem – perplexity and incomprehension (2, 130f.; 3, 48) and an impossible figure of reading as an access to immortality (3, 111), a reading into which the reader dies.

This latter explanation for the stilling of narrative is, of course, related to our notion of Romantic posterity as the posthumous life of writing, and might be approached through the figure of the dead hand of Saturn with which 'Hyperion' opens. There are two hands in the opening twenty lines of 'Hyperion', both of which strongly figure negation: first there is the admonitory hand of the Naiad – 'the Naiad 'mid her reeds / Press'd her cold finger closer to her lips' (1, 13–14). This deadened hand at the start of the poem interdicts speech, language, poetry and prefigures the dead hand of Saturn four lines later:

> Upon the sodden ground
> His old right hand lay nerveless, listless, dead,
> Unsceptred   (1, 17–19).

In poems written two years later, Keats twice figured the hand as a synecdoche for poetry and thereby suggested the inevitability of the failure of 'Hyperion'. As I have suggested, in the Introduction to the present study, 'This living hand' lives through the death of its audience. Similarly, the opening to 'The Fall of Hyperion' figures the hand as the still-life or living-death of poetry and of the relationship between text and audience:

> Whether the dream now purposed to rehearse
> Be poet's or fanatic's will be known
> When this warm scribe my hand is in the grave.
>
> ('The Fall', 1, 16–18)

The Induction to 'The Fall' reads the dead hand of the opening to 'Hyperion' – just as the whole of 'The Fall' may be understood as a reading of the earlier poem[13]: the later poem explicitly refigures the relationship of poetic death to audience in 'Hyperion'. In the Induction to 'The Fall', the death of the poet and his status as 'poet' or 'fanatic' is implicitly related to the 'death' of the reader not only because of the way that the lines allow no reading other than that mediated by 'This living hand', but also because there is already within these lines a question of the life or death of the audience: 'Who alive can say / "Thou art no poet; may'st not tell thy dreams"?' (1, 11–12). If there is no one *alive* who can judge on the poetic merits of the poem, then the explicit request for such judgement and its deferral to a time after the death of the writer might also be read as a reading or 'saying' deferred until after the death of the reader.

The crucial difference between 'Hyperion' and 'The Fall of Hyperion', then, is this: 'Hyperion' figures death as a pre-condition for inspiration, it is a poem crucially concerned with the notion of dying into poetic creation, a mortal creativity; 'The Fall', on the other hand, is crucially concerned to figure *reading* as an activity irreducibly bound up with death. And it is through 'The Fall' that we can read the death of the audience in 'Hyperion'. In what follows, I shall attempt to elaborate the figured reader in 'The Fall' and implicitly to read 'Hyperion' through this figured reading.

FAULTURE

The poems which Keats wrote in the interval between abandoning 'Hyperion' and rewriting the poem later in 1819 provide ample evidence for his developing aesthetics of poetic reception. All of the five spring odes, are, to different degrees, critiques of the reciprocity of art/beauty and its audience. However much Keats identifies himself as a poet in these poems, it is also clear that the narrator-poet also constitutes an audience, and that the poems all plot an aesthetics of response. If, as is usually assumed, the move from 'Hyperion' to 'The Fall of Hyperion' marks a move from Milton to Dante, we may find more evidence of aesthetic reception in Keats's new 'intertext': in *The Divine Comedy*, Dante is a reader *par excellence*. In the episode from *The Inferno* which Keats knew best, the story of Paolo and Francesca from Canto Five, which Hunt rewrote in *The Story of Rimini* and which Keats responded to in his 'Dream' sonnet, Dante provides a listener who both weeps and faints in empathic reaction to Francesca's tale. This concentration on an aesthetics of reception, and specifically on the receptivity of listeners is fully explored in 'The Fall of Hyperion'.

Unlike the minor alterations, the pragmatic and socially (in-) decorous revisions to 'The Eve of St Agnes', Keats's rewriting of 'Hyperion' amounts to a comprehensive doctoring of its earlier form.[14] The rewriting of 'Hyperion' as 'The Fall of Hyperion' results in a central inquiry into the nature of the poet-reader relationship. Although critics tend to insist on reading 'The Fall' as an allegory of the birth of poetic creativity, such a birth is crucially mediated by the notion of reading: despite critics' attempts to elide or suppress this point, the narrator is primarily figured as a 'dreamer' – and a dreamer who watches and reacts, who provides an audience for a 'tragedy' – while the question of the narrator's status as a creator or poet is explicitly and repeatedly placed in suspense. And while 'The Fall' seeks to assert the irreducible conflation of poetic reading with poetic writing, the extant narrative produces a dying into reading. Similarly, critics have tended to read the discussion of the relative merits of poets, dreamers, etc., in the Induction in terms of the question of the extent to which Keats intends to value each one. In fact, of course, these important opening lines are effective precisely to the extent that their confusions are *not* elided. The 'meaning' of the lines, deeply problematic and internally inconsistent, produces a series of questions too often ignored in discussions of this opening.[15] What are the narrative strategies brought into play here? To what extent are the concerns of the passage generated by their audience?

> Fanatics have their dreams, wherewith they weave
> A paradise for a sect; the savage too
> From forth the loftiest fashion of his sleep

Guesses at heaven: pity these have not
Trac'd upon vellum or wild Indian leaf
The shadows of melodious utterance.
But bare of laurel they live, dream, and die;
For Poesy alone can tell her dreams,
With the fine spell of words alone can save
Imagination from the sable charm
And dumb enchantment. Who alive can say
'Thou art no poet; may'st not tell thy dreams'?
Since every man whose soul is not a clod
Hath visions, and would speak, if he had lov'd
And been well nurtured in his mother tongue.
Whether the dream now purposed to rehearse
Be poet's or fanatic's will be known
When this warm scribe my hand is in the grave.   (1, 1–18)

The interpretive shift which is needed here is that which would move from hermeneutics to pragmatics. In fact, whatever the confusions of thought in the Induction, the lines have demonstrably produced a reception of 'The Fall of Hyperion' which is defined within the terms presented by the Induction itself. The Induction offers the reader an explicit commentary on the poem to follow, a commentary which both directs readers' attention and provides evaluative comment. It asserts, most fundamentally (and logically prior to any thematic or analytical statement), a social function for poetry, an acknowledgement of the pragmatic, public nature of poetic discourse and, at the same time, a recognition of the fundamental importance of the relationship between poet and audience: if the audience judges well, then the poem exists as a poem, if they judge against it, the dream is a 'fanatic's'. This is a radical redescription not only of the poet's role, but of the very nature of poetic discourse and of the definition of 'literature': the poem can only exist as poetry with the consent of its audience.[16] This may explain the significance of 'rehearse': only when the audience receives and approves the poem will it be 'performed'. The last line of the Induction is an accurate metaphor for the nature of literary production in an age of mechanical reproduction, where the living hand of the poet, his hand-writing, is 'dead' as it is read in its printed form: the line lucidly marks the gap between writing and reception. Usually taken as an attempt to define the poet against the dreamer/fanatic, the Induction also vitally asserts the public nature of the poetry.

This assertion of the pragmatic basis of poetic expression is also implicitly asserted by the alterations in narrative form made in rewriting 'Hyperion', the most notable of which is the alteration made in narratorial voice from third to first person. Through this alteration in voice, the narrator becomes the reader-surrogate, and the narrative of the Titans is mediated through his reactions to the story: Keats's rewriting of the poem recognizes the limitations of the earlier poem's attempt to isolate poetry from its audience. As many critics have recognized, 'Hyperion' seems to be deeply ambivalent about its sympathy towards the Titans and the Olympians: the poem fractures and halts in its movement from the tragic to the Apollonian.[17] The disnarrated which characterizes the form of 'Hyperion' is another expression of this ambivalence. The first-person narration of 'The Fall', then, allows for an altered focus of narrative and an altered emphasis on the events: instead of the question of sympathy for the Titans or the Olympians, the emphasis falls on the narrator's reactions to events – a shift which organizes the narrative around the question of response. What this reader-narrator makes possible is, precisely, the alterity to which 'Hyperion' continually alluded: the story which Keats writes now is the alternative, the supplementary story.

In 'Hyperion', the crucial mechanics of the transition from one character to another, from one episode to another, is constituted by disjunction, resulting in a narrative form which seems to reflect the picture of the fallen Titans as broken statues strewn around the poem: thematic *disjecta membra* are actualized in narrative form. In 'The Fall', by contrast, these limitations, these fault-lines in the narrative texture, become the transitions between levels of framing and are motivated by the subjective experience of the narrator (from consciousness to sleep, from solitude to dialogic exchange, from talk to vision, from *discours* to *histoire*, etc.). Thus, instead of breaking off from one line of narrative and moving to another, 'The Fall' is crucially structured around the 'faultures' of narration.[18] It is within the spaces formed by the disjointed articulations of narration, that 'The Fall' is narrated, just as it is the *supplementary* narrative of response that becomes critical. This is a movement from immobility to movement, from the totalities of narrative or history to the dispersal of event or process, from continuity to disjunction, from place to space, and thus from failure to faulture.

The framing structure of 'The Fall' is the most complex of all of

Keats's narratives.[19] Eventually in 'The Fall', the several layerings of frame look like this:

Induction > garden > dream > vision > 'Hyperion'[20]

The Induction (1, 1–18) frames the whole poem; the first scene within the garden (1, 19–57) is a vision which is interrupted by sleep and opens out into another embedding in the dream of the struggle of the narrator to become a poet or reader (1, 58–256); this leads to a greater visionary potential, represented in the vision of Moneta's face which I have classified as a further embedding, as 'vision', because the narrator seems to be on a qualitatively different narratorial level (1, 256–90); this visionary potential opens out into Moneta's narration of the immortal struggle which, referring to Keats's first attempt, I have labelled 'Hyperion' (1, 291–end). Such rigorously complex embedding provides an unstable, liminal quality to the poetry, which continually threatens to slide, through a 'faulture', on to a different plane of narration, just as Moneta's narrations continually slide into the narrator's 'vision'. At the same time, such a technique radically distances the *histoire* from 'the world' and from the reader, who must view the tale through the various implicit commentaries of embedded narrative level:[21] like the poet-narrator (the reader's surrogate), the reader must struggle through various thresholds before he or she is able to approach the story of 'Hyperion'. This is, on one level, a typically Romantic manoeuvre, asserting epistemological dislocation and authorial suspension and, in contrast to the first 'Hyperion', suggests ways in which that poem's desire for coherence, for narrative form, and, by implication, for a negation of audience, has evolved into a poetics inhabiting the unstable interstice of text and audience.

The major episode of reading in 'The Fall' is that in which the figured reader, the narrator-poet, reads Moneta's face. For Helen Vendler, Moneta's eyes figure the inspiration of the poet, asserting an aesthetic which explicitly denies audience:[22]

> Half closed, and visionless entire they seem'd
> Of all external things – they saw me not,
> But in blank splendour beam'd like the mild moon,
> Who comforts those she sees not, who knows not
> What eyes are upward cast. (1, 267–71)

If we read Moneta's face with Vendler as a figure for poetic inspiration and a denial of audience, it becomes clear that Keats's text is itself a transgression of precisely this law of authorial ignorance or disdain: how would it be possible to read Moneta's face as a negation of audience in poetic creativity if 'The Fall of Hyperion' does not itself engage with precisely this question? In as much as 'The Fall' presents an implicit ideology of the poet detached from and ignorant of its audience, the poem itself must fall outside of this definition of poetry because of its explicit engagement at this point with the question of reading. But audience is not only figured by this 'figural' ideology of authorial ignorance. We have already seen that the Induction presents the poem as constituted by its audience. At the same time the notion of the unbridgeable ontological gap between poet and reader apparently presented by the face of Moneta is also transgressed by the scene itself which, despite many critics' apparent blindness to the point, is constituted as a figure of reading.[23] It is clearly the case that the narrator explicitly *reads* Moneta's face:

> As I had found
> A grain of gold upon a mountain's side,
> And twing'd with avarice strain'd out my eyes
> To search its sullen entrails rich with ore,
> So at the view of sad Moneta's brow,
> I ached to see what things the hollow brain
> Behind enwomed   (1, 271–7)

We have already seen, in particular in relation to 'Isabella' and 'The Eve of St Agnes', ways in which the inspirational or hallucinatory eyes of the poet always already presuppose, figure, or demand the eyes of readers: here the blind, unseeing eyes of inspired Poetry lead inexorably to a 'straining out' of the reader's eyes. Keats's letter to Shelley, which exhorts the older poet to '"load every rift" of your subject with ore' (*Letters*, vol. II, p. 323) is an obvious counterpart to these rich entrails, and in 'The Fall' the poet is exhorting his readers, by the use of a reader-surrogate, to 'strain [their] eyes': if Keats's poetry is 'loaded with ore', the task of the reader must be to extract the wealth embedded within it. Earlier, the voice of Moneta had declared that if the narrator cannot ascend the steps 'thy bones / Will wither in few years, and vanish so / That not the quickest eye could find a grain / Of what thou now art' (1, 110–13): the poet who is no poet will lack all reception, will be invisible to the public eye. Thus the 'faultures' by which the narrative is organized, the liminal stratifications of narrative embedding, provide rich pickings for the eyes of avaricious readers.

What 'The Fall' would seem to present, then, is a figure of poetry which is not self-identical: that is, the role of the reader is presented in 'The Fall' as a shattering of the self-identical, hermetic inspiration of poetry. The face of Moneta may, as Vendler and others have read it, produce an ideology of solipsistic, self-enclosed and self-referential poetic making, and we might (mis)read the word 'disinterested' as Keats's word for this process (see *Letters*, vol. I, pp. 205, 293; vol. II, pp. 79, 129, 279). But at the same time this figure of poetry demands to be read, demands to be read as a figure of reading, and as such threatens to shatter the illusion of aesthetic isolation. As such, 'The Fall' figures the activity of reading as a transgression of the poetic text.

In fact, reading back from the vision of Moneta, we find that the narrator-reader has been figured as both transgressive and guilt-ridden from the first: in particular, his journey towards this vision has involved an explicit transgression of borders and boundaries (of text, topography, narrative level, consciousness, etc.). Indeed, as I have suggested, the unstable location of the narrator-reader is precisely in these spaces between levels, at these transgressive junctures which we have named 'faultures'. Reading in 'The Fall' is thus figured as transgressive, as solecistic, while at the same time, poetry is itself constructed by such reading.

If reading in 'The Fall' is transgressive, the poem also emphasizes its difficulty – not only in terms of the hermeneutic difficulties of ignorance, confusion, bewilderment of 'Hyperion', but also in the way that reading is strenuous and physically and emotionally draining. In particular, the narrator's struggle towards Moneta which I have been 'reading', is figured as a struggle *against* the condition of the fallen Saturn:

> I strove hard to escape
> The numbness; strove to gain the lowest step.
> Slow, heavy, deadly was my pace: the cold
> Grew stifling, suffocating, at the heart;
> And when I clasp'd my hands I felt them not. (1, 127–31)

Charles Rzepka has suggested that '[t]he issue in "The Eve of St Agnes", as in much of the poetry of Wordsworth and Coleridge, can best be stated as the problem of defining, selecting, or controlling one's audience, and the social context of one's art and artistic self-representation, so as to make the image of the poet (or poet-lover) prevail as an objective, agreed-upon reality'.[24] Episodes such as the vision of Moneta must be understood to have been phenomenally successful in controlling the audience through its figuration of poetic inspiration, its presentation of a particular configuration of the ideology of poethood, while at the same time presenting a transgressive undermining of precisely that audience response. Rzepka's assertion of the importance of audience for the Romantics comes in response to his question 'Can one *make* one's dream of oneself real?', to which he replies, 'Only, perhaps, by making the reality of others one's dream'.[25] But we might answer the question slightly differently in relation to our reading of 'The Fall': one can make one's dream real – as Moneta does – by making others dream it. The reality of the imagination, the reality of Adam's dream, is constituted by the audience for that dream: the reality of the dream is not constructed by the dreamer, who knows that it is only a dream. Rather, the reality of the dream is constructed by the transgressive reading of the dreamer's audience.

CHAPTER 9

'To Autumn'

The criticism of 'To Autumn' has articulated a clear discrepancy between the apparent denial of historical and political analysis in the poem and the events of the second decade of the nineteenth century, including economic and political crisis, the suspension of Habeas Corpus, the Spa Fields riot, Luddism, sporadic but widespread food riots in rural areas, and, most specifically, the Peterloo Massacre of August 1819, just one month before the composition of Keats's poem. The apparent silence of 'To Autumn' on the subject of politics tends to be read as evidence of a Keatsian desire to abstract poetic language from history, a desire to write perfected language into which the disruptions of history do not intrude. 'To Autumn' has been read as a poem of perfection, a poem in which language is perfected in form and in the exclusion of history. A. C. Swinburne classed it with 'Ode on a Grecian Urn' as the 'nearest to absolute perfection' of Keats's odes;[1] more recently, Walter Jackson Bate has called 'To Autumn' 'one of the most nearly perfect poems in English', Aileen Ward has remarked that it is Keats's 'most perfect and untroubled poem', and Douglas Bush has stated that the poem is 'flawless in structure, texture, tone, and rhythm'.[2] This 'perfection' of language, a perfection apparently undaunted by contemporary political events, has led politically minded critics to describe 'To Autumn' as an escape from history. Attempting to account for the discrepancy between the perfected language of the poem and the contemporary disruptions of politics, Jerome McGann, for example, has analysed 'To Autumn' as 'an attempt to "escape" the period which provides the poem with its context'.[3] Similarly, in a recent essay which has perceptive things to say about politics in Keats's poetry, Vincent Newey has argued that 'To Autumn' 'celebrates a capacity quite opposite to that of political engagement'.[4] In this chapter, I attempt to situate 'To Autumn' within its political context of agrarian economics in the early nineteenth century in order to suggest ways in which the perfected critical response to 'To Autumn' is both figured by the text and, crucially, disrupted by the subtextual pressures of politics on the poem. Figures of reading become, literally, economic figures and the silencing of politics and history in 'To Autumn' is repeated in the silence of critical response to the implicit political 'subtext' of the poem.[5]

'To Autumn', then, is embedded within both the context of a Keatsian anxiety over the economics of writing which I have outlined in my discussion of the letters written between May and September (see Chapter 2, above), and a more general anxiety of economics in England in 1819. The Keatsian rhetoric of harvesting in 'To Autumn' may be read both as a figure of political discourse and as a self-description of poetry and poetic making. On a number of occasions in his poems and letters, Keats inscribed the economics of harvesting within the terms of the economics of poetic writing: in a letter of July 1819, for example, in reference to the publication of his poetry, Keats says 'the very corn which is now so beautiful, as if it had only ⟨taken⟩ took to ripening yesterday, is for the market: So, why shod I be delicate.' (*Letters*, vol. II, p. 129). The rhetoric of gleaning also provides an amphibology of harvesting and writing in a number of poems, most clearly expressed in the desire to glean the poet's 'teeming brain' in 'When I have fears that I may cease to be'.[6] 'To Autumn', as a poem of harvesting, represents Keats's most fully worked nexus of such homologies: among other things the poem is an articulation of the politics and economics both of agriculture and of writing.

In this chapter I shall depart somewhat from the dual focus of this book – narrative and audience, what I term 'figures of reading' – in order to suggest ways in which Keats's most 'perfected' of poems engages with the discourses of politics and economics. Implicit in such a reading is the recognition that increasingly during 1819 the question of writing for a living, and thus of finding a public, becomes more and more urgent. But this chapter also presents an exercise in reading 'against the grain': by reading 'To Autumn' intertextually, through intertexts which fracture the surface poise of the poem, I shall suggest that one way to read a poem which so signally represses solecism is to make of reading itself a solecism.

As I have suggested, 'To Autumn' has been read as a poem of perfection, a poem which suppresses the cacophonous noises of history: it is a poem which seems to exclude the language of politics from its rhetoric, to silence the noise of history, politics, economics. Without such purchase on the text, readers stand powerless in front of the irrefragable beauty of language, they are left to luxuriate in the fecund textuality of words, and, in the face of such poetry, critics generally speak in languid autumnal tones, in extended nostalgic periods, intoning the litany of perfection, the organic, the whole. To historicize Keats's poem, however, would be to read against the grain, to listen to the fractious intertextual cacophony of history, politics, economics, noises which Autumn seems to silence. Our analysis of Keats's letters in terms of the relationship between writing, work, and economics in Chapter 2, suggests that, on one level, 'To Autumn' was generated out of the ideological tensions to which the writer in the early nineteenth century was subject. Written just before the letters announcing his abandonment of the notion of writing for money, 'To Autumn' may be read as a crucial text in Keats's developing economics of writing. The perfection of language which critics have discerned in the poem is fractured by the economics of writing.

Part of the perfection of language in 'To Autumn' involves a density of intertextuality, an inclusion of other voices into a univocal exclusivity of Keatsian voice, which both textures and textualizes the poem. Although, as Helen Vendler has noted, 'To Autumn' denies specific allusion,[7] the echoes that critics have heard in the poem are legion: they include, for example, echoes from Virgil, Shakespeare, Spenser, Milton, Thomson, Wordsworth, Coleridge, Chatterton. Rather than disrupting the univocality of Keats's poem, these echoes are seen as texturing the poem's literariness and homogenizing its monolithic voice – the voice of the literary. Keats's 1816 sonnet 'How many bards gild the lapses of time' provides, in itself, an intertextual commentary on the intertextuality of 'To Autumn'. The earlier poem explicitly argues for the 'pleasing chime' of the literary tradition – a music which 'occasions' 'no confusion, no disturbance rude' – as a generating impulse for writing, and compares such music to 'the unnumber'd sounds that evening store[s]' which 'Make pleasing music, not wild uproar'. The sonnet interacts fruitfully with the later ode in a number of ways, not least in the economics of the opening line's 'gild' (a word which, as I show below, will be erased in/by 'To Autumn'), and in the 'lapses of time', the discontinuities of history, which such gilding suppresses. But Keats's crisis of writing during the summer and autumn of 1819 means that such an aesthetics of literary perfection/exclusion is deeply fractured by the intrusive discourses of economics. By focusing on a different set of 'intertexts', it is possible to describe 'To Autumn' as an intervention in a series of discourses, literary and political, which both disrupt the poem's 'perfection' and situate it within the political events of autumn 1819.

There is, then, a double intertextuality of 'To Autumn': an intertextuality of the literary, and an intertextuality – still mediated to a large extent by literary texts – of the historical. The literary intertextuality of 'To Autumn' posits an ideology of literary language as separated from history precisely through its exclusion of other voices: the literary is presented as a closed and enclosed discursive space immune to the infringements of other discourses. In this model of intertextuality the text is enclosed, an enclosure bounded by the limits of a specifically literary history. The boundaries of the literary exclude the illicit incursions of transgressive (non-literary) language into the space of poetry. The poem's historical intertextuality, on the other hand, involves the antagonistic intertexts which the poem's literariness attempts to suppress – the texts of economics, history, politics. The fractures in the poem's literary logic – the famous syntactical suspension in stanza one, the thematic laziness of the workers in stanza two, the semantic ambivalence of the word 'conspiring', the use of the apostrophic convention in a poem which otherwise refuses the outworn formulations of the eighteenth-century ode[8] – all suggest fault-lines which mark the repression of history by textuality. By attending to a number of intertextual echoes we might discern a number of ideological fault-lines in Keats's poem in which we might trace the text's engagement with the discourses of history.

The politics of 'To Autumn' are most explicitly articulated within the terms of the contemporary politics of agriculture. The politics of agriculture had potentially revolutionary implications in the early nineteenth century due to the repeated minor uprisings of rural workers agitating against the 1815 corn law, enclosures, and generally against oppressive economic conditions. In 'To Autumn', however, these matters are displaced into the mythological figure of Ceres. A number of critics have recently suggested that Ceres, the goddess of corn and harvests, is a pervasive absent presence in 'To Autumn', a presence which is unstated, unspecified, and disseminated throughout both the pastoral tradition and Keats's poem.[9] The agrarian politics of the early nineteenth century are mediated by the unnamed mythological discourse 'Ceres': by looking closely at this mythological substitution, we may be able to position 'To Autumn' within contemporary political discourses.

Keats's contemporary poem 'Lamia' offers an intriguing insight into the significance of Ceres in the lines 'and the store thrice told / Of Ceres' horn' (part 2, lines 186–7). The phrase 'Ceres' horn', which is an expansion of the word 'cornucopia' (literally, 'horn of plenty') represents an example of Keats's generative solecisms. Ceres, goddess of abundant food (particularly corn) is not, in any of Keats's sources, nor in the mythological tradition, described as possessing a horn: the cornucopia, in fact, belongs to an entirely unrelated deity, Amalthea.[10] Keats's reference to 'Ceres' horn' is, then, a kind of corny illicit pun on cornucopia, which is 'thrice told' in that 'cornucopia' may be translated into 'Ceres' horn' in three different ways: plenty of corn; horn of plenty; Ceres' [corn's] horn. Unravelling this ravelled pun we find a tautology in the association of 'Ceres' horn' with cornucopia: Ceres = corn (by metonymy); horn = cornus (by translation); so the pun reads 'Corn's (Ceres') corn[us] (horn)' – and 'copia' is omitted except in the copious linguistic play involved. Ceres' horn is thrice-told as well as thrice-counted in this cornucopia of linguistic compression.

Within the context of an economic analysis of 'To Autumn', this paronomastic play on Ceres is significant because of the figure's relationship with property, law, and the politics of agriculture. In classical mythology, Ceres represents not only agrarian plenitude but also the transition from a pre-monetary and, indeed, communistic, economy to a fully commercial and proto-capitalist economy of monetary exchange, a transition which brought with it the institution of the law. The seventeenth-century encyclopaedist Andrew Tooke explains this in his *Pantheon* in a passage which reverberates with significance for the discourse of agricultural politics in the early nineteenth century:

This you may learn from *Ovid*, who tells us that *Ceres* was the first that made laws; provided wholesome food; and taught the art of husbandry, of ploughing and sowing. For before her time, the earth lay rough and uncultivated, covered with briars, and unprofitable plants; when there were no proprietors of land, they neglected to cultivate it; when nobody had any ground of his own, they did not care to fix landmarks: but all things were common to all men, till *Ceres* who had invented the art of husbandry, taught men how to exercise it; and then they began to contend and dispute about the limits of those fields, from the culture of which they reaped so much profit: and hence it was necessary that laws should be enacted to determine the rights and properties of those who contended. For this reason *Ceres* was named the foundress of laws.[11]

Ceres, then, represents the origins of lawful and economic exchange and of topographical boundaries, and we might gloss Keats's illicit paronomastic play on cornucopia in 'Lamia' as a subtextual, and perhaps subliminal, revolt against such order, exchanging the illicit coinage of puns for the true currency of etymology: Keats presents the reader with a 'Pun mote' (*Letters*, vol. II, p. 214). If, as seems to be the case, Ceres is the pervasive unstated presence in 'To Autumn', then the perfected language of pastoral description is invaded by political questions of lawful exchange, agricultural boundaries, private property and labour relations. That critics have noted Ceres' pervasive but unnamed presence in 'To Autumn' is suggestive: Keats appropriates the mythology but explicitly excludes the nominal property of the mythological originator of private property. Indeed, this denial of Ceres' name is particularly remarkable in a poet who, as John Clare wryly commented, 'keeps up a constant a[l]lusion or illusion to the grecian mythology' and who 'behind every rose ... looks for a Venus & under every laurel a thrumming Apollo' (*Heritage*, pp. 155, 156). The exclusion of Ceres' proper name – her property – in the poem represents a transgression of the law of property.

Furthermore, the association of the origins of law with the demarcation of boundaries in the mythology of Ceres is particularly significant in a poem based on the boundary season, autumn.[12] Between the eighteenth-century analysis of the origins of property (mythologized in Ceres) and the contemporary controversy over enclosures, there is a homology in the movement from a communistic pre-agrarian past before the law of Ceres and its transmutation into 'modern' agriculture on the one hand, and the movement from common agricultural usage to the privatization of land in enclosures on the other. Other things being equal (and the history of enclosures is, of course, far more complex than this reduction allows), enclosure reproduces the structure of the mythological origins of (agricultural) private property, the bounding of land ownership.[13] As a boundary, however, autumn is unbounded, as the poem's notorious ambivalence over the precise temporal location of the season suggests: the poem is located within both summer and autumn, and points forward to winter, it is located at the beginning as well as at the end of harvest, the bees in stanza one are dislocated in their sense of time, and the lambs in stanza three are ambivalent sheep. Similarly, these temporal transgressions of bounding-lines are repeated in the topographical violation of boundaries as the poem moves out in space from the cottage to the garden to the fields to the hills and finally upwards to the unbounded skies. This movement, in itself, suggests a denial of enclosure, a political gesture of defiance against the appropriation of public property in the contemporary enclosure movement.

It is, of course, the second stanza of 'To Autumn', with its images of rural workers, which most clearly articulates the discourse of agricultural labour relations. Although the unstated figure of the goddess Ceres activates the discourses of labour, property, lawful exchange, and legal boundaries, it is possible to hear in 'To Autumn' the noise of the politics and economics of agriculture in a hitherto unnoticed verbal echo of Pope's *Epistle to Bathurst*. It has been well documented that, in preparing to write 'Lamia' in the summer of 1819, Keats had been rereading Dryden's poetry to get the feel of a 'flint-worded' poet (*Letters*, vol. II, p. 214).[14] But the fact that Keats appears to quote Pope at least three times in the letters of that summer (*Letters*, vol. II, pp. 133, 164, 201), including a quotation from *Eloisa to Abelard* on the day he wrote 'To Autumn', strongly suggests that he was also reading the poet who had previously been something of a Keatsian *bête noire*. Pope's *Epistle to Bathurst*, one of his 'Moral Essays' whose 'Argument' is subtitled 'Of the Use of Riches', satirically examines the knotty question of whether, as the Argument has it, 'the invention of Money has been more commodious, or pernicious to Mankind'.[15] In particular, Pope attacks the extremes of Avarice and Prodigality. A personification occurs at a key point in Pope's poem in order to satirize avaricious hoarding:

> Riches, like insects, when conceal'd they lie,
> Wait but for wings, and in their season, fly.
> Who sees pale Mammon pine amidst his store,
> Sees but a backward steward for the Poor   (lines 171–4[16])

Although the first two lines might provide a secondary echo of the last stanza of 'To Autumn', which moves from insects to flight, the third line offers an echo which, in rhythm and verbal cadence, is a precise model for the opening to stanza two of Keats's poem:

Who sees pale Mammon pine amidst his store

in Pope is translated into the rhetorical question of

Who hath not seen thee oft amid thy store?

in Keats. 'Seeing' this hidden intertext within the Keatsian store of
Romantic luxuriance allows us to discern a rich economic and
political subtext within Keats's overtly naturalistic and 'disinterested' poem: it alerts us to the fact that the turbulent, fractious
subtext of 'To Autumn' involves a problematic relationship between,
on the one hand, the capital accumulation of stanza one – loading,
bending, filling, swelling, budding – a kind of 'natural' accumulation which constitutes a displaced representation of financial
accumulation, and, on the other hand, work and its negation in
stanza two – expressed in the phrases 'sitting careless', 'sound
asleep', 'thy laden head', 'with patient look / Thou watchest'.

The echo of Pope's Moral Essay not only activates the subtextual
economics of 'To Autumn' but also suggests an ideological explanation of aristocratic accumulation: 'pale Mammon' who
'pine[s] amidst his store' is a 'backward steward for the Poor'.
Similarly, the representation of rural leisure is double-edged in that
not only are the workers incongruously leisurely but their lassitude
reflects the seasonal nature of the work and the fact that their
relaxation will soon become unemployment: if the bees are seduced
into believing that warm days will never cease, the workers have
similarly confused the seasons.[17] Just as the full granaries will soon
start to empty, the warm days will soon turn cold. The third stanza
already – even within the frame of this pressingly plenitudinous and
affluent poem – marks a declining repletion (or, indeed, an over-
repletion) in its diction ('soft dying', 'wailful', 'mourn', 'lives or
dies') and imagery. Indeed, we might argue that it is precisely
because of the plenitude, the generosity, of autumnal days, that work
is left undone, just as Keats's poem, with its slow, lush, plenitudinous
generosity almost convinces its readers that the work of history may
be abandoned in aesthetic contemplation. And, indeed, the act of
writing 'To Autumn' was specifically recorded by Keats as a
leisurely affair, engendered by a walk which constituted a break from
writing – a holiday not only from the more serious business of
rewriting 'Hyperion' but also from work proper.

But the silent intertextual echo of Pope's Mammon also suggests that money may be silenced, may be barred from Keats's poem in significant ways, and we might ask what is invested in this silent barring of money from 'To Autumn'. Money is explicitly suppressed by Keats in an alteration to line twenty-five: 'barred clouds bloom' was, in the first draft of the poem, altered from 'a gold cloud gilds': the alteration – from 'gold' to 'barred', from 'gilds' to 'bloom' – bars the noisy intrusion of economics into the poem. The suppressed word 'gilds' threatens to open up a number of semantic seams in 'To Autumn': one archaic sense of 'gild' is a noise or clamour;[18] 'gild' also involves the payment of taxes and the covering of an object with a thin layer of gold, as well as the common metaphorical development of this latter sense in the idea of giving a specious brilliance to an unworthy object. These noisy economic sememes of 'gild', however, are literally barred – they are crossed out – by the final text: they are explicitly barred by the word 'barred'. The verb 'to bar' is associated with exclusion, with the law, with property, with limiting, confining, and enclosing: in order to read these sememes of 'barred' in Keats's poem, however, we must read the text as a palimpsest – literally, because 'barred ... bloom' is written over 'gold ... gilds'[19] – we must transgress the space of words in the poem, and deny the law of authorial exclusion. Similarly, 'barred' gives us a key to the poem's attempted exclusivity of intertextuality, its barring of heterogeneous noises from its perfected surface – a barring which is represented phonetically by the alteration from the harsh noise of the velar to the softer harmony of the bi-labial plosives, and which is represented throughout the poem by Keats's notoriously mellifluous harmonics. And to say, as we might want to, that 'barred clouds bloom' is simply more beautiful, more perfect, than 'a gold cloud gilds', is both to register the aesthetic force of the 'natural' plenitude which structures the poem and, at the same time, to beg the question of the poem's engagement with the economics of the aesthetic.

John Clare's poetry provides an interesting commentary on the relationship between law, wealth, and enclosure in the early nineteenth century which helps to illuminate the subtextual economics of Keats's poem. In a number of poems,[20] Clare comments nostalgically on the damage done by enclosures to the rural scene, but he also writes perceptively on the economic matrix of values that produces such ecological damage. In the early poem 'Helpstone', for example, Clare laments the destruction caused by enclosures and comments:

Acursed wealth o'er bounding human laws
Of every evil thou remainst the cause
Victims of want those wretches such as me
Too truly lay their wretchedness to thee
Thou art the bar that keeps from being fed
And thine our loss of labour and of bread   (lines 127–32)

Although 'Helpstone', written in 1812, was not published until 1820, reading Keats's poem through the perspective of Clare's helps to elucidate the complex ideological matrix in the verbal cluster 'wealth', 'bounding', 'laws', 'victims', 'bar', 'fed', 'labour', 'bread', explicit in Clare's poem, and fracturing the surface poise in Keats's: if one of the subtextual pressures of 'To Autumn' is the refusal of the physical, economic, and legal limitations of enclosure, we might read Keats's poem as in some sense correlative with the explicit denunciation of the transgression of humanitarianism and the picturesque which Clare's poem articulates. In 'The Mores' Clare is even more explicit in his locution 'lawless laws' (line 178), a formulation which expresses the fundamental injustice of enclosures (fundamental because the rationale for enclosure – private property and legal ownership – deconstructs itself in its gesture of legalizing such appropriation; the change from public to private ownership reveals the arbitrary basis of private property: Clare's point is that the arbitrary legality of enclosures deconstructs the very concept of legality upon which laws are founded). As Robert Malcolmson has noted, the justification for private property seems to have undergone a conceptual shift during the eighteenth century (generated, in part at least, by the enclosure movement), from the notion of use-right to that of absolute property ownership: Malcolmson points out that it is in practices such as gleaning that the conflict between the two conceptions of rights is most clearly articulated.[21] Clare's 'lawless laws' points to the fact that from one perspective, at least, enclosures involved the institution of, for example, gleaning as robbery through, precisely, robbery – as E. P. Thompson has commented, 'Enclosure (when all the sophistications are allowed for) was a plain enough case of class robbery, played according to fair rules of property and law laid down by a Parliament of property-owners and lawyers'.[22]

Although the mythological figure of Ceres, representing copious luxury, property, proper boundaries, and the law, is ambiguously absent from 'To Autumn', Keats explicitly includes the reciprocal figure of the anonymous gleaner in stanza two. The figure of the gleaner activates the vocabularies of want, the appropriation of property, the violation of proper boundaries, and the transgression of the law. The affluence suggested by the richness of literary language in the poem is undercut by the discourse of gleaning: the pressures of linguistic plenitude, the wealthy luxuriance of language, are counterpointed by this explicit reference to the plight of the poor.

When we examine the contemporary discourse of gleaning, then, we discover a final intertextual pressure on the perfected language of 'To Autumn'. Gleaning was particularly controversial in the autumn of 1819 due to a contemporary controversy over its legality. It was an ancient custom, ideologically overdetermined by the biblical story of Ruth, producing a symbolic significance which reinforced its practical importance for the diet of agricultural workers. The gleaner was a common figure in poetry and painting up to and indeed throughout the nineteenth century as a signifier of the balancing of avarice and charity. Although gleaning was sanctioned by the Bible and traditionally permitted by landowners, at the end of the eighteenth century landowners began to claim that gleaning transgressed laws of property, and started to bring prosecutions against gleaners. The nineteenth century saw numerous attempts by landowners to restrict the practice through the use of the law, by prosecution for trespass and theft. The inclusion of the gleaner figure in stanza two of 'To Autumn', together with the stanza's silence over the political question of gleaning, may be understood to mark a reappropriation of the figure for poetry and simultaneously for agricultural workers.[23] By presupposing the legitimacy of the gleaner figure for poetry, Keats also assumes the legality of gleaners. At the same time, however, Keats's representation of the gleaner – as with other nineteenth-century pictorial representations of this pastoral figure[24] – involves a nostalgic objectification and elision of the suffering which gleaning involved: not only was gleaning generated by poverty, but physically it was extremely demanding.[25] The poised steadiness of Keats's gleaner only hints – with 'laden', and perhaps with the assertion of steadiness in its negated implication of unsteadiness, weariness, fatigue – at the physical exertions involved in gleaning.

I would like to suggest that gleaning is the constitutive trope in an intertextual reading of 'To Autumn': indeed, the older word 'leasing' expresses the whole gamut of concerns in my reading of Keats's poem – as a legal term 'leasing' involves the letting of property and at the same time a legally binding or constricting contract; as a synonym for gleaning it involves the (re)appropriation of others' property; etymologically the word also signifies reading. In 'To Autumn' Keats gleans anterior texts, exterior discourses: the Keatsian text is, like all texts, a tissue of gleanings. The opposition of the unnamed Ceres to the anonymous gleaner figures the poem's play of property: such an opposition may itself be read as an allegory of intertextual interpretation. In its various manifestations and transformations in the work of critics such as M. M. Bakhtin, Julia Kristeva, Roland Barthes and Michael Riffaterre, intertextuality tends to demand a dual reading: on the one hand it is understood as a strategy of dissemination, a radical dispersal of origins, and on the other hand it seems to be constituted by a precise specificity of intertextual location and filiation:[26] in 'To Autumn' this play of absence and presence is figured in the dual nominality of the unnamed Ceres and the anonymous gleaner. And the duality of Ceres and the gleaner also reminds us that the gleanings of intertextuality constitute an illicit appropriation of others' property – that, as T. S. Eliot would have it, 'mature poets steal'.[27] Keats's text no longer properly demarcates itself and is no longer properly demarcated: as the extending boundaries of the last stanza suggest, it eliminates all textual boundaries. The poem is unbounded in a movement which refuses (en)closure as it enacts the structure of illicit appropriation implicit in intertextuality.

'To Autumn' ends with noise, and with the question of noise: 'Where are the songs of spring?' The noises made in the third stanza by gnats, sheep, hedge-crickets, birds, are the attenuated sounds of buzzing, bleating, whistling, twittering, noises which Keats enumerates as poetically illicit – they are not the noises of spring nor are they the noises of the literary tradition – and which are specifically presented as an alternative music. These noises provide a final model for our intertextual reading of the poem. If textuality is to be defined in terms of intertextuality, then we should recognize that poems include the noise made by textual imposters in the literary tradition, imposters which impose illicit sounds on poetry. Similarly, we should recognize that, because, as Roland Barthes says 'any text is an intertext' and 'any text is a new tissue of past citations'[28] – because textuality is intertextuality – in their turn, poems constitute just such illicit noises, the tintinnabulous noises of language disempowered, made by poetic language within the discourse of history. By attending to the disruptive intertextual noises of history, politics, economics we find that the attempt to silence the noise of history in 'To Autumn', rather than an escape from the historical, is itself a strategic silencing, a silencing which echoes most profoundly the political effacement, which we might call the 'noise', of the oppressed. And the recuperative reading which is figured in intertextuality should also be understood to figure the political dynamics of 'To Autumn'. The peculiar resistance to the political which has been read into 'To Autumn' can be disfigured by the transgressions which constitute the politics of intertextuality in the poem: in order to read the politics of 'To Autumn' we must transgress the boundaries of authorial property, we must refuse to be figured within, or by, the bounds of the text.

Epilogue: allegories of reading ('Lamia')

Charles Brown's well-known account of the composition of Keats's 'Ode to a Nightingale' constructs an exemplary drama of poetic production which figures the Romantic desire for a separation of poetic composition from publication:

In the spring of 1819 a nightingale had built her nest near my house. Keats felt a tranquil and continual joy in her song; and one morning he took his chair from the breakfast-table to the grass-plot under a plum-tree, where he sat for two or three hours. When he came into the house, I perceived he had some scraps of paper in his hand, and these he was quietly thrusting behind the books. On inquiry, I found those scraps, four or five in number, contained his poetic feeling on the song of our nightingale. (*KC*, vol. II, p. 65)

Concealing his poem behind some books, Keats makes his work fugitive, removing it from both the communicative and the commercial circuits of public poetry. Given what we know of Brown's brusque character, we are not surprised, perhaps, that Keats's sensibility curled like a leaf on a hot palm after writing his most intense poem of psychic, inner, 'private', conflict.[1] But the drama should also be read within the terms of the Romantic ideology of poetic creation, whereby writing is understood to be a function of 'personal' or 'private' self-expression (thus the 'scraps' are said to 'contain' Keats's 'poetic feeling'). In this sense this little allegory of writing may be understood to have been played out within the terms constructed by the Romantic ideology and it may be reread as a construction of the Romantic Poet: the Romantic Poet, moved to inspiration by the bird's song, removes himself from society (the breakfast table) and retreats into the solitude of nature (the garden); after writing one of the most important and influential poems in the English language, the poet then secretes the poem amongst some books in a gesture which marks the intertextuality of writing, symbolically inserting it into the literary tradition while at the same time effacing its individuality; a friend or audience then recovers the poem from obscurity and reads it as an expression of poetic 'feeling'. In this narrative, the act of concealment adds to its value (Keats hides the poem because it is so 'personal', and it is both this subjectivity and the implied fear of exposure which marks it as valuable).[2] By removing the poem from the public circuits of communication and commerce, Keats is, in fact, aggrandizing it: its value, within the terms of the Romantic ideology of the isolated poet and of non-commercial poetry, is enhanced. Rather than the poet presenting the poem to his friend, it is important that Brown 'finds' the poem in order that Keats's poetic integrity may be established. And the structure of this drama is very similar to that which figures in the Romantic construction of posterity, the establishment of posthumous reputation, in which the value of a poet, such as Chatterton or Kirke White, is not 'discovered' until after his death.

In 'Lamia', Keats narrates a similar drama of private creation and articulates a mortal fear of publication. 'Lamia' presents Keats's last and most explicit allegory of reading, an allegory which problematizes the relationship between private poetic creation or imaginative construction and its public reception, and presents us, once again, with the posthumous life of writing. Our readings of Keats's earlier poems allow us to understand 'Lamia' almost too easily in terms of reading: Lycius becomes a tragic reader and Lamia the text. Moreover, the congruence of Lamia's name with the poem itself suggests that Lycius's reading of the snake-woman is strategically congruent with a certain reading of the poem so that the deathly mechanism of reading in the poem also configures the way that reading is itself determined by 'Lamia'.

'Lamia', then, presents Keats's most explicit and at the same time most problematic allegory of reading. This point has already been recognized by critics: R. H. Fogle has commented that '"Lamia" appears to lend itself to allegorical interpretation', and Garrett Stewart has remarked that the poem 'seems to invite allegorical reading'.[3] And this is indeed the case: since its publication, 'Lamia' has generated a series of allegorical readings. In most cases, such allegorical readings focus on ways in which the three characters in the poem, Lamia, Lycius, and Apollonius may be said to represent something other than themselves. The various allegories constructed

by critics tend to interconnect with each other in complex ways and
they tend to be disrupted by the allegory of Hermes and the Nymph
in the opening section. Nevertheless, critics' characterological allegories of 'Lamia' can be schematically if reductively summarized as
follows:[4]

Lamia	Lycius	Apollonius
Fanny Brawne	Keats	Charles Brown[5]
Poetry	Poet	Philosopher[6]
Poem	Keats/Poet	Reviewers[7]
Illusion/Dream	Dreamer	Reason/Reality Principle[8]
Id	Ego	Superego[9]
Text	Reader	Public[10]

Not all allegorical readings employ such a threefold division: Leon
Waldoff, for example, reads the poem as an allegory of castration
anxiety; Bruce Clarke reads it as 'the fable of a poet's inability to
protect his own psyche ... from efficient reduction by the negativity of
his own spirit'; Terence Hoagwood reads it in terms of the notion
that a 'private discourse of illusion is always produced *by* and *within*
a social reality'; and Marjorie Levinson reads it as 'an allegory about
the evolution of value forms and their corresponding social forms'.[11]
It would be possible to extend these allegorical readings and, in
particular, to extend Wolfson and Rzepka's allegory of reading, by
reading the poem in terms of audience, such that while Lamia (and
'Lamia') figure the desired (textual) object, Lycius, Apollonius, and
the public, or Lycius's friends, each figure different ways of reading
or different types of audience: Lycius, in this reading, would figure
the enthralled, seduced, enticed, entrapped or entrammelled reader;
Apollonius would figure the critical or allegorical reader; and the
public, who are 'maz'd, curious and keen' (part 2, line 156) would
figure both what Rzepka characterizes as 'the cheap tastes and
infantile raptures of [Keats's] literary public', and the material
conditions of publication themselves.[12]

This kind of reading, involving the elaboration of figures of
reading, could then be grafted on to traditional readings of the major
questions surrounding 'Lamia', such as the question of the relationship between the introductory episode of Hermes and the
Nymph and the main narrative itself, or the apparently undecidable
issue of whether, in writing the poem, Keats intends to parody

imagination or to condemn reason.[13] An elaboration of the figure of allegorical reading would suggest that in constructing an allegorical reading of Lamia (the woman, Lamia = a snake, a lamia), Apollonius brings both the poem and Lamia's fiction to an end. But it would also suggest that Apollonius's allegorical reading is itself generated by the solecism of the private made public and that what it destroys is not the 'text' of Lamia (which only ever exists in Lycius's imagination or reading), but rather Lycius's enthralled reading. One of the many interesting aspects of this hypothetical allegory of allegorical readings is that it would be implicitly self-destructive in that it would suggest the destructiveness of 'allegorical' reading, while at the same time attempting to present its own allegorical reading as more truthful or accurate than others. Indeed, as a critique of allegorical reading, this reading would engage with the problem which any criticism of criticism *per se*, or of theory *per se*, encounters: as soon as we encounter a call for reading without the complexities, sophistications, sophistries and distortions of 'criticism' or 'theory', then we have already begun to excavate the buried *figure* of reading within any reading. Reading, this suggests, is always already figured.

This point might be suggested most economically by a short digression. In March 1819, Keats wrote a letter to his young sister Fanny. The letter includes one of Keats's most concise and most evocative figures of reading:

> I must confess even now a partiality for a handsome Globe of goldfish – then I would have it hold 10 pails of water and be fed continually fresh through a cool pipe with another pipe to let through the floor – well ventilated they would preserve all their beautiful silver and Crimson – Then I would put it before a handsome painted window and shade it all round with myrtles and Japonicas. I should like the window to open onto the Lake of Geneva – and there I'd sit and read all day like the picture of somebody reading. (*Letters*, vol. II, p. 46)

The words 'fresh' and 'cool' come from Keats's exemplary poem of reading, 'This pleasant tale is like a little copse' – 'The honied lines do freshly interlace, / To keep the reader in so sweet a place ... / ... he feels the dewy drops / Come cool and suddenly against his face' – reminding us of the sensuous luxury within which Keats tends to figure reading. The desire for reading in Keats is the desire for the self-identity of sensuous experience. But this sensuousness of reading is fissured by the duplicity of reading read, of figured reading, because reading is presented not *as reading* but as a picture of somebody reading. Reading is self-divided, figured – at the same time the action of reading and the perception or reading of that reading. Reading in Keats is not reading but the picture of somebody reading.[14]

Caught within the 'trap' of reading – the desire for the sensuous self-identity of the 'experience' of reading and the recognition that reading is always self-divided, a representation of itself – we might then return to 'Lamia' in order to examine the ways in which such a reading would figure reading(s) of the poem. In particular, we might focus briefly on two aspects of Lamia in the poem: her name and the figure of the hand. It is possible to read Lamia (in the dazzling descriptions of the serpent-woman) as a figure for the poem itself: Lamia is also, in some sense, 'Lamia', and 'Lamia' is a lamia, a seductive trap, not what it seems.[15] As this might suggest, however, the congruence of Lamia's name with the poem produces a series of paradoxes which threaten to disturb the whole question of naming, of language, and of reading. Lamia's name is itself a crux of inter-pretation because of its inconsistent use (at part 2, lines 88–9, Lycius asks Lamia for her name; Lamia does not reply, but later, at part 2, line 254, Lycius uses it anyway).[16] Indeed, Lycius's request for Lamia's name is itself tautologically problematic: 'Hast any mortal name, / Fit appellation for this dazzling frame?' (2, 88–9). The lines suggest the tautology of naming while at the same time suggesting that naming Lamia might also be naming 'Lamia' ('this dazzling frame'). The vexed question of naming, however, is only one aspect of the problematics of language in 'Lamia'. To the extent that Lamia figures the text of 'Lamia', we might understand Lycius's fear over the dissolution of his dream-woman to produce a rich allegory of reading. Lamia dissolves twice – into the shape of a woman at part 1, lines 146–70, and again at the end of the poem when her looks dissolve in the look of Apollonius. Lamia's initial metamorphosis is repeatedly figured as a kind of melting – 'her elfin blood in madness ran, / Her mouth foam'd, and the grass, therewith besprent, / Wither'd at dew so sweet and virulent ... A deep volcanian yellow took the place / Of all her wilder-mooned body's grace; / And, as the lava ravishes the mead, / Spoilt all her silver mail, and golden brede ... she / Melted and disappear'd' (1, 147–66). And with this destructive melting and dissolving, her voice and language dissolve:

> And in the air, her new voice luting soft,
> Cried, 'Lycius! gentle Lycius!' – Borne aloft
> With the bright mists about the mountains hoar
> These words dissolv'd: Crete's forests heard no more. (1, 167–70)

These words dissolve, such that melting, dissolution is the condition of language in 'Lamia': Lamia is language, a construct of language, and her words, like her body, constantly threaten to melt, to dissolve so that neither Crete's forests, nor Keats's audience hear any more. Words in 'Lamia', like Lamia herself, constantly threaten to dissolve in the irreducible instability of the signifier: the question of how to name Lamia is also the question of how to name 'Lamia', that is how it is possible for language not to dissolve upon our ears. And it is words, voiced by Lamia, which ravish Lycius, and which we fear to lose in Lamia's melting:

> 'So sweetly to these ravish'd ears of mine
> Came thy sweet greeting, that if thou shouldst fade
> Thy memory will waste me to a shade: –
> For pity do not melt!' (1, 268–71)

Lycius voices the fear of the loss of the voice, of the language, of the body of Lamia and, as a figure of reading, also voices the potential melting, the dissolution, of language in reading. Melting, though, is both constitutive of Lamia – how she came to be in the first place – and constitutive of reading as figured by Keats – the melting 'dewy drops' of language which make the reader melt. The dissolution of the signifier is unstoppable in reading. Figures of reading might themselves be read as generative or productive of the dissolution of Lamia and of 'Lamia'.

Finally, the hot cold hand of 'This living hand' and 'The Fall of Hyperion' is figured in 'Lamia' as the icy grip of the snake-woman and the text on Lycius and the reader:

> Lycius then press'd her hand, with devout touch,
> As pale it lay upon the rosy couch:
> 'Twas icy, and the cold ran through his veins;
> Then sudden it grew hot, and all the pains
> Of an unnatural heat shot to his heart. (2, 249–53)

It is at this point that Lycius first names Lamia: with the hot icy unnatural touch of her hand, Lycius is given the gift of speech or the gift, more accurately, of reading, an indeterminate, unenlightened non-allegorical reading: 'Lamia, what means this?' (2, 254). And finally, as Lamia dissolves and Lycius dies with her, her hand 'gives' meaning, signifies:

> she, as well
> As her weak hand could any meaning tell,
> Motion'd him to be silent.   (2, 301-3)

The significance of the hand, the hot-cold, living-dead hand of poetry is silence (an interdiction of speech which is transgressed by reading and by Apollonius). In 'Lamia', as in 'The Fall of Hyperion' and 'This living hand', Keats presents the synecdochic dead hand of poetry as a figure for the death of the reader.

If this kind of reading were accepted for 'Lamia', however, it would have to consider its own relationship with the reading of Apollonius: it would have to figure itself in Apollonius's reading and recognize that allegorical reading is figured in 'Lamia' as destructive. Lycius is a loving reader who ignores the meaning or allegory of Lamia and is instead enthralled, entrammelled in the text, while Apollonius is a critical reader who understands Lamia as not identical with herself, as an allegory.[17] As we have seen, 'Lamia' prefigures, constructs and irreducibly determines its own critical reception as allegorical, while at the same time irreducibly determining such a reading as destructive or impossible. And the point which we would be making here is not quite the same as, or at least not *only*, the kind of allegorical reading which notes the destructiveness in 'Lamia' of philosophy, reason, criticism, or allegorical reading, because this reading would assert both the necessity, the inevitability, and the impossibility of allegorical reading. By this account, the posthumous life of writing would be shown to have been figured in and by the text of 'Lamia' so that a reading of the poem would be deferred to a place and a time beyond its own.

Notes

INTRODUCTION: FIGURES OF READING

1 See John Bayley's comment that all of Keats's 'greatest poetic effects are founded on [a] kind of instability, deep inside their verbal texture', in 'Sexist', *London Review of Books*, 9, 22 (10 December 1987), p. 23. As an anonymous contemporary reviewer said, Keats 'is continually shocking our ideas of poetical decorum, at the very time when we are acknowledging the hand of genius' (*Heritage*, p. 160). Here, and throughout this study, I draw more or less explicitly on a tradition of Keats criticism which emphasizes the disruptive forces of his poetry, and which includes Bayley's description of Keats's disconcerting but enriching vulgarity in *The Uses of Division: Unity and Disharmony in Literature* (London, Chatto and Windus, 1976), pp. 107–56, Christopher Ricks's notion of the liberating and 'humanizing' embarrassments of Keats's poetry in *Keats and Embarrassment* (Oxford University Press, 1976), and Marjorie Levinson's analysis of the class-determined 'badness' of his poetry, in *Keats's Life of Allegory: The Origins of a Style* (Oxford, Basil Blackwell, 1988). My contribution to this tradition involves a re-description of Keatsian solecism. The opposition referred to here between Keats's 'sensuousness' and his 'thought' also has a distinguished critical history, of which Hermione de Almeida's collection, *Critical Essays on John Keats* (Boston, G. K. Hall, 1990), is only the most recent emanation. Almeida comments that her selection of essays proposes 'to assert the intellectual life and philosophical tenor and currency of Keats' (p. 1): in this respect, the collection curiously elides what might be understood to be the contemporary version of 'philosophical tenor' ('literary theory') in literary criticism of Keats in the work of, for example, Paul de Man, Eugenio Donato, Richard Macksey, Richard Rand, Martin Aske, Marjorie Levinson and Paul Hamilton – none of whom earns a place in Almeida's book.

2 Barbara Herrnstein Smith, 'Narrative Versions, Narrative Theories', in W. J. T. Mitchell, ed., *On Narrative* (University of Chicago Press, 1981), p. 228. Jean-François Lyotard provides a useful informal definition of narrative pragmatics as 'all the complicated relations that exist between

a speaker and what he is talking about, between the storyteller and his listener, and between the listener and the story told by the story-teller' ('Lessons in Paganism' in Andrew Benjamin, ed., *The Lyotard Reader*, Oxford, Basil Blackwell, 1989, p. 125).

3 Solecism may be understood to include de Manian 'catachresis' – the aporia of, for example, grammar and rhetoric, or reference and inscription: my use of the word 'solecism', however, would also seek to suggest the explicitly social (political, historical) nature of such scandal. More recently, Michael Riffaterre, in a discussion of 'six universals of literariness' ('Relevance of Theory/Theory of Relevance', *Yale Journal of Criticism*, 1, 2 (1988), pp. 163–76), has named catachresis the first 'universal'. As Riffaterre comments, 'Catachresis is *the* sign for inappropriateness, and that should do so long as we remember that inappropriateness at the level of common parlance becomes perfect appropriateness at the literary level' (p. 167).

4 Lyotard uses the word 'tortures' to describe the different 'games' which are 'inflicted' on language (including the game of literature), in Jean-François Lyotard and Jean-Loup Thébaud, *Just Gaming*, tr. Wlad Godzich (Manchester University Press, 1985), p. 50.

5 More to the point, this is precisely how Keats has consistently been read: see, for example, John Gibson Lockhart's attack on Keats as a member of the 'Cockney School of Poetry', in *Blackwood's Edinburgh Magazine* (*Heritage*, pp. 97–110); Marjorie Levinson is only the most recent critic to frame Keats's poetry within such (quasi-)biographical terms, in *Keats's Life of Allegory*.

6 See, for example, Peter Brooks, *Reading for the Plot: Design and Intention in Narrative* (Oxford University Press, 1984), p. 103; D. A. Miller, *Narrative and Its Discontents: Problems of Closure in the Traditional Novel* (New Jersey, Princeton University Press, 1981), p. ix; and Barbara Herrnstein Smith, *Poetic Closure: A Study of How Poems End* (University of Chicago Press, 1968), p. 35.

7 Jonathan Culler, 'Story and Discourse in the Analysis of Narrative', in *The Pursuit of Signs: Semiotics, Literature, Deconstruction* (London, Routledge and Kegan Paul, 1981), pp. 169–87. See also Brooks, *Reading for the Plot*, pp. 28–9, Gerald Prince, *Narratology: The Form and Functioning of Narrative* (Berlin, Mouton, 1982), pp. 157–8, and Gérard Genette, 'Vraisemblance et motivation', in *Figures II: Essais* (Paris, Seuil, 1969), pp. 96–7. Culler's argument is that although the 'meaning' of a text is usually considered to be determined by the events of the narrative, in fact these events can be shown to be determined by 'discursive requirements' (p. 186): as Brooks puts it, 'prior events, causes, are so only retrospectively, in a reading back from the end' (p. 29). Culler's version of this argument has been questioned in a recent essay by Seymour Chatman, 'On Deconstructing Narratology', *Style*, 22 (1988), pp. 9–17: but even if we accept Chatman's suggestion that Culler 'seems

to confuse psychological and logical orderings of events' (p. 15), it is possible to read the aporetic double logic of narrative as determining the space between text and audience.

8 I refer to Paul de Man's well-known but highly ambivalent statement in *Allegories of Reading: Figural Language in Rousseau, Nietzsche, Rilke, and Proust* (New Haven, Yale University Press, 1979, p. 245), that 'the impossibility of reading should not be taken too lightly'. The question which this assertion raises is: how do we take the word 'taken'? This itself is a question of reading: what does he *mean* here? The phrase produces, in short, its own allegory of the possibilities and impossibilities of reading.

9 Paul Ricoeur, *Time and Narrative*, trs. Kathleen McLaughlin and David Pellauer (3 vols., University of Chicago Press, 1985), vol. II, p. 39; see also Prince, *Narratology*, p. 157; Peter J. Rabinowitz, *Before Reading: Narrative Conventions and the Politics of Interpretation* (Ithaca, Cornell University Press, 1987), p. 108; and Paul Goodman, *The Structure of Literature* (University of Chicago Press, 1954), p. 14 ('in the beginning anything is possible; in the middle things become probable; in the ending everything is necessary'). See also Roland Barthes, 'Introduction to the Structural Analysis of Narratives', in *The Semiotic Challenge*, tr. Richard Howard (Oxford, Basil Blackwell, 1988), pp. 108–9, on 'the mainspring of narrative activity', the confusion between causality and consecutiveness ('consecution and consequentiality'), which apparently governs narrative under the rule of *post hoc, ergo propter hoc*. The idea dovetails with that – crucial to any notion of narrative – of 'motivation' (see Wallace Martin, *Recent Theories of Narrative*, Ithaca, Cornell University Press, 1986, p. 66), and it might also be read as a form of Freudian *Nachträglichkeit* or 'deferred action'.

10 Jean Ricardou, 'Belligérance du texte', in Claudine Gothot-Mersch, ed., *La production du sens chez Flaubert* (Paris, Union Générale d'Editions, 1975), pp. 85–102.

11 Roland Barthes, *S/Z* (Paris, Seuil, 1970), p. 82; Patricia A. Parker, *Inescapable Romance: Studies in the Poetics of a Mode* (New Jersey, Princeton University Press, 1979), p. 4: '"Romance" is characterized primarily as a form which simultaneously quests for and postpones a particular end, objective, or object'.

12 On the 'consumer boom' in eighteenth-century England, see Neil McKendrick, John Brewer and J. H. Plumb, *The Birth of a Consumer Society: The Commercialization of Eighteenth-Century England* (London, Europa Publications, 1982), esp. pp. 165–73 on the book trade. More generally, see Roy Porter, *English Society in the Eighteenth Century*, 2nd edn. (Harmondsworth, Penguin, 1990); and see below, ch. 1, note 27.

13 Lyotard and Thébaud, *Just Gaming*, p. 9.

14 See Philip W. Martin, *Byron: A Poet Before His Public* (Cambridge University Press, 1982), p. 38.

15 Percy Bysshe Shelley, *The Letters of Percy Bysshe Shelley*, ed. Frederick L.
    Jones (2 vols., Oxford University Press, 1964), vol. II, p. 388.
16 The paradigmatic twentieth-century discussion of the notion of Ro-
    mantic writing as 'self-expression' is that by M. H. Abrams in *The
    Mirror and the Lamp: Romantic Theory and the Critical Tradition* (Oxford
    University Press, 1971); see also John Barrell, *The Political Theory of
    Painting from Reynolds to Hazlitt: 'The Body of the Public'* (New Haven,
    Yale University Press, 1986), on the 'privatization' of social and
    aesthetic theory and practice during the eighteenth century 'under the
    pressure of commercial capitalism' (p. 339). But see Jerome J. McGann,
    The Romantic Ideology: A Critical Investigation (University of Chicago Press,
    1983), p. 131, on the distinction between Romantic *ideology* and
    Romantic *work*: 'The grand illusion of Romantic *ideology* is that one may
    escape [the] world through imagination and poetry. The great truth of
    Romantic *work* is that there is no escape, that there is only revelation (in
    a wholly secular sense)'.
17 See Sigmund Freud, 'The Uncanny', in *The Standard Edition of the
    Complete Psychological Works of Sigmund Freud*, tr. James Strachey *et al.* (24
    vols., London, Hogarth, 1981), vol. XVII, p. 241.
18 Margaret Homans, 'Keats Reading Women, Women Reading Keats',
    SiR, 29 (1990), 360.
19 *Ibid.*, 362.
20 De Man, *Allegories of Reading*, p. 77.
21 Jonathan Culler, 'The Identity of the Literary Text', in Mario J. Valdés
    and Owen Miller, eds., *Identity of the Literary Text* (University of Toronto
    Press, 1985), p. 14.
22 Timothy Clark, *Derrida, Heidegger, Blanchot: Sources of Derrida's Notion and
    Practice of Literature* (Cambridge University Press, 1992), pp. 7–8;
    compare de Man, *Allegories of Reading*, pp. 161–2.
23 The most important general studies of the question of the relationship
    between Romantics and readers/audiences are Jon P. Klancher, *The
    Making of English Reading Audiences, 1790–1832* (Madison, University of
    Wisconsin Press, 1987), and Tilottama Rajan, *The Supplement of Reading:
    Figures of Understanding in Romantic Theory and Practice* (Ithaca, Cornell
    University Press, 1990), to which any discussion of the topic will be
    indebted. For more specific studies, see, on Wordsworth, David Perkins,
    Wordsworth and the Poetry of Sincerity (Cambridge, Mass., Harvard
    University Press, 1964), ch. 6; D. D. Devlin, *Wordsworth and the Poetry of
    Epitaphs* (London, Macmillan, 1980), ch. 1; Michael Baron, 'Speaking
    and Writing: Wordsworth's "Fit Audience"', *English*, 32 (1983), pp.
    217–50; Kurt Heinzelman, *The Economics of the Imagination* (Amherst,
    University of Massachusetts Press, 1980), ch. 7; Gene W. Ruoff,
    'Wordsworth on Language: Towards a Radical Poetics for English
    Romanticism', *The Wordsworth Circle*, 3 (1972), pp. 204–11; Willard
    Spiegelman, *Wordsworth's Heroes* (Berkeley, University of California

Press, 1985), pp. 219–39; Geoffrey Jackson, 'Nominal and Actual Audiences: Some Strategies of Communication in Wordsworth's Poetry', *The Wordsworth Circle*, 12 (1981), pp. 226–31; Don H. Bialostosky, *Making Tales: The Poetics of Wordsworth's Narrative Experiments* (University of Chicago Press, 1984); L. J. Swingle, *The Obstinate Questionings of English Romanticism* (Baton Rouge, Louisiana State University Press, 1987), pp. 93–107; Susan Edwards Meisenhelder, *Wordsworth's Informed Reader: Structures of Experience in His Poetry* (Nashville, Vanderbilt University Press, 1988); Richard G. Swartz, 'Wordsworth, Copyright, and the Commodities of Genius', *Modern Philology*, 89 (1992), pp. 482–509. On Keats, see esp. Aileen Ward, '"That Last Infirmity of Noble Mind"': Keats and the Idea of Fame', in Donald H. Reiman *et al.*, eds., *The Evidence of the Imagination: Studies in the Interaction Between Life and Art in English Romantic Literature* (New York University Press, 1978); R. S. White, *Keats as a Reader of Shakespeare* (London, Athlone, 1987); Donald C. Goellnicht, 'Keats on Reading: "Delicious Diligent Indolence"', *JEGP*, 88 (1989), pp. 190–210; Susan J. Wolfson, *The Questioning Presence: Wordsworth, Keats, and the Interrogative Mode in Romantic Poetry* (Ithaca, Cornell University Press, 1986), esp. ch. 13; Charles J. Rzepka, *The Self as Mind: Vision and Identity in Wordsworth, Coleridge, and Keats* (Cambridge, Mass., Harvard University Press, 1986), ch. 4; and Homans, 'Keats Reading Women', pp. 341–70. On Shelley, see Stephen C. Behrendt, *Shelley and His Audiences* (Lincoln, University of Nebraska Press, 1989); on Byron, see Philip W. Martin, *Byron*; on Blake, see Morris Eaves, 'Romantic Expressive Theory and Blake's Idea of the Audience', *PMLA*, 95 (1980), pp. 784–801, and Paul Mann, 'Apocalypse and Recuperation: Blake and the Maw of Commerce', *ELH*, 52 (1985), pp. 5–10. More generally on the Romantics and audience, see Clifford Siskin, *The Historicity of Romantic Discourse* (New York, Oxford University Press, 1988), pp. 106ff., and Karl Kroeber, *British Romantic Art* (Berkeley, University of California Press, 1986). Studies of other nineteenth-century poets include Dorothy Mermin, *The Audience in the Poem: Five Victorian Poets* (New Brunswick, Rutgers University Press, 1983); Ian Jack, *The Poet and His Audience* (Cambridge University Press, 1984); Lee Erickson, *Robert Browning: His Poetry and His Audiences* (Ithaca, Cornell University Press, 1984).

24 Wolfgang Iser, *The Act of Reading: A Theory of Aesthetic Response* (Baltimore, The Johns Hopkins University Press, 1978); see, for example, Meisenhelder, *Wordsworth's Informed Reader* and Goellnicht, 'Keats on Reading'. In the present study, I would wish to distinguish the notion of 'figures of reading' from any notion of 'implied readers' which act simply as directions for use or rules of engagement for what is then hypothesized as the 'real' reader.

25 See, for example, Behrendt, *Shelley and His Audiences*; Baron, 'Speaking and Writing', pp. 217–50; Devlin, *Wordsworth and the Poetry of Epitaphs*;

Wolfson, *The Questioning Presence*. In order to discriminate between the apparently private, personal nature of the 'reader' in the first category and the public impulse of audience in the second, I have tended to make a distinction between 'readers' and 'audiences', but this distinction should itself, as Klancher suggests, be understood as a construct of the early nineteenth century (*The Making of English Reading Audiences*, p. 11).

26 See, for example, Spiegelman, *Wordsworth's Heroes*, and Mermin, *The Audience in the Poem*. Theoretical work on this topic includes, for example, Gerald Prince, 'Introduction to the Study of the Narratee', in Jane P. Tompkins, ed., *Reader-Response Criticism: From Formalism to Post-Structuralism* (Baltimore, The Johns Hopkins University Press, 1980), pp. 7–25; Lucien Dällenbach, *The Mirror in the Text*, tr. Jeremy Whiteley (Cambridge, Polity, 1989); and Ross Chambers, *Story and Situation: Narrative Seduction and the Power of Fiction* (Manchester University Press, 1984). A number of other categories may also be discerned, including the study of poets' proposed or desired audiences; the reception which the poetry actually received after its publication; the study of poets themselves as readers; and studies of Romantic poets' theorizations of the act of reading: these categories are all dealt with to some extent in Klancher, *The Making of English Reading Audiences*, which book constitutes an important analysis of the *construction* of audience by the Romantics in their prose writing.

27 See Behrendt, *Shelley and His Audiences*, for an example of the first category, and Meisenhelder, *Wordsworth's Informed Reader*, for an example of the second.

28 Frances Ferguson, *Wordsworth: Language as Counter-Spirit* (New Haven, Yale University Press, 1977), p. xiv.

29 Compare Keats's 'To My Brother George', lines 73–4: 'Yet shall my spirit lofty converse hold / With after times'.

30 See Tilottama Rajan, *The Supplement of Reading*, for a ground-breaking discussion of Romantic (hermeneutic) reading in these terms. It should be noted, however, that Rajan's notion of 'supplement' involves, finally, a *completion* of the text rather than, as in my account, an opening up or uncanny exposure of the necessary but undecidable incompletion of the Romantic literary text. In this respect, the pathos of the Romantic configuration of reading involves the tragic recognition that the supplement of reading, rather than completing the text, might stand in its place, both concealing and exposing its incompletion.

31 See, for example, Jacques Derrida, 'Signature Event Context', in *Margins of Philosophy*, tr. Alan Bass (Brighton, Harvester, 1982), pp. 315–16: 'All writing, therefore, in order to be what it is, must be able to function in the radical absence of every empirically determined addressee in general. And this absence is not a continuous modification of presence; it is a break in presence, "death", or the possibility of the "death" of the addressee, inscribed in the structure of the mark ... ' And he adds that 'What holds for the addressee holds also, for the same

reasons, for the sender or the producer'. For Derrida, then, a written sign is 'a mark which remains' (p. 317). What Derrida proposes is an account of writing in general, whereas my suggestion for the Romantic construction of posterity involves a historically specific configuration of the audience as inscribed in certain Romantic texts. To the extent that we accept his propositions, we might conceive of Derrida's notion of writing as being an explication of Romanticism or as itself prefigured and as such determined by the Romantic ideology. It is in its conception of posthumous *life* that the present study might most clearly be seen to diverge from the most important recent study of Keats, Marjorie Levinson's *Keats's Life of Allegory*. While Levinson brilliantly elaborates the exemplary particularity of Keats's life in his writing, the present book attempts to put into suspense the very possibility of that 'life' as an origin in order to suggest ways in which it is bound up with death and with the posthumous life of writing. As such, the present study would suggest the impossibility of reading either Keats's life or his poetry except through his 'tragic' death at the age of twenty-five and in terms of a necessary inscription of (that) death in his writing, in his very 'style'. 'The posthumous life of writing' alludes to a letter describing Keats's death by Joseph Severn, the friend who watched Keats die, to John Taylor, Keats's publisher, dated 6 March 1821: 'Each day he would look up in the doctors face to discover how long he should live – he would say – "how long will this posthumous life of mine last" – that look was more than we could ever bear – the extreme brightness of his eyes – with his poor pallid face – were not earthly' (*KC*, vol. I, p. 224).

32 Shelley, *Letters*, vol. I, p. 216.

33 *Shelley's Poetry and Prose*, eds. Donald H. Reiman and Sharon B. Powers (New York, Norton, 1977), p. 373; compare Shelley, *Letters*, vol. II, pp. 262–3. See my paper, 'Shelley in Posterity', in Stuart Curran and Betty T. Bennett, eds., *Shelley: Poet and Legislator of the World* (Baltimore, The Johns Hopkins University Press, forthcoming), for a more detailed analysis of Shelley's writing in this respect.

34 William Wordsworth, *The Prelude 1799, 1805, 1850*, eds. Jonathan Wordsworth *et al.* (New York, Norton, 1979), Book 5, lines 45–9 (1805).

35 In quoting 'This living hand' I have reproduced the punctuation from the holograph manuscript: see Jack Stillinger, ed., *The Poems of John Keats* (London, Heinemann, 1978), p. 723. (In the manuscript the word 'heart' in line five appears above the line between 'thine' and 'own' and is spelt 'heat'.)

36 *Works*, vol. XVII, pp. 197–9; see also 'On Posthumous Fame, – Whether Shakespeare was Influenced by a Love of it' (*Works*, vol. IV, pp. 21–4).

37 Brooke Hopkins, 'Keats and the Uncanny: "This living hand"', *The Kenyon Review*, n.s., 11, 4 (1989), pp. 28–40.

38 As well as Hopkins, see, for other recent readings of the poem, Culler, 'Apostrophe', in *The Pursuit of Signs*, pp. 153–4; Lawrence Lipking, *The Life of the Poet: Beginning and Ending Poetic Careers* (University of Chicago

Press, 1981), pp. 180–84; Timothy Bahti, 'Ambiguity and Indeterminacy: The Juncture', *Comparative Literature*, 38 (1986), pp. 218–23; and Richard Macksey, 'Keats and the Poetics of Extremity', *MLN*, 99 (1984), pp. 853–4.
39 Hopkins, 'Keats and the Uncanny', p. 38.
40 *Ibid.*
41 Paul de Man, 'Introduction' to John Keats, *Selected Poetry* (New York, The New American Library, 1966), p. xii.

1 : NARRATIVE AND AUDIENCE IN ROMANTIC POETICS

1 *Shelley's Poetry and Prose*, p. 485.
2 For discussions of the Romantics and narrative, see Karl Kroeber, *Romantic Narrative Art* (Madison, University of Wisconsin Press, 1966); and 'Trends in Minor Romantic Narrative Poetry', in James V. Logan *et al.*, eds., *Some British Romantics: A Collection of Essays* (Ohio State University Press, 1966), pp. 269–92; Jay Clayton, *Romantic Vision and the Novel* (Cambridge University Press, 1987), esp. ch. 1; Lionel Stevenson, 'The Mystique of Romantic Narrative Poetry', in W. Paul Elledge and Richard L. Hoffman, eds., *Romantic and Victorian* (Rutherford, Fairleigh Dickinson University Press, 1971); Jack Stillinger, 'The Plots of Romantic Poetry', *College Literature*, 12 (1985), pp. 97–112; Hermann Fischer, *Romantic Verse Narrative: The History of a Genre*, tr. Sue Bollans (Cambridge University Press, 1991); Tilottama Rajan, 'The Erasure of Narrative in Post-Structuralist Representations of Wordsworth', in Kenneth R. Johnston *et al.*, eds., *Romantic Revolutions: Criticism and Theory* (Bloomington, Indiana University Press, 1990), pp. 350–70. Considerations of individual poets include Brian Nellist, 'Shelley's Narratives and "The Witch of Atlas"', in Miriam Allott, ed., *Essays on Shelley* (Liverpool University Press, 1982), pp. 160–90; Ian Reid, 'Prospero Meets Adam Smith: Narrative Exchange and Control in *The Prelude*', *Textual Practice*, 1 (1987), pp. 169–91; Gene W. Ruoff, 'The Sense of a Beginning: *Mansfield Park* and Romantic Narrative', *The Wordsworth Circle*, 10 (1979), pp. 174–86; Beth Nelson, *George Crabbe and the Progress of Eighteenth-Century Narrative Verse* (Lewisburg, Bucknell University Press, 1976); Angus Easson, 'Statesman, Dwarf and Weaver: Wordsworth and Nineteenth-Century Narrative', in Jeremy Hawthorn, ed., *The Nineteenth-Century British Novel* (London, Edward Arnold, 1986), pp. 17–29; Bialostosky, *Making Tales*.
3 Such condemnations, directed particularly at the popular novel, are extremely common: see, for example, Richard Payne Knight, *An Analytical Inquiry into the Principles of Taste*, 4th edn. (London, 1808), pp. 450–55. For studies of such attacks in the eighteenth and early nineteenth centuries, see Richard D. Altick, *The English Common Reader: A Social History of the Mass Reading Public, 1800–1900* (University of Chicago Press,

1963), pp. 110–28, 231–4; John Tinnon Taylor, *Early Opposition to the English Novel: The Popular Reaction from 1760–1830* (New York, Columbia University Press, 1943); and Michael Munday 'The Novel and its Critics in the Early Nineteenth Century', *SP*, 79 (1982), pp. 205–26.

4 Jean-François Lyotard, *The Différend: Phrases in Dispute*, tr. G. Van den Abbeele (Minneapolis, University of Minnesota Press, 1988).

5 See my essay '"Devious Feet": Wordsworth and the Scandal of Narrative Form' (*ELH*, 59, 1992, pp. 145–73), for a discussion of interruptions or blockages to narrative as constitutive of Wordsworthian narration.

6 Ricoeur, *Time and Narrative*, vol. 1, p. x; compare M. H. Abrams, *Natural Supernaturalism: Tradition and Revolution in Romantic Literature* (London, Oxford University Press, 1971) on 'the Romantic plot of the circular or spiral quest' (p. 193).

7 Tilottama Rajan, *The Supplement of Reading*, pp. 280–81.

8 Roy Park, ed., *Lamb as Critic* (London, Routledge and Kegan Paul, 1980), p. 187.

9 Compare Hazlitt's criticism of Canto Four, that 'there is no plot, no story, no interest excited, no catastrophe. The general reflections are connected together merely by the accidental occurrence of different objects' (Reiman, B5, p. 2336).

10 Ioan Williams, ed., *Sir Walter Scott on Novelists and Fiction* (London, Routledge and Kegan Paul, 1968), p. 226.

11 For a contemporary appraisal of 'internalized' narrative form, see an anonymous article, 'Thoughts on Novel Writing', *Blackwood's Edinburgh Magazine*, 4 (January 1819), pp. 394–6. On Wordsworth and the internalization of narrative, see Clayton, *Romantic Vision*, pp. 106–7 and ch. 5 *passim*; on this as a central feature of Romantic narrative, see, for example, Kroeber, 'Trends in Minor Romantic Narrative Poetry', p. 291, Harold Bloom, 'The Internalization of Quest Romance', in *The Ringers in the Tower: Studies in Romantic Tradition* (University of Chicago Press, 1971), pp. 13–35, and Stuart Curran, *Poetic Form and British Romanticism* (New York, Oxford University Press, 1986), p. 182.

12 Kroeber, *Romantic Narrative Art*, p. 84.

13 Bruce R. McElderry, ed., *Shelley's Critical Prose* (Lincoln, University of Nebraska Press, 1967), p. 91.

14 *Ibid.*, p. 90.

15 Clayton, *Romantic Vision*, p. 48; 'the otherness of narrative' is from p. 13.

16 Leigh Hunt, ed., *Classic Tales, Serious and Lively, with Critical Essays on the Merits and Reputations of the Authors* (2 vols., London, 1807), vol. 1, pp. 213–14.

17 Lee Erickson, 'The Poets' Corner: The Impact of Technological Changes in Printing on English Poetry, 1800–1850', *ELH*, 52 (1985), p. 894.

18 Brian Nellist's suggestion that 'we might accept on empirical grounds

the priority of story for the Romantic poet and its comparative unimportance for the Augustan poet' ('Shelley's Narratives', p. 160) is, however, too simplistic: see John W. Draper, 'The Metrical Tale in XVIII-Century England', *PMLA*, 52 (1937), p. 390: 'At first sight, this prevalence of narrative [in early nineteenth-century poetry] seems to be an utter departure from the preceding hundred years... but a closer examination, especially of minor writers, shows that the eighteenth century had an unbroken tradition of such writings'; and see Nelson, *George Crabbe*, p. 20, who lists, amongst others, Prior, Parnell, Congreve, Swift, Pope, Gay, Thomson, Shenstone, Cowper, Goldsmith, Burns, Blake and Percy as exponents of the verse-tale in one form or another.

19 See Klancher, *The Making of English Reading Audiences*, p. 12, on audience as an 'otherness within one's own discourse'.

20 See, for example, Harold Bloom, *Poetry and Repression: Revisionism from Blake to Stevens* (New Haven, Yale University Press, 1976); W. Jackson Bate, *The Burden of the Past and the English Poet* (London, Chatto and Windus, 1971). The 'anxiety of influence' and the 'anxiety of audience' are not, of course, mutually exclusive: as Hazlitt points out in his essay 'On Posthumous Fame', 'The love of fame is a species of emulation' (*Works*, vol. IV, p. 22).

21 See Coleridge's comments on this as an anxiety of audience: 'Modern Poetry characterized by the Poets ANXIETY to be always *striking*'; he compares such poetry to Claudian, in whose poetry we can observe 'the anxious craving Vanity! every Line, nay, every word *stops*, looks full in your face, & asks & *begs* for Praise' (*CN*, 2728); and he claims that 'In the present age the Poet proposes to himself as his main Object & most characteristic of his art, new and striking Images, incidents that interest the Affections or excite the curiosity of the Reader' (*CN*, 2599). See Chambers, *Story and Situation*: this book provides an important analysis of narrative form in terms of 'point', 'tellability', narrative contract, the notion of the effect of the reader on narrative production, narrative seduction and *mise en abyme*. See also Marie Maclean, *Narrative as Performance: The Baudelairean Experiment* (London, Routledge, 1988); Alexander Gelley, *Narrative Crossings: Theory and Pragmatics of Prose Fiction* (Baltimore, The Johns Hopkins University Press, 1987); and, on 'point', Prince, *Narratology*, pp. 158–62: these critics tend to draw on the work of William Labov in particular *Language in the Inner City: Studies in the Black English Vernacular* (Oxford, Basil Blackwell, 1972), ch. 9. For the importance of 'point' in literary texts, see also Northrop Frye, *Anatomy of Criticism: Four Essays* (New Jersey, Princeton University Press, 1973), p. 52; and E. M. Forster, *Aspects of the Novel* (Harmondsworth, Penguin, 1982), p. 42. For a sceptical survey of such concerns, see Seymour Chatman, 'What Can We Learn From Contextualist Narratology', *Poetics Today*, 11 (1990), pp. 309–28.

22 Prince, *Narratology*, p. 149.

23 See Michael McKeon's argument for the epistemological reorientation of narrative as a key function in the birth of the novel, the growth of which he shows to be due to a dialectical progression from 'romance idealism' through 'naïve empiricism' to 'extreme skepticism' in *The Origins of the English Novel: 1600–1740* (Baltimore, The Johns Hopkins University Press, 1987); and see Nellist, 'Shelley's Narratives', p. 162. This 'epistemological suspension' in the early nineteenth century might be understood as a reaction against what Thomas Love Peacock defined as 'the taste of the present day': 'Information, not enquiry – manners, not morals – facts, not inferences' ('An Essay on Fashionable Literature' (1818), in Howard Mills, ed., *Memoirs of Shelley and Other Essays and Reviews*, London, Rupert Hart-Davis, 1970, p. 101).

24 Many early nineteenth-century writers and critics, of course, deprecated and professed to spurn such considerations: Shelley, for example, in his preface to *Laon and Cythna*, remarked that '[i]t is the misfortune of this age, that its Writers, too thoughtless of immortality, are exquisitely sensible to temporary praise or blame. They write with the fear of Reviews before their eyes' (McElderry, *Shelley's Critical Prose*, p. 50).

25 Linda Zionkowski, 'Bridging the Gulf Between: The Poet and the Audience in the Work of Gray', *ELH*, 58 (1991), p. 339. Compare Coleridge's early expression of the need for what he later calls a 'clerisy' and 'the opinion of a Public' as 'Perdition' (*CN*, 2395).

26 Jane P. Tompkins, 'The Reader in History: The Changing Shape of Literary Response', in Tompkins, ed., *Reader-Response Criticism*, p. 214.

27 For a similar argument, see Alvin Kernan, *Printing, Technology, Letters and Samuel Johnson* (New Jersey, Princeton University Press, 1987), pp. 294–5. Bertrand Harris Bronson comments that when author and audience are unknown to each other, 'the heart of the problem' is 'how to establish … a … reciprocity of emotional, intellectual, moral response with a person or persons never seen' ('Strange Relations: The Author and His Audience', in *Facets of the Enlightenment: Studies in English Literature and Its Contexts*, Berkeley, University of California Press, 1968, p. 309); see also A. S. Collins, *The Profession of Letters: A Study of the Relation of Author to Patron, Publisher, and Public, 1780–1832* (London, Routledge, 1928); Erickson, 'Poets' Corner', p. 893 and *passim*; and Fischer, *Romantic Verse Narrative*, pp. 47–53, on the changes in the reading public in the early nineteenth century. See John Feather, *A History of British Publishing* (London, Croom Helm, 1988) and Eric Halévy, *England in 1815*, 2nd edn., trs. E. I. Watkin and D. A. Barker (London, Ernest Benn, 1949), pp. 490–524, on publishing and the condition of the writer in the early nineteenth century; Amy Cruse, *The Englishman and His Books in the Early Nineteenth Century* (London, Harrap, 1930), on readers and reading; Tim Chilcott, *A Publisher and His Circle: The Life and Work of John Taylor, Keats's Publisher* (London, Routledge and Kegan Paul, 1972), pp. 201–2, on the heterogeneity of the audience

for poetry at the time; Lewis A. Coser, *Men of Ideas: A Sociologist's View* (New York, The Free Press, 1970), pp. 37–49; and J. W. Saunders, *The Profession of English Letters* (London, Routledge and Kegan Paul, 1964) on the 'literary schizophrenia' which this situation produced (p. 159). More generally on the question of the uncertainty of audience as constitutive of modernity, see Lyotard and Thébaud, *Just Gaming*, pp. 8–14.

28 The extent of Coleridge's ambivalence on this point, however, may be judged by his fears about 'promiscuous' readers, the kind of Coleridgean readers who abuse their position, who misread, either by (deliberate) misinterpretation, or by an unsystematic and eclectic choice of works, by annotation, by uncontextual (mis-)quotation, by plagiarism, etc.

29 John R. Nabholtz, '*My Reader, My Fellow Labourer*': *A Study of English Romantic Prose* (Columbia, University of Missouri Press, 1986), p. 4; Coleridge often both wrote and read as if he were in conversation, and he often expressed frustration when writing that he could not make physical gestures (see *CN*, 2322; *CL*, vol. II, pp. 872, 966; vol. IV, p. 571); Taylor (*Early Opposition to the English Novel*, p. 11) quotes Charles Dickens's essay 'Our English Watering Place' in which Dickens remembers the habit of making marginal annotations to novels in the early nineteenth century – as if the reader were conversing with the writer. This type of reciprocal reading seems to have been institutionalized in contemporary rhetoric text books: they function both as handbooks of study and appreciation of the great writers, and as advice for public speaking/writing – reading automatically leads to writing. See Peter de Bolla, *The Discourse of the Sublime*: *Readings in History, Aesthetics and the Subject* (Oxford, Basil Blackwell, 1989), ch. 10.

30 Coleridge, *The Friend*, ed. Barbara E. Rooke (2 vols., New Jersey, Princeton University Press, 1969), vol. I, p. 20.

31 See Erickson, 'The Poets' Corner', p. 907.

32 T. N. Talfourd, 'An Attempt to Estimate the Poetical Talent of the Present Age', *The Pamphleteer*, 5 (London, 1815), pp. 443–4.

33 See 'The Four Ages of Poetry', in David Bromwich, ed., *Romantic Critical Essays* (Cambridge University Press, 1987), p. 211; see also Peacock's letter to Shelley of December 1820, in Shelley, *Letters*, vol. II, p. 245.

34 For recent analyses of the nature of the literary contract, see Roland Barthes, *S/Z*, tr. Richard Miller (Oxford, Basil Blackwell, 1990), pp. 88–90; Martin Price, *Forms of Life: Character and Moral Imagination in the Novel* (New Haven, Yale University Press, 1983), ch. 1; Chambers, *Story and Situation*, pp. 8–9 and *passim*; and on Wordsworth and contract, see Heinzelman, *The Economics of the Imagination*, pp. 207ff. Prince (*Narratology*, pp. 159–60) relates the concept of narrative 'point' to that of 'narrative contract': because of the contextualized phenomenon of 'point', an 'economic' exchange takes place between narrator and narratee. Christopher Prendergast elaborates some important reserva-

tions concerning the metaphor because of its illusion of an agreement freely entered into between autonomous subjects (*The Order of Mimesis: Balzac, Stendhal, Nerval, Flaubert*, Cambridge University Press, 1986, pp. 36–41).

35 William Wordsworth, *The Prelude* (1805), book 4, lines 341–4; see also, Wordsworth's 'Idiot Boy', lines 337–8.

36 Mark A. Weinstein, ed., *The Prefaces to the Waverley Novels* (Lincoln, University of Nebraska Press, 1978), p. 3.

37 David Simpson, *Irony and Authority in Romantic Poetry* (London, Macmillan, 1979), p. xi.

38 Compare Edward Mangin's *An Essay on Light Reading* (London, 1808), p. 7: 'The writer and the reader of an ordinary novel seem to have entered into a mutual agreement as to the quality of the ingredients used in its composition'.

39 Edwin W. Marrs, ed., *The Letters of Charles and Mary Lamb* (3 vols., Ithaca, Cornell University Press, 1975), vol. 1, pp. 265–6. But see *Peter Bell*, lines 196–200, where Wordsworth plays with the idea of impoliteness in story-telling.

40 Labov, *Language in the Inner City*, ch. 9.

41 Hugh Murray, *Morality of Fiction* (Edinburgh, 1805), p. 44. Compare Robert Dodsley's comments of forty years earlier: 'The very article of giving instruction supposes at least, a superiority of wisdom in the adviser; a circumstance by no means favourable to the ready admission of advice. 'Tis the peculiar excellence of Fable [in comparison to Tales] to *wave* this air of superiority: it leaves the *reader* to collect the moral; who by thus discovering more than is shewn him, finds his principle of self-love *gratified*, instead of being *disgusted*' (*An Essay on Fable*, 1764, Los Angeles, William Andrews Clark Memorial Library, 1965, pp. lix–lx). In 1762 John Newbery made a similar point in *The Art of Poetry on a New Plan* (2 vols., London, 1762), vol. 1, p. 157. By contrast, however, John Charles O'Reid (alias Josiah Conder), in a discussion of the iniquities of modern criticism in *Reviewers Reviewed* (Oxford, 1811), p. 11, argued that such arrogant behaviour is unbecoming to a humble *reader*. See Michael Fried's discussion of the importance in eighteenth-century aesthetics of the visual arts, following Diderot, of the *absorption* of figures in painting: Fried argues 'that starting around the mid-1750s in France (and only there) the inescapableness of beholding, or say the primordial convention that paintings are made to be beheld, became deeply problematic for the enterprise of painting precisely to the extent that the latter took upon itself the task of striving to defeat what Diderot called theater, and that the irruption of that internal conflict or contradiction was something new in the history of the art' (*Courbet's Realism*, University of Chicago Press, 1990, p. 13): this is a summary of the argument presented in Fried's earlier book, *Absorption and Theatricality: Painting and Beholder in the Age of Diderot* (Berkeley, University of California Press,

1980). Despite Fried's stricture on the geographical specificity of his comments, Wendy Steiner has convincingly applied Fried's ideas in *Absorption and Theatricality* specifically to absorbed figures in Keats, in *Pictures of Romance, Form Against Context in Painting and Literature* (University of Chicago Press, 1988), pp. 77–90. The important paradox which Fried brings out is that it is precisely when figures (for example figures of reading) seem to be absorbed in sleep, natural scenery, an aesthetic object, or in our case a book – and when the painting or text thereby seems to ignore *its* beholder or reader – it is precisely at this point that the text or picture may be understood to be most carefully intent on absorbing the gaze of its audience.

42 Edmund Burke, *A Philosophical Enquiry into the Origin of our Ideas of the Sublime and Beautiful*, ed. J. T. Boulton (London, Routledge and Kegan Paul, 1958), pp. 58–64. See Peacock, 'An Essay', p. 98: 'There is a systematical cant in criticism [in the periodicals] which passes with many for the language of superior intelligence; such, for instance, is that which pronounces unintelligible whatever is in any degree obscure, more especially if it be really matter of deeper sense than the critic likes to be molested with'. But 'obscurity' is common enough in much of the avant-garde poetry published in the period, and may be seen to have had its precursors in, for example, the eighteenth-century rhapsodic odes of Gray and Collins; Patrick Parrinder points out that the 'stylistic obscurity of Gray's odes is wholly deliberate' and that such obscurity was 'clearly intended to overawe the reader' (*Authors and Authority: A Study of English Literary Criticism and its Relation to Culture, 1750–1900*, London, Routledge and Kegan Paul, 1977, p. 35).

43 The most famous expressions of this are Shelley's comments on the poet as nightingale singing to please himself in 'A Defence of Poetry' (*Shelley's Poetry and Prose*, p. 486) and John Stuart Mill's comment that 'eloquence is *heard*, poetry is *overheard*' (John Stuart Mill, *Essays on Poetry*, ed. F. Parvin Sharpless, Columbia, University of South Carolina Press, 1976, p. 12). This tradition has been continued in twentieth-century criticism of the Romantics: see, for example, Abrams, *The Mirror and the Lamp*, pp. 25–6: the audience for the Romantic poet is 'reduced to a single member, consisting of the poet himself' (p. 25); but as Jack comments in *The Poet and His Audience*, p. 169, 'Mill's view ... betray[s] a complete failure to consider the facts of the case, the actual history of poetry'; see also Eaves, 'Romantic Expressive Theory', pp. 784–801, and Siskin, *The Historicity of Romantic Discourse*, p. 96 and *passim*, on what Siskin refers to as the 'increasingly problematic relationship of author to audience' (p. 96). This has, of course, been much commented on: see, for example, Terry Lovell, *Consuming Fiction* (London, Verso, 1987), p. 28, and Jerome J. McGann, *Social Values and Poetic Acts: The Historical Judgment of Literary Work* (Cambridge, Mass., Harvard University Press, 1988), p. 76. Marilyn Butler makes it a reason for the standard argument that

Romantic poetics concentrate on the artist rather than the audience (*Peacock Displayed: A Satirist in His Context*, London, Routledge and Kegan Paul, 1979, p. 4); but Butler seems to be repeating a common fallacy: not only does the discourse of Romanticism focus almost neurotically upon the role of the reader or audience, but there is no simple division between eighteenth-century and Romantic poetics, but rather a gradual and complex reorientation which precludes neither audience nor, as Butler implies, narrative (but see her *Romantics, Rebels, and Reactionaries: English Literature and its Background, 1760–1830*, Oxford University Press, 1981, pp. 71–2).

44 Lucien Dällenbach, 'Reflexivity and Reading', *NLH*, 11 (1980), p. 441; Dällenbach defines *mise en abyme* as 'doublings which function as mirrors or microcosms of the text' and views the trope as 'a factor in the readability of the text' (p. 435); for 'reading interludes', see Gerald Prince, 'Notes on the Text as Reader', in Susan Suleiman and Inge Crosman, eds., *The Reader in the Text: Essays on Audience and Interpretation* (New Jersey, Princeton University Press, 1980), pp. 225–40.

45 Chambers, *Story and Situation*, ch. 2. At its simplest, and most common, a figure of reading is the representation of a surrogate reader within a text, from whom the 'real' reader may take his or her cue. Alvin Kernan has linked the use of such a trope historically to the alienation of reader and writer due to the development of print technology in the eighteenth century, when 'author figures and readers, or models of readers, appearing as characters in the work become literary commonplaces in an attempt to bridge the separation of author and reader in the actual world' (*Printing, Technology, Letters*, p. 225). See Scott's description of this effect in his review of *Frankenstein* (*Sir Walter Scott on Novelists*, p. 261); and see Beth Newman, 'Narratives of Seduction and the Seductions of Narrative: The Frame Structure of *Frankenstein*', *ELH*, 53 (1986), pp. 141–63, for a reading of this novel which coincides in some respects with my conception of the figured reading of Romantic poetry. One of the most successful of these figured readers (which are not restricted to the act of reading), is that of the wedding guest in Coleridge's 'The Rime of the Ancient Mariner': as a contemporary reviewer noted, 'The opening of the Poem is admirably calculated to arrest the reader's attention, by the well-imagined idea of the Wedding Guest, who is held to hear the tale, in spite of his efforts to escape' (Reiman, A1, p. 128). Deconstruction would tend to figure *mise en abyme* as an aporia, an impossibly paradoxical opening in and of the text: see, for example Anna Whiteside, 'The Double Bind: Self-referring Poetry' in Anna Whiteside and Michael Issacharoff, eds., *On Referring in Literature* (Bloomington, Indiana University Press, 1987), p. 30; but compare Dällenbach, 'Reflexivity and Reading', p. 440: 'mise en abyme, the most powerful textual signal and aid to readability, can (1) use artifice to repragmatize the text, (2) seal directly or indirectly the text's vanishing points, (3) condense the

text in order to provide a surview, and (4) render the text more intelligible by making use of redundancy and an integrated metalanguage'.

46 A number of critics have noted the tendentious nature of Wordsworth's theory: see, for example, W. J. B. Owen, *Wordsworth as Critic* (University of Toronto Press, 1969), pp. 188–228; Devlin, *Wordsworth and the Poetry of Epitaphs*, pp. 37–41; Perkins, *Wordsworth and the Poetry of Sincerity*, p. 155.

47 Compare Wordsworth's remarks on 'improving posterity' (*MY*, vol. I, p. 195).

48 Wordsworth later admits Pope's contemporary popularity (see *Prose*, p. 400).

49 As David Perkins comments in *The Quest for Permanence: The Symbolism of Wordsworth, Shelley and Keats* (Cambridge, Mass., Harvard University Press, 1959), p. 148, 'To assert that one writes for posterity is ... senseless except as a statement of hope'.

50 See Devlin, *Wordsworth and the Poetry of Epitaphs*, p. 43. See Klancher, *The Making of English Reading Audiences*, pp. 134–50, esp. pp. 148–50, for an important consideration of Wordsworth's theorization of audience in 1800 and 1815: as Klancher comments, for Wordsworth in 1815, 'Literature ... never addresses itself to the social present but realizes its audience only at the end of time' (p. 149). Compare Wordsworth's comments in a letter to John Wilson on his audience as 'human nature' rather, presumably, than human beings (*Prose*, pp. 310–12).

2 : KEATS'S LETTERS

1 Jacques Derrida, *The Post Card: From Socrates to Freud and Beyond*, tr. Alan Bass (University of Chicago Press, 1987), p. 444.

2 Richard Woodhouse, *KC*, vol. I, p. 92.

3 See Jacques Derrida, 'Telepathy', tr. Nicholas Royle, *The Oxford Literary Review*, 10 (1988), pp. 3–41, on the way that epistolary communications construct their addressees.

4 Significantly, Keats decides not to write a preface at all in the end. For another example of the rhetoric of belligerent language, see *Letters*, vol. I, p. 157: 'with the armour of words and the Sword of Syllables I hope to attack you in a very short time'.

5 Later, the letter actually formulates the projected response of Georgiana, representing her reading of the letter – in a pastiche of *Tristram Shandy* as much as Georgiana herself – as irritable, impatient and distracted by domestic affairs: see Homans, 'Keats Reading Women', pp. 351–2, for a discussion of this passage. See also *Letters*, vol. II, p. 173, for a repetition of the distinction between writing 'to' and writing 'at'.

6 See Susan J. Wolfson, 'Keats the Letter-Writer: Epistolary Poetics', *Romanticism Past and Present*, 6, 2 (1982), pp. 43–61.

7 In addition to my discussion of this topic in Chapter 1, above, see, on

Keats and the book market, Chilcott, *A Publisher and His Circle*; John Barnard, *John Keats* (Cambridge University Press, 1987), pp. 8–11; and Goellnicht, 'Keats on Reading', pp. 190–93; for a Freudian reading of Keats's reactions to reviews, see Harold E. Briggs, 'Keats's Conscious and Unconscious Reactions to Criticism of *Endymion*', *PMLA*, 60 (1945), pp. 1106–29.

8 See, for example, Chilcott, *A Publisher and His Circle*, p. 201.

9 This is a reversal of Mario L. D'Avanzo's argument that the Romantic poets' insecurity about their audiences resulted in the 'inward' turn of their poetry (*Keats's Metaphors for the Poetic Imagination*, Durham, N.C., Duke University Press, 1967, pp. 4–6).

10 See Ward, 'Keats and the Idea of Fame', p. 318, who suggests that the *Blackwood's* campaign against the 'Cockney' poets of the previous autumn made Keats aware for the first time of 'the force of literary politics intervening in the ideal relationship between poet and audience in which he had previously trusted': Ward's essay is a useful consideration of Keats on fame, but needs to be supplemented by a fuller consideration of the tensions in Keats's notions of his audiences as produced in letters and poems; see also Barnard, *John Keats*, pp. 11–14, for a brief analysis of Keats's relations with the public.

11 Stillinger, ed., *The Poems of John Keats*, p. 739.

12 *Ibid.*

13 John Marston, *The Fawn*, ed. Gerald A. Smith (London, Edward Arnold, 1965), p. 6.

14 The reference to Marston should remind us that hostility towards audiences is neither new nor original with the Romantics. For a discussion of earlier expressions of hostility, see Debra Belt, 'The Poetics of Hostile Response, 1575–1610', *Criticism*, 33 (1991), pp. 419–59. In fact Belt discusses a number of historical and technological innovations at the end of the sixteenth century prefiguring those of the late eighteenth and early nineteenth centuries, which suggest that a comparison of the rhetoric of hostility in the two periods would be revealing.

15 See *Prose*, pp. 387–93. See Ward, 'Keats and the Idea of Fame', p. 319, for a similar comparison.

16 Elizabeth L. Eisenstein, *The Printing Press as an Agent of Change: Communications and Cultural Transformations in Early-Modern Europe* (2 vols., Cambridge University Press, 1979), vol. I, p. 156. Chilcott, *A Publisher and His Circle*, p. 207, argues that the 'scarcely veiled hysteria' of some reviewers 'effectively killed' sales of *Endymion*; but see certain comments by a reviewer of the anonymous *Patronage, A Poem* in *The London Magazine* (Baldwin's) 2, 12 (December 1820), p. 628: 'Keats has been bitterly assailed, but he has also been gallantly supported. We observe his publishers place the attack made upon him by the Quarterly, the very foremost amongst the critical testimonies to his merit, – and in so doing they act spiritedly and rightly'.

17 On Keats and posterity/fame, see Ward, 'Keats and the Idea of Fame';

Chilcott, *A Publisher and His Circle*, p. 44; and Briggs, 'Conscious and Unconscious Reactions', p. 1108. On the Romantic construction of the distinction between the reader and the audience, see Klancher, *The Making of English Reading Audiences*, p. 11; Hazlitt has an eloquent passage on fame and immortality at the beginning of his lecture 'On the Living Poets', in *Lectures on the English Poets* (*Works*, vol. v, pp. 143–5): 'Fame', he declares, 'is the recompense not of the living, but of the dead' (p. 143). Hazlitt also makes the important distinction in this essay, between 'fame' and 'popularity'. For Keats's comments on the possibility of immortal fame in the letters, see *Letters*, vol. I, pp. 141, 160, 394; vol. II, pp. 5, 25, 263, 293.

18 See also *Letters*, vol. II, p. 121.

19 On Keats's indolence, creative and otherwise, see remarks in *Letters*, vol. I, pp. 214, 231, 232, 351, 413; vol. II, pp. 37, 42, 51, 55, 77, 78–9, 83, 106, 224, 227, 231, 239. For discussions of Keats and indolence, see Luisa Conti Camaiora, '"Idle Fever" and "Diligent Indolence": Opposing Principles in Keats', *Rivista di Letterature Moderne e Comparate*, 28 (1975), pp. 165–84; Lore Metzger, *One Foot in Eden: Modes of Pastoral in Romantic Poetry* (Chapel Hill, University of North Carolina Press, 1986), pp. 212–35; William F. Zak, 'The Confirmation of Keats's Belief in Negative Capability: The "Ode on Indolence"', *KSJ*, 25 (1976), pp. 55–64; and Helen Vendler, *The Odes of John Keats* (Cambridge, Mass., Harvard University Press, 1983), on the 'Ode to Indolence' as an expression of the aesthetic ideology of indolence (pp. 20–39). More generally, see Eisenstein, *The Printing Press as an Agent of Change*, vol. I, p. 156, and Clyde De L. Ryals, 'The Nineteenth-Century Cult of Inaction', *Tennessee Studies in Literature*, 4 (1959), pp. 51–60, on the nineteenth-century aesthetic ideology of idleness. Outside of these months, Keats's idea that he could undertake paid work (other than writing) appears in *Letters*, vol. I, pp. 276–7; vol. II, pp. 70, 77, 84, 219, 230, 237. The possibility of writing for money is more difficult to discern outside of the June–September 'window', but appears in *Letters*, vol. II, pp. 17 and 229.

20 See Nigel Cross, *The Common Writer: Life in Nineteenth-Century Grub Street* (Cambridge University Press, 1985), pp. 38–47, on imprisonment as an 'occupational hazard' (p. 39) for the professional writer. All of this talk about working for a living may be understood to have been generated by Keats's precarious financial position at the time: earlier in his life, although constantly troubled by a lack of money, he was able to shrug it off with a joke: see *Letters*, vol. I, pp. 141, 142; by April 1819, however, he is rather more serious when he lists the 'mortal pains' of 'civilised Life' as 'Bailiffs, Debts and Poverties' (*Letters*, vol. II, p. 101).

21 By comparison, Keats's references to diligence/hard work prior to June 1819 are sparse: see *Letters*, vol. I, pp. 154, 188, 412 (the latter two are imperative in mood rather than recording any achievement).

22 For the details of Keats's financial affairs, see Robert Gittings, *The Keats*

Inheritance (London, Heinemann, 1964); K. K. Ruthven, 'Keats and Dea Moneta', *SiR*, 15 (1976), pp. 450–57; and W. Jackson Bate, *John Keats* (Cambridge, Mass., Harvard University Press, 1963), chs. 20–21.

23 The best reader-response study of Keats is, of course, Ricks's *Keats and Embarrassment*; the most thorough consideration of Keats as a reader is White's, *Keats as a Reader of Shakespeare*. As White points out, Keats 'regards reading as a collaborative activity, in which the writer supplies potential meanings embodied in a text, and the reader brings a receptive, open ear' (p. 68). For comments on Keats and the reciprocity of reading, see, in particular, pp. 65, 99, 195, 226, 227. See also Goellnicht, 'Keats on Reading', pp. 190–210, for a recent account of Keats's 'poetics' of reading along the lines of recent theorists, in particular Wolfgang Iser. Wolfson, *The Questioning Presence*, also devotes ch. 8 of her book to such considerations; finally, see Ward, 'Keats and the Idea of Fame', p. 328, on the 'vitally reciprocal relationship' between poet and reader, and between poet and tradition. Levinson, *Keats's Life of Allegory*, has recently argued against the notion of a 'reciprocity' of Keats's poetry and audiences: 'where the textual labor does develop reciprocities... these are not, typically, *audience* reciprocities' (p. 36), and 'Keats's social relations were so much more primitive than that [*sic*] of the other Romantics, one learns very little... from research into reception, actual and anticipated' (p. 38), but, as I understand it, Levinson does little to justify either statement.

24 See *Letters*, vol. I, pp. 149–51, 156–7, 157–60.

25 The trope of reader as lover is, of course, extremely common in the history of literary response; see Stephen Kellman, *Loving Reading: Erotics of the Text* (Hamden, Conn., The Shoe String Press-Archon Books, 1985).

26 See Goellnicht, 'Keats on Reading', pp. 194–6, for a pertinent consideration of this important letter.

27 D. A. Pearsall, 'Introduction' to *The Floure and the Leafe* (London, Thomas Nelson, 1962), p. 38.

28 Compare 'The Eve of St Mark', a poem which figures reading as obsessional and escapist: Bertha reads a book which 'Had taken captive her two eyes / Among its golden broideries' (lines 27–8). Wallace Martin, *Recent Theories of Narrative*, p. 158, quotes Jean-Paul Sartre, in *What is Literature?*, on literary words as traps: 'On the one hand, the literary object has no substance but the reader's subjectivity... But on the other hand, the words are there like traps to arouse our feelings and to reflect them toward us... Thus, the writer appeals to the reader's freedom to collaborate in the production of his work'.

29 See White, *Keats as a Reader of Shakespeare*, pp. 223–4, for a consideration of this important passage.

30 Jacques Derrida, *Mémoires for Paul de Man*, revised edn. (New York, Columbia University Press, 1989), p. 99.

31 Quoted in White, *Keats as a Reader of Shakespeare*, p. 152.

32 Lipking, *The Life of the Poet*, p. 195. As Lawrence Lipking has commented, the whole poem 'suspends' from line seven (p. 8): Lipking presents an acute reading of the poem (pp. 3–11) and, in particular, of the word 'breathe' (pp. 7–8).

33 For examples of hallucination or trance and poetry, see 'To My Brother George', lines 25ff.; 'Sleep and Poetry', lines 69–84, 125–54, and *passim*; 'Dear Reynolds, as last night I lay in bed'; 'As Hermes once took to his feathers light'; 'Ode to a Nightingale'; 'Ode on Indolence'; 'Lamia'; and so on. These examples suggest that it is not only writing – inspiration – which is a form of hallucination, but Keats's sense of and experience of reading.

3: THE EARLY VERSE AND *ENDYMION*

1 John Spencer Hill, ed., *Keats: The Narrative Poems* (London, Macmillan, 1983), p. 63. See Fischer, *Romantic Verse Narrative*, pp. 163–85, on Keats as a poet who 'occupies a central place in [the] history of the dissolution and ramification of the romantic tale in verse genre' (p. 185); and Perkins, *The Quest for Permanence*, on the idea that even in 1819, Keats 'may not have been ready…to write narrative verse', and on 'the embarrassments of narrative for a poet with Keats's skeptical, uncommitted habit of mind' (pp. 297, 298). For summaries of the criticism of Keatsian narrative, see Miriam Allott '"Isabella", "The Eve of St Agnes", and "Lamia"', in Kenneth Muir, ed., *John Keats: A Reassessment* (Liverpool University Press, 1958), pp. 39–41; and Jaqueline Zeff, 'Strategies of Time in Keats's Narratives', *SEL*, 17 (1977), pp. 621–37. The most extended discussion of Keats in relation to narrative is Judy Little's conceptually limited analysis, *Keats as a Narrative Poet: A Test of Invention* (Lincoln, University of Nebraska Press, 1975).

2 Ricardou, 'Belligérance', p. 85.

3 Butler, *Peacock Displayed*, p. 299. Keats's letters provide ample evidence, if any were needed, for an interest in the mechanics of narration: discussing the difference between Scott's and Smollett's novels in terms of a 'romantic' as opposed to a 'levelling' sensibility (*Letters*, vol. I, pp. 199–200); declaring that Hyperion 'will shape his actions' like a god, as opposed to Endymion, who was 'led on, like Buonaparte, by circumstance' (*Letters*, vol. I, p. 207); promising to send George and Georgiana Keats a prose tale which he will write 'on account of the activity of my Mind; of its inability to remain at rest' (*Letters*, vol. I, p. 401); telling stories to explain a point (*Letters*, vol. I, p. 150); paying close attention to reviews of Godwin's novels (*Letters*, vol. II, pp. 24–5); discussing the nature of plot and incident in Charles Brockden Brown's *Wieland* (*Letters*, vol. II, p. 173), etc.

4 See Bate, *John Keats*, p. 73: 'the primary inspiration of this virile,

relatively unbookish poet is intensely literary'; and see de Man, 'Introduction' to John Keats, *Selected Poetry*, p. xi: 'In reading Keats, we are ... reading the work of a man whose experience is mainly literary'.

5 Martin Aske comments of 'I stood tip-toe' that 'it is not the stories themselves but the very possibility of their *telling* which becomes crucial to the poet' (*Keats and Hellenism: An Essay*, Cambridge University Press, 1985, p. 52); Aske's reading of the early poems as an attempt to compensate for the 'loss' of antiquity with a plenitude of narration (ch. 2) might be compared with Levinson's account of the way in which the resistance to narrative in the early poems becomes the 'throbbing suspension' of the later poems (*Keats's Life of Allegory*, p. 245). As Levinson comments, 'when we conceive the resistance to narrative sequence as a refusal – we call it "poise"' (p. 246).

6 Josiah Conder was the first to remark upon this lack of a story (*Heritage*, p. 64), but it has often been pointed out; most recently, for example, by Levinson, in *Keats's Life of Allegory*, pp. 243–4.

7 Bate, *John Keats*, p. 73; the idea that Keats's only subject was poetry is, again, a commonplace in Keats criticism: see, for example, Jack Stillinger, *The Hoodwinking of Madeline and Other Essays on Keats's Poems* (Urbana, University of Illinois Press, 1971), p. 13; Stuart M. Sperry, *Keats the Poet* (New Jersey, Princeton University Press, 1973), p. 72; Levinson, *Keats's Life of Allegory*, p. 243.

8 See Bate, *John Keats*, p. 70, on Keats's need for some audience, and, in consequence, his writing for his family and friends; Barnard, *John Keats*, p. 24, posits a rather more calculated reason for such personal 'audiences': 'Those poems addressed to named or un-named individuals ... suggest that an audience of immediate friends and practising artists, occupying a specific socio-literary position, already exists'.

9 As Claude Lee Finney suggests of 'Calidore', Keats's 'power of description had developed beyond his power of narration' (*The Evolution of Keats's Poetry*, 2 vols., Cambridge, Mass., Harvard University Press, 1936, vol. I, p. 105). Levinson has commented on Keats's inability to 'get his hero into action' (*Keats's Life of Allegory*, p. 245).

10 This technique is often used with great effect by later novelists, of course, and employed by Keats himself with great tact for the rhythms of readerly excitement in 'The Eve of St Agnes' (where the present tense is used in stanzas 2, 10, 26, 36 and 41), and – rather differently – when he suspends the tense of the first stanza of 'To Autumn' in a dangling participle, or when he prefaces the present tenses of 'Ode to a Nightingale' with a subjunctive which holds the whole poem in animated suspense. On 'the use of the conditional and subjunctive throughout the [1817] volume', Barnard comments that it 'signals a fundamental honesty – the poet's large assertions are promissory' (*John Keats*, p. 19); see also Hubert Heinen, 'Interwoven Time in Keats's Poetry', *Texas Studies in Literature and Language*, 3 (1961), p. 383. It is

significant, however, that Hazlitt criticized Pope's translation of *The Iliad*, because 'he continually changes the tenses in the same sentence for the purpose of the rhyme, which shews either a want of technical resources, or great inattention to punctilious exactness' (*Works*, vol. v, p. 75).

11 See Ricardou, 'Belligérance', pp. 85–102.

12 As Little (*Keats as a Narrative Poet*, p. 14) comments, 'In the extant lines of these fragments ['Calidore' and the 'Induction'] there is no suspense, no expectation set up, no contrast or conflict suggested which could give the meandering narrative any direction'.

13 Emile Benveniste, 'The Correlations of Tense in the French Verb', in *Problems in General Linguistics*, tr. M. E. Meek (Florida, University of Miami Press, 1971), p. 206. For a discussion of similarities in English, see Ann Banfield, *Unspeakable Sentences: Narration and Representation in the Language of Fiction* (Boston, Routledge and Kegan Paul, 1982): Banfield defines the aorist – which she suggests is roughly equivalent to the English simple past – in terms of 'its lack of a PRESENT and an ADDRESSEE/HEARER' (p. 154); see also, Banfield's 'Ecriture, Narration and the Grammar of French', in Jeremy Hawthorn, ed., *Narrative: From Malory to Motion Pictures* (London, Edward Arnold, 1985), pp. 1–22, for a discussion of 'impersonality' in this context.

14 Ricoeur, *Time and Narrative*, vol. ii, p. 63.

15 *Ibid.*, pp. 68–9; as Gérard Genette comments, in 'Boundaries of Narrative', *NLH*, 8 (1976), p. 9, the differences between the use of the past and the present tenses which Benveniste defines 'dovetail sharply into an opposition between the objectivity of narrative and the subjectivity of discourse'.

16 See Michel Beaujour, 'Some Paradoxes of Description', *Yale French Studies*, 61 (1981), p. 33, on 'description's seemingly uncheckable tendency to turn into micro-narratives. The static scenes depicted are fictitiously and surreptitiously endowed with motion...'; Alan Liu, *Wordsworth and the Sense of History* (Stanford University Press, 1989), pp. 119ff., on the narrativity of the loco-descriptive in Wordsworth; and see Paul de Man, *Allegories of Reading*, pp. 160–61, on the way that 'all denominative discourse has to be narrative'.

17 For a detailed thematic account of this poem along these lines, see Seraphia D. Leyda, 'The Structure of Keats's "I stood tip-toe upon a little hill"', in M. L. Johnson and S. D. Leyda, eds., *Reconciliations: Studies in Honor of Richard Harter Fogle* (Universität Salzburg, 1983), pp. 111–28.

18 See Keats's later comment on *Endymion* that 'it was read by some dozen of my friends, who lik'd it; and some dozen whom I was unacquainted with, who did not' (Stillinger, ed., *The Poems of John Keats*, p. 739).

19 Roland Barthes, *S/Z*, p. 82; Brooks, *Reading for the Plot*, p. 92.

20 Patricia Parker, 'Shakespeare and Rhetoric: "Dilation" and "De-

lation" in *Othello*', in Patricia Parker and Geoffrey Hartman, eds., *Shakespeare and the Question of Theory* (New York, Methuen, 1985), pp. 61–2; see also Parker's 'Dilation and Delay: Renaissance Matrices', *Poetics Today*, 5 (1984), pp. 519–35. My reading of *Endymion* in this section also owes much to Parker's analysis of the poem's 'strategy of deferral and dilation' in an earlier consideration of delay in narrative, in *Inescapable Romance* (p. 182).

21 See, for example, *Prose*, p. 373; 'Invention' still tends to be valued below imagination: see James Kissane, 'The Authorization of John Keats', *KSJ*, 37 (1988), p. 61, who says that 'Keats saw *Endymion* essentially as "a test, a trial of my Powers of Imagination"', but ends the quotation here, omitting Keats's vital rider 'and chiefly of my invention which is a rare thing indeed'. John Jones suggests that what Keats 'means by Invention is never very clear; without exactly denying its long and respectable neo-classic past he overlays it with the opaque semi-privacy ... of the word which is becoming, for a season, a Keats word' (*John Keats's Dream of Truth*, London, Chatto and Windus, 1980, p. 128).

22 Samuel Johnson, *Rasselas, Poems, and Selected Prose*, ed. Bertrand H. Bronson, 3rd edn. (New York, Holt Rinehart and Winston, 1971), p. 496.

23 See Edward S. Le Comte, *Endymion in England: The Literary History of a Greek Myth* (New York, Columbia University Press, 1944), p. 152: 'The Endymion myth is slight ... In a large frame it is lost ... It provides too little in the way of incident ... The poems of Drayton and Keats seem overluxuriant and digressive largely because their subject is too small for the frame'; Judy Little makes much the same point (*Keats as a Narrative Poet*, pp. 41–2).

24 George Gascoigne, 'Certayne Notes of Instruction', quoted by Murray W. Bundy, in '"Invention" and "Imagination" in the Renaissance', *JEGP*, 29 (1930), p. 539.

25 See Barnard, *John Keats*, p. 40, on the 'pull between narrative and Keats's predilection for static "pictures"'. Patricia Parker speaks of 'The movement which in *Endymion* takes the form of a tension between questing and the expanding circumference of embowered moments' (*Inescapable Romance*, p. 194). Early in her book, Parker characterizes Romance as 'a form which simultaneously quests for and postpones a particular end, objective, or object' (p. 4): Barthes's 'dilatory space', however, seems to make this the organizing principle of all narrative. For a discussion of the problematics of the notion of invention with relevance for the question of early Keatsian narrative, see Jacques Derrida, 'Psyche: Inventions of the Other', tr. Catherine Porter, in Derek Attridge, ed., *Acts of Literature* (New York, Routledge, 1992), pp. 310–43.

26 Parker, *Inescapable Romance*, p. 181.

27 Stillinger, ed., *The Poems of John Keats*, p. 102.

28 For examples in other poems, see 'Isabella', line 478; 'The Eve of St

Agnes', line 151; 'Hyperion', book 1, line 318, book 2, line 247; 'Lamia', part 2, line 120. See Jones, *John Keats's Dream of Truth, passim*, for a fuller consideration of Keats on space/time. See also Zeff, 'Strategies of Time', p. 628, on the conflation of space with time; Arthur H. Bell on space imagery, in '"The Depth of Things"': Keats and Human Space', *KSJ*, 23 (1974), pp. 77–94; and Ruth Salvaggio, 'Time, Space, and the Couplet', *PQ*, 62 (1983), p. 105, on the 'interaction of time and space' in Keats's couplets, which is 'the very subject of the verse'.

29 The structure of a pun is itself a kind of compressed solecism of space-time: a pun works by the temporal and spatial coincidence of two 'signifieds' in one 'signifier'.

30 Sperry, *Keats the Poet*, p. 90. See, for example, Edward B. Hungerford, *Shores of Darkness* (New York, Columbia University Press, 1941), p. 107, on the poem's 'remarkable meandering of the narrative'; Parker, *Inescapable Romance*, p. 177, on the poem's 'wandering structure', a labyrinth whose form is 'related to the theme of the fruitfulness of wandering, of the more circuitous route'; Wolfson, *The Questioning Presence*, p. 228, on the 'errant, or wandering, course of the narrative'; and Aske, *Keats and Hellenism*, p. 69, on the pleasure of wandering in texts.

31 Brooks, *Reading for the Plot*, p. 104; see Francis Jeffrey (*Heritage*, p. 203) and Aske, *Keats and Hellenism*, ch. 3, on the idea of the arabesque in relation to the narrative form of *Endymion*.

32 Wolfson, *The Questioning Presence*, p. 233.

33 On 'subplots' (Barnard, *John Keats*, p. 40, calls them 'inset stories'), see Sperry, *Keats the Poet*, p. 108: 'the larger meaning of the poem ... lies in the way such episodes ... play off against and qualify each other'.

34 See, for example, Clarisse Godfrey, '"Endymion"', in Muir, ed., *Reassessment*, p. 31; Leon Waldoff, *Keats and the Silent Work of Imagination* (Urbana, University of Illinois Press, 1985), p. 41.

35 Brooks, *Reading for the Plot*, p. 104.

36 See Peter George Patmore's comment in his review of the poem, that 'as a tale, this work is nothing. There is no connecting interest to bind one part of it to another. Almost any two parts of it might be transposed, without disadvantage to either, or to the whole' (*Heritage*, p. 137). Compare Aske, *Keats and Hellenism*, p. 64, on *Endymion* as 'a text obeying something like the fragmentary mode of lyrical associationism, a flowing story whose floral excesses question the hitherto privileged assumptions of coherence and unity'. Nevertheless, there have been numerous attempts to plot a unity for the poem: see, for example, Charles I. Patterson, 'The Monomyth in the Structure of Keats's *Endymion*', *KSJ*, 31 (1982), pp. 64–81; and Barry Gradman, *Metamorphosis in Keats* (Brighton, Harvester, 1980), ch. 2.

37 See Ricardou's discussion of what he calls the 'diégétisation' of

description: by employing adverbs of time and verbs of action used metaphorically in description, an 'illusory chronology' is produced – what Ricardou calls a 'récit fallacieux' ('Belligérance', p. 92).

38 See Aske, *Keats and Hellenism*, pp. 66–7, and Gene M. Bernstein 'Keats' "Lamia": The Sense of A Non-Ending', *Papers on Language and Literature*, 15 (1979), pp. 175–80, on 'Lamia' and mazes/labyrinths.

39 See Le Comte, *Endymion in England*, p. 168: Keats tells the Glaucus story 'straightforwardly and with newfound restraint. He is trying his hand, for the first time, at pure narrative'. Curiously, although, as Leon Waldoff comments, 'Book III is central to Endymion's quest' (*Keats and the Silent Work of Imagination*, p. 54), Judy Little claims that Glaucus's story constitutes 'a rather bulky digression', and that 'Internally, this book is the most poorly managed of the four' (*Keats as a Narrative Poet*, p. 53): these opposing views present an intriguing paradox in terms of the reception of the Glaucus 'episode' and its centrality or marginality.

4: 'ISABELLA'

1 Herbert Wright, *Boccaccio in England from Chaucer to Tennyson* (London, Athlone, 1957), pp. 331–478; Hazlitt, *Works*, vol. v, p. 82: see also Coleridge's comment that 'we owe... the happy art of narration' to Boccaccio (*Lectures 1808–1819 on Literature*, ed. R. A. Foakes, 2 vols., London, Routledge and Kegan Paul, 1987, vol. II, p. 92).

2 Reynolds's translation from Boccaccio, 'The Garden of Florence', was eventually published separately in his book, *The Garden of Florence* (London, 1821).

3 See Kurt Heinzelman, 'Self-interest and the Politics of Composition in Keats's *Isabella*', *ELH*, 55 (1988), pp. 159–93, on 'Isabella' as 'a crisis point in Keats's economic thinking about the question of literary achievement' and as a poem 'about a poet pondering whether his success or failure as a modern poet can be determined solely in aesthetic terms' (p. 160). On 'inwardness' in Keats, see Jones, *John Keats's Dream of Truth*.

4 Barnard, *John Keats*, p. 78.

5 On the effect of the stanza form on the poem, see Edward Thomas, *Keats* (London, T. C. and E. C. Jack, 1916), p. 49: 'The stanza form ... was a discipline that forbade loose running on: it exhibited the poet's choiceness of detail better than the couplets of *Endymion*, and, at the same time, each stanza being complete in itself gave more excuse for it ... although a story was involved, 'Isabella' became, with the help of the *adagio* stanza, a very still poem'. Susan Wolfson suggests that one impulse for the choice was the comic effect achieved by the ottava rima of Byron's *Beppo* (*The Questioning Presence*, pp. 285–6); for other comments on the stanza form, see Ernest de Sélincourt, *The Poems of John Keats* (London, Methuen, 1951), p. 460; M. R. Ridley, *Keats' Craftsmanship: A*

Study in Poetic Development (London, Methuen, 1965), pp. 18–22; Barnard, *John Keats*, pp. 76–7.

6 See Wolfson's comment (*The Questioning Presence*, p. 282) on the 'disturbing alignment of how we read with how the brethren conduct their business' in the repetition of the word 'rich' in stanzas 13 and 14; see also Heinzelman, 'Self-interest', p. 162 and *passim*. See 'Lamia', part 1, lines 394–7, for a similar trope.

7 An 1807 version of Boccaccio's story by Charles Kirkpatrick Sharpe, 'Lorenzo and Isabella' (in *Metrical Legends*, Oxford, 1807), makes this even clearer: the poem begins with a conventional modesty topos explaining that 'private sorrows have the readier art / To wound us near, and wring the feeling heart' (p. 77), and comments, through the speech of one of the brothers, that 'public knowledge doubles private guilt' (p. 80).

8 And the 'core of the story': see Leigh Hunt's review, 'but to return to the core of the story. – Observe the fervid misery of the following [stanzas 46–8]' (*Heritage*, p. 172).

9 On the question of the scandalous nature of stanzas 46–8, see, for example, Finney, *The Evolution of Keats's Poetry*, p. 379; Eve Leoff, *A Study of John Keats's 'Isabella'* (Universität Salzburg, 1972), pp. 176–7; Jones, *John Keats's Dream of Truth*, pp. 15–16.

10 Wolfson, *The Questioning Presence*, p. 287.

11 See Garrett Stewart, *Reading Voices: Literature and the Phonotext* (Berkeley, University of California Press, 1990), for a discussion of ways in which 'silent' reading 'voices' the text. On the thematics of 'voice' in 'Isabella', see, for example, Leoff, *A Study of John Keats's 'Isabella'*, pp. 153–4.

12 As Ross Chambers has argued, 'it is a rare narrative that does not include a representation of some communicational act ... and it is axiomatic that the understandings of human communication which underlie the representation of the act must also in some sense and to some degree apply to the communicational act which is the story itself' ('Narrative Point', *Southern Review*, 16, 1983, p. 62).

13 For 'moves', see Thomas G. Pavel, *The Poetics of Plot: The Case of English Renaissance Drama* (Manchester University Press, 1985), pp. 17–24; for a discussion of 'kernels', see Roland Barthes, 'Introduction to the Structural Analysis of Narratives', pp. 106–11, in which he uses the terms 'neuclei' or 'cardinal functions'.

14 Although Jones (*John Keats's Dream of Truth*, p. 15) has put the poem on to the plane of the pathological by suggesting that in reading 'Isabella' we have to decide 'whether the object under contemplation is the work of a sick erotic fancy, or something very like such a work on the surface and very different underneath', critics generally have elided or repressed the incestuous possibilities of the poem (Heinzelman, 'Self-interest', p. 172, however, contrasts the brothers' motivation in Keats's poem with

the motivation of the brother in Barry Cornwall's contemporary version of the narrative, 'A Sicilian Story', and suggests that Cornwall's version articulates the 'incestuous possibility' of the story). In this way, the critical reception of the poem would seem to repeat the displacements involved in the poem itself: most recent readings have concentrated on the political aspects of the poem without recognizing the crucial importance of *sexual* politics. It is no doubt significant that Leigh Hunt's *The Story of Rimini* was often considered to be, amongst other things, 'incestuous' – see, for example, *Heritage*, p. 98. For a discussion of the Romantics and the 'incest theme', see Eino Railo, *The Haunted Castle: A Study of the Elements of English Romanticism* (London, George Routledge, 1927), ch. 8.

15 As Heinzelman comments ('Self-interest', p. 193), 'most critics have deplored this image of the kiss'; but see Ricks, *Keats and Embarrassment*, pp. 97–9.

16 See Anthony John Harding, 'Speech, Silence, and the Self-Doubting Interpreter in Keats's Poetry', *KSJ*, 35 (1986), p. 92, for a similar reading. The ghost-effect of Lorenzo's haunting voice is also an effect of a displaced intertextuality: while the voice of Boccaccio's Lorenzo is not described, the ghostly voice which Keats invokes specifically echoes that of Ulysses in Canto 26 of Dante's *Inferno*, and the revenant's appearance uncannily resembles the ghost of Hector as it appears to Aeneas in Virgil's *Aeneid*, Book 2, lines 268–97.

17 The major critical debate around 'Isabella' has centred on the question of the potential sentimentality of the poem – itself a question of solecism and implicitly connected to my discussion of the poem's relationship with audience – as John Barnard has commented, 'Keats's anxieties about *Isabella, The Eve of St Agnes*, and 'La Belle Dame' turned on his fear of serious readers, and reviewers in particular, finding them sentimental' (*John Keats*, p. 68). Finney, *The Evolution of Keats's Poetry*, pp. 373–4, sees Keats as reverting to 'Hunt's "poetic luxury" or sensuous sentimentality' (p. 374); Stillinger, *The Hoodwinking of Madeline*, pp. 31–45, describes 'Isabella' as an 'anti-Romance'; Tilottama Rajan, *Dark Interpreter: The Discourse of Romanticism* (Ithaca, Cornell University Press, 1980), p. 101, suggests an inherent 'emotional indeterminacy' in Keats's romances; Leoff, *A Study of John Keats's 'Isabella'*, p. 73, suggests that 'The accusation of sentimental ... attributes a superficiality to the writer that really lies with the reader'; Allott, '"Isabella", "The Eve of St Agnes", and "Lamia"', p. 51, comments that at 'this stage of his development Keats's effort to write a more "social" kind of poetry throws into relief his difficulty in reconciling discordant elements'; Louise Z. Smith, 'The Material Sublime: Keats and *Isabella*', *SiR*, 13 (1974), p. 305, suggests that 'Isabella' 'offers a constant balance of sentiment and detachment' through 'digression and juxtaposition'. It was, of course, Keats himself who began this tradition, by suggesting

that 'Isabella' was 'mawkish': see *KC*, vol. 1, p. 90, where Richard Woodhouse both reports Keats's ideas about the poem, and suggests that sentimentality or mawkishness depends on the frame of mind of the reader at the time of reading.

18 For a somewhat similar reading of Keats's 'crime', see Heinzelman, 'Self-interest', p. 167; and see pp. 174–6 on Keats's anxieties over his divergences from Boccaccio.

19 See Wolfson, *The Questioning Presence*, pp. 277–88.

20 Roland Barthes, 'The Reality Effect', in *The Rustle of Language*, tr. Richard Howard (Oxford, Basil Blackwell, 1986), p. 141.

21 The crime of luxury is explicitly configured in the 'political' stanzas 14–18, but the 'luxury' of these political comments is in turn configured in stanzas 19 and 20, as an offence against the 'simplicity' of Boccaccio's text.

22 'Ode to Psyche', line 43.

23 Earlier, in a kind of reverse encryptment of the later sepulchral eyes, Isabella had 'a quick eye' (line 51).

24 See Chapter 5, below, for a discussion of 'sight-lines' in 'The Eve of St Agnes'.

25 See Matthew Arnold's comment on 'Isabella' that 'almost in every stanza there occurs one of those vivid and picturesque turns of expression, by which the object is made to flash upon the eye of the mind' (*Heritage*, p. 327).

26 See lines 491–2 on the 'melodious chuckle in the strings / Of her lorn voice'.

27 Claude Lévi-Strauss suggests the way in which sexuality itself conforms to my description of solecism in his 'Introduction' to *The Elementary Structures of Kinship*, rev. edn., trs. James Harle Bell and John Richard von Sturmer (Boston, Beacon, 1969), p. 12: 'Man's [*sic*] sexual life is itself external to the group, firstly, in being the highest expression of his animal nature, and the most significant survival of instinct, and secondly, in that its ends are to satisfy individual desires, which, as is known, hold little respect for social conventions ... However, if the regulation of relationships between the sexes represents an overflow of culture into nature, in another way sexual life is one beginning of social life in nature, for the sexual is man's only instinct requiring the stimulation of another person'. It is in my analysis of Keatsian solecism as mediated at this point by Lévi-Strauss's notion of sexuality as inhabiting the liminal and transgressive space of the private and the social, that I would most strongly and at the same time most tentatively begin to diverge from Marjorie Levinson's reading of Keatsian poetics in *Keats's Life of Allegory*: according to Levinson, it is only in 'Lamia' that 'For the first time, Keats tries to *relate* social facts to private life, production to consumption, outside to inside, work to love' (p. 222), but I hope that my study shows how much earlier in his poetic career Keats was

attempting to relate the 'private' to the 'social', and how much we might lose in an elision of this aspect of his poetry.

28 But don't expect to have uncovered a *cryptonymic* account of 'Isabella' within this reading, for a summary of which I would ask you to turn your eyes away, to look elsewhere, outside of this reading, to, in the first place, Nicolas Abraham, 'The Shell and the Kernel', *Diacritics*, 9 (1979), pp. 16–28, 'Notes on the Phantom: A Complement to Freud's Metapsychology', *Critical Inquiry*, 13 (1987), pp. 287–92, and 'The Phantom of Hamlet or the Sixth Act: Preceded by the Intermission of "Truth"', *Diacritics*, 18 (1988), pp. 2–19; Nicolas Abraham and Maria Torok, *The Wolf Man's Magic Word: A Cryptonymy*, tr. Nicholas Rand (Minneapolis, University of Minnesota Press, 1986); Jacques Derrida, 'Foreword: *Fors*: The Anglish Words of Nicolas Abraham and Maria Torok', in *The Wolf Man's Magic Word*, pp. xi-xlviii; Esther Rashkin, 'Tools for a New Psychoanalytic Literary Criticism: The Work of Abraham and Torok', *Diacritics*, 18 (1988), pp. 31–52; Nicholas Royle, 'Cryptaesthesia: The Case of *Wuthering Heights*', in *Telepathy and Literature: Essays on the Reading Mind* (Oxford, Basil Blackwell, 1991).

29 Stillinger, *The Hoodwinking of Madeline*, p. 37.

5: 'THE EVE OF ST AGNES'

1 'To My Brother George', line 35.

2 Stuart A. Ende, *Keats and the Sublime* (New Haven, Yale University Press, 1976), ch. 2, discusses Keats and sight in relation to the sublime; more recently, Waldoff, *Keats and the Silent Work of Imagination*, pp. 71–6, has discussed sight in 'St Agnes', although he confines his analysis to Porphyro's vision and ignores the vision of Madeline and of the reader, and, moreover, focuses his argument on the question of the relationship between seeing and imagining; Ian Jack, *Keats and the Mirror of Art* (Oxford University Press, 1967), pp. 191–5, also comments on sight in the poem but similarly fails to follow the discussion through to the 'vision' of the reader. The fullest consideration of Keats and vision is, perhaps, that of Helen E. Haworth, 'Keats and the Metaphor of Vision', *JEGP*, 67 (1968), pp. 371–94, but Haworth seems to conflate the crucial distinction between the visual and the visionary. Both G. J. Finch, 'Wordsworth, Keats, and "the language of the sense"', *Ariel*, 11, 2 (1980), pp. 23–36, and John Barnard, 'Keats's Tactile Vision: "Ode to Psyche" and the Early Poetry', *KSMB*, 33 (1982), pp. 1–24, have explicitly argued for the priority of touch in Keats's poetry; on the importance of the tactile as contrasted with the visual in 'St Agnes', see Walter Jackson Bate, *The Stylistic Development of Keats* (New York, Humanities Press, 1962), pp. 94–5.

3 See Jack Stillinger, 'The Plots of Romantic Poetry', p. 102; Waldoff, *Keats and the Silent Work of Imagination*, p. 63.

4 See Steven Greenblatt's idea of the transformation of sexual friction into the friction of words in Shakespeare's comedies, in *Shakespearean Negotiations: The Circulation of Social Energy in Renaissance England* (Oxford University Press, 1988), ch. 3. Although the frictions I delineate in this paragraph are conceived on a different level in that they attempt to take account of the (erotic) frictions between reader and text, we might argue that it is the displaced frictions of sexual desire – correlative with the heat created by sexual/verbal foreplay/by-play which Greenblatt recognizes in Shakespearean comedy – that ultimately control the form of Keats's poem.

5 Michel Beaujour, 'Some Paradoxes of Description', pp. 27–59: 'As the multifaceted mirror of Desire, description bears only an oblique and tangential relationship to things, bodies and spaces. This is the reason why description is so intrinsically bound up with Utopia, and with pornography' (pp. 58–9). See Earl R. Wasserman, *The Finer Tone: Keats' Major Poems* (Baltimore, The Johns Hopkins University Press, 1953), pp. 97–137; Stillinger, *The Hoodwinking of Madeline*, pp. 67–93.

6 The other cruxes may be said to be the physical consummation of this visible vision at stanza 36 – a consummation which is, in itself, sublimated into the language of sight – and the displaced consummation of the inedible, the visual feast in stanza 30.

7 For a reading of the violence of Porphyro, see Beverly Fields's analysis of the poem in terms of the Philomel myth in 'Keats and the Tongueless Nightingale: Some Unheard Melodies in "The Eve of St Agnes"', *The Wordsworth Circle*, 14 (1983), pp. 246–50, on the 'repressed violence' of the poem and Porphyro's 'rage' (p. 247), the 'fantasy of eroticized destructiveness' and 'the terrifying aspects in the figure of Porphyro' (p. 249).

8 Waldoff, *Keats and the Silent Work of Imagination*, p. 73, makes a similar distinction between Porphyro's seeing and Madeline's; and compare Richard Cronin, *Colour and Experience in Nineteenth-Century Poetry* (London, Macmillan, 1988), p. 71, on Madeline's eyesight.

9 Stillinger, *The Hoodwinking of Madeline*, p. 86; see also Michael Ragussis, 'Narrative Structure and the Problem of the Divided Reader in *The Eve of St Agnes*', *ELH*, 42 (1975), pp. 383–4.

10 See Laura Mulvey's influential essay 'Visual Pleasure and Narrative Cinema', *Screen*, 16, 3 (1975), pp. 6–18, for an analysis of the female as spectacle and the male as mover of narrative in film, which seems to correspond well with the dynamics of the gaze in 'St Agnes'.

11 Ende, *Keats and the Sublime*, p. 40 (referring to 'peerless' in 'Ode on Melancholy').

12 Sperry, *Keats the Poet*, p. 207, comments finely on this feature of the narrative form of 'St Agnes': 'Throughout the poem we find Keats using the imagery of sculpture to express the way feeling is arrested or repressed, then liberated and fulfilled in a new onrush of emotion'.

13 See also W. M. Rossetti in Hill, ed., *Keats: The Narrative Poems*, pp. 63–4;

and see Robert Gittings, *John Keats* (Harmondsworth, Penguin, 1985), p. 410.

14 See Levinson, *Keats's Life of Allegory*, pp. 108–9, for an analysis of how the poem demands a critical fixation on the surface figuration; but see Stillinger, 'The Plots of Romantic Poetry', pp. 102–3, on the necessity of considering the effects of *discours* in order to overcome the problem of the confusions of plot.

15 In the following discussion of description, I am indebted to certain 'structuralist' analyses of the function and functioning of description in narrative: see Genette, 'Boundaries of Narrative', pp. 5–8; Philippe Hamon, 'What is a Description?', in Tzvetan Todorov, ed., *French Literary Theory Today: A Reader* (Cambridge University Press, 1982), pp. 147–78, and 'Rhetorical Status of the Descriptive', *Yale French Studies*, 61 (1981), pp. 1–26; and Beaujour, 'Some Paradoxes of Description', pp. 27–59. Recently, Alexander Gelley has argued against the rigid subordination of description to narration in the structuralist analysis, and has attempted to theorize the (phenomenological/pragmatic) 'distinctive mode of descriptive cognition' (*Narrative Crossings*, p. 13). Gelley does not, however, seek to collapse the distinction between narrative and description which I discuss.

16 See Michael Riffaterre, 'Descriptive Imagery', *Yale French Studies*, 61 (1981), p. 125; and see Barnard, 'Keats's Tactile Vision', p. 3: 'the reader does not literally "see" a picture created from words ... It is more helpful to examine visual effects in poetry through the linguistic and rhetorical techniques used to create those effects'. My reading of the incommensurability of figurative language with 'seeing' might be compared with Jean-François Lyotard's analysis of the disruptive force of the figure: Lyotard suggests that 'whatever is language is dedicated to communication between interlocutors, while the figure ... has to jam that communication', and that 'language, at least in its poetic usage, is possessed, haunted by the figure' ('The Dream-Work Does Not Think', in Benjamin, ed., *The Lyotard Reader*, p. 30).

17 For an extended reading of stanza one, see Levinson, *Keats's Life of Allegory*, pp. 133–159, esp. pp. 136 and 143 on the visuality of the stanza.

18 This question is generated again by the deleted 'See, while she speaks his arms encroaching slow' at line 314.

19 I am concerned here with 'motivation' in the sense discussed by the Russian Formalists: it might be argued that stanza 9 provides an explanation of Porphyro's motivation ('That he might gaze and worship all unseen; / Perchance speak, kneel, touch, kiss', lines 80–81) which includes not only looking but more tactile experiences as well. But what is extraordinary about Porphyro's plot is his desire to look rather than his (more conventional) desire for physical consummation – it will at least be granted that it is Porphyro's hidden gaze which leads to this consummation.

20 See Paul de Man's notion of 'inscription', expressed most explicitly in

'Hypogram and Inscription: Michael Riffaterre's Poetics of Reading', *Diacritics*, 11, 4 (1981), pp. 17–35: de Man argues, against Riffaterre's 'evasion' of prosopopoeia, that this figure 'undoes the distinction between reference and signification on which all semiotic systems... depend' (p. 34) such that what is important 'is not the assertion of non-referentiality, which is obvious, but the implied assertion of semantic determination of which non-referentiality is the specular negation' (p. 34). Similarly, in the title essay of *The Resistance to Theory* (Manchester University Press, 1986), de Man states, categorically, that he does not deny 'the referential function of language' (p. 11) but rather 'its authority as a model for natural or phenomenal cognition': it is precisely the seductions of such an (apparent) authority that I am attempting to describe in the present essay, such that the mechanics of the language of the text are repeated in the mechanics of reading, or, to put it another way, it is not only the case that we 'see' like Porphyro (and in some senses, of course, we don't) but also that the problematic structure of descriptive language in 'St Agnes' is generated by and at the same time generates the problematic structure of the reader's 'vision' – the hallucination of reading.

21 Compare Hamon's argument that description in nineteenth-century realism has to be motivated by a character's status as, for example, a spy ('What is a Description?', p. 150).

22 *Ibid.*, p. 159.

23 Jack, *Keats and the Mirror of Art*, p. 193.

24 See Levinson, *Keats's Life of Allegory*, p. 162: 'Stanza 24 is the shielded scutcheon at the center of the poem' (see also p. 119); and see Tilottama Rajan, *Dark Interpreter*, p. 111, on Keats's use of 'self-duplicating structure[s]' in the poem. Recently John Kerrigan, in 'Keats and Lucrece', *Shakespeare Survey*, 41 (1989), pp. 103–18, has written fruitfully on Keats's modernizing of Shakespearean blazonry in his response to *Lucrece* in 'St Agnes' (see esp. p. 108).

25 Hamon, 'What is a Description?', p. 162.

26 Dedication to *The Corsair*, in *Lord Byron: The Complete Poetical Works*, ed. Jerome J. McGann (7 vols., Oxford University Press, 1980–1993), vol. III (1981), p. 49.

27 See W. M. Rossetti's argument that the octave stanza of 'Isabella' accounts for the narrative energy of the poem, while the Spenserian stanza of 'St Agnes' accounts for the fact that it is 'hardly a narrative' (in Hill, ed., *Keats: The Narrative Poems*, pp. 62–3); for comments on the effect of the stanza form in 'St Agnes', see also Bate, *John Keats*, pp. 91–2; and Levinson, *Keats's Life of Allegory*, pp. 132, 186 (note 40).

28 Riffaterre, 'Descriptive Imagery', p. 125.

29 See Stillinger, *The Hoodwinking of Madeline*, pp. 67–93, for a reading of Porphyro as a voyeur; both Fields ('Keats and the Tongueless Nightingale', pp. 246–50) and Kerrigan ('Keats and *Lucrece*', pp.

111–13) suggest the possibility of reading 'The Eve of St Agnes', through the Philomel myth, in terms of rape. For a recent example of critical resistance to such ethical considerations, see Cronin's discussion of the poem (*Colour and Experience*, pp. 69–80), which repeatedly refuses both 'meaning' (see p. 74) and ethics: most remarkable, perhaps, is Cronin's assertion that Madeline 'is neither the object of our moral concern nor the victim of our irony. She is just beautiful' (p. 75). This is immediately followed by a quotation from the scene of her undressing – precisely the scopophilic scandal that threatens to undermine this kind of reading: Cronin's objectification of Madeline in the assertion that she is 'just beautiful' is precisely the kind of response 'The Eve of St Agnes' both demands and puts into question. On this point, see Ricks, *Keats and Embarrassment*, p. 89: 'the case for some of Keats's most impassioned poetry is essentially the case for a purified and liberated scopophilia: for a contemplating which is more than permissible since it is so enabling and free of anxiety, and yet is still felt to be surprising because it includes a sense of possible guilt, shabbiness, or prurience held off by an unmisgiving largeness of mind'.

30 Robert Gittings, *John Keats: The Living Year* (London, Heinemann, 1978), pp. 79–81.

31 *Letters*, vol. II, p. 46; see the Epilogue, below, for a discussion of this important letter.

32 Ricks, *Keats and Embarrassment*, p. 91.

33 See, for example, Jeffrey Baker, *John Keats and Symbolism* (Brighton, Harvester, 1986), p. 58, on the 'relieved tension' of the description.

34 Compare Cronin's comment on the meal that it is 'a feast so fairy that it is eaten just by being pronounced' (*Colour and Experience*, p. 75), and Karl Kroeber's assertion that it 'literally makes a reader's mouth water if he reads it aloud' (*British Romantic Art*, p. 205).

35 Wasserman, *The Finer Tone*, pp. 109–11.

36 Clifford Adelman, 'The Dangers of Enthrallment', in Allan Danzig, ed., *Twentieth Century Interpretations of 'The Eve of St Agnes'* (Englewood Cliffs, Prentice-Hall, 1971), pp. 113–14, suggests that 'The fact that [Porphyro] is "seen" as a star indicates that his being is a function of the disposition of the perceiver. Both the narrator and Madeline, if only for a moment, have seen him simultaneously exist in the world of the immortal dream and that of mutability', but this elides the question of the identity of the narrator, and the curious narratorial doubling of Porphyro which must take place for a narrator to 'see' this image.

37 Many critics have developed a comment by Keats on the colouring of the poem: 'I wish to diffuse the colouring of St Agnes eve throughout a Poem in which Character and Sentiment would be the figures to such drapery' (*Letters*, vol. II, p. 234): see R. H. Fogle, 'A Reading of Keats's "The Eve of St Agnes"', *College English*, 6 (1945), p. 327; C. F. Burgess, '"The Eve of St Agnes": One Way to the Poem', *English Journal*, 54

(1965), pp. 391–2; Stillinger, 'The Plots of Romantic Poetry', pp. 102–3. On Porphyro as 'tainting', see Martin Aske, 'Magical Spaces in "The Eve of St Agnes"', *Essays in Criticism*, 31 (1981), p. 203.

38 Jean H. Hagstrum, *The Romantic Body: Love and Sexuality in Keats, Wordsworth, and Blake* (Knoxville, University of Tennessee Press, 1985), p. 52.

39 See Barnard, *John Keats*, p. 89, and Ragussis, 'Narrative Structure', p. 389; 'hazardous magic' is from John Scott's review of Keats's 1820 volume: 'the magical delicacy of the hazardous picture' (*Heritage*, p. 224). For a discussion of one 'hazard' of 'St Agnes', the possibility of its subtextual engagement with the discourse of prostitution, see Wendy Steiner, *Pictures of Romance*, pp. 62–6; and see my '"Fragment of Castle-builder" and Keats's Use of Sexual Slang', *English Language Notes*, 28, 2 (1990), pp. 49–50.

6: 'LA BELLE DAME SANS MERCI'

1 Wasserman, *The Finer Tone*, p. 65. Compare Steiner's comment, in *Pictures of Romance*, p. 59, that 'virtually every one of Keats's masterpieces is concerned with redefining imaginative activity in terms of the visual arts and with saving vision from stasis and enthrallment'.

2 Sperry, *Keats the Poet*, pp. 231–2, 235.

3 The terms 'impaction' and 'rarefaction' are borrowed from Martin Nystrand, who defines such usages as 'dysfunctional' language, in 'An Analysis of Errors in Written Communication', in Martin Nystrand, ed., *What Writers Know: The Language, Process, and Structure of Written Discourse* (New York, Academic Press, 1982), pp. 57–74; see also *The Structure of Written Communication: Studies in Reciprocity Between Writers and Readers* (New York, Academic Press, 1986), p. 74; D. S. Neff makes a similar distinction in a study of 'Lamia', 'Overdetermination and Ambiguity: Narrative Strategies in Keats's *Lamia*', *Research Studies*, 52 (1983), pp. 138–145.

4 See Derrida, *Acts of Literature*, pp. 44–8, for such a description of the literary.

5 Quotations from 'La Belle Dame sans Merci' are from a transcript made by Charles Brown: I also refer to the first publication of the poem in the *Indicator* (10 May 1820) as 'the *Indicator* version' (from the footnotes in Stillinger's edition): as I shall attempt to show, the alterations to the published version of the text, which emphatically reduce the poem's mystery, might be understood to provide evidence for Keats's anxiety of audience.

6 Simpson, *Irony and Authority*, p. 16.

7 There is also a sense in which love cannot be told in ordinary language; see Keats's letter to Fanny Brawne: 'My sweet Girl I cannot speak my love for you' (*Letters*, vol. II, p. 131).

8 Thus 'language strange' can be seen as an example of what Gerald Prince has called 'reading interludes', aspects of texts which 'read' themselves and direct the reading of the reader, in 'Notes on the Text as Reader', pp. 225–40.

9 For criticism of Keatsian diction, see, for example, *Heritage*, p. 183. The vehement criticism that met Coleridge's use of archaic diction in 'The Ancient Mariner' was part of this debate and something that no doubt alerted Keats to the dangers of such usage (see J. R. de J. Jackson, ed., *Coleridge: The Critical Heritage*, London, Routledge and Kegan Paul, 1970, pp. 53, 55–6, 58, 317). For the conventionality of 'old' English in the broadside ballad of the eighteenth century, see Albert B. Friedman, *The Ballad Revival: Studies in the Influence of Popular on Sophisticated Poetry* (University of Chicago Press, 1961), p. 269. Friedman argues that the tensions discernible in 'La Belle Dame' involve its being compromised as a ballad by its 'participation in romance' (pp. 299–300); according to Friedman, what Keats wanted was to evoke the 'rich and sensuous texture' of romance literature.

10 François Matthey, *The Evolution of Keats's Structural Imagery* (Berne, Francke, 1974), p. 178.

11 Simpson, *Irony and Authority*, p. 18.

12 *Ibid.*, pp. 15–16.

13 Theresa M. Kelley, 'Poetics and the Politics of Reception: Keats's "La Belle Dame sans Merci"', *ELH*, 54 (1987), p. 336.

14 See Jerome J. McGann's argument in 'The Meaning of the Ancient Mariner', in *The Beauty of Inflections: Literary Investigations in Historical Method and Theory* (Oxford University Press, 1985), p. 163, that Coleridge 'had to establish a text which displayed several textual "layers"… and the poem's lexicon is the ultimate carrier of this set of textual layers' and that 'the archaic diction is only significant in its relation to the more modern dictions'.

15 See Simpson's argument for the poem's 'epistemological and ontological suspension' (*Irony and Authority*, pp. 15ff.) and Perkins's assertion in *The Quest for Permanence*, that 'the poem is not only uncertain but a poem about uncertainty' (p. 263).

16 See McGann, *The Beauty of Inflections*, p. 34: McGann argues that 'wretched wight' signals an ironic distance between the poet and his subject: I would argue that 'knight at arms' also achieves this distancing even if the 'wight' is more overtly ironic.

17 Their nature is ambiguous: see, for example, Susan J. Wolfson 'The Language of Interpretation in Romantic Poetry: "A Strong Working of the Mind"', in Arden Reed, ed., *Romanticism and Language* (London, Methuen, 1984), p. 35.

18 Eric Partridge defines a 'Lady of the lake' as a mistress and a 'laker lady' as 'an actor's whore' in *A Dictionary of Slang and Unconventional English*, 8th edn., ed. Paul Beale (London, Routledge, 1984); Keats

makes a sexual joke out of the expression in a letter to his brother Tom on 17 July 1818 (*Letters*, vol. I, p. 333; but see Robert Gittings, ed., *Letters of John Keats*, Oxford University Press, 1970, pp. 129 and 402, note 4, for the corrected text). Relevant in this context is Dorothy Van Ghent's suggestion in *Keats: The Myth of the Hero* (New Jersey, Princeton University Press, 1983), that 'we can read the ballad of the Belle Dame in terms of a purely subjective libido-symbolism' (p. 129).

19 Samuel Johnson, *A Dictionary of the English Language* (2 vols., New York, Ams Press, 1967). See Wolfson, 'The Language of Interpretation', p. 36, who emphasizes the importance of etymologies in this poem and uses a similar argument to mine: 'The adjectives "haggard" and "woe-begone"... begin to play against this vacancy of information... by hinting at anterior events'.

20 Miriam Allott, ed., *The Poems of John Keats* (London, Longman, 1970), p. 502. The lily and the rose can be found in similar contexts in literary ballads of the eighteenth century. See David Mallett, 'William and Mary' (1724), lines 7, 15 and 19; Thomas Tickel, 'Colin and Lucy' (1725), lines 6 and 9; William Julius Mickle, 'Cumnar Hall' (1784), line 34, in Anne Henry Ehrenpreis, ed., *The Literary Ballad* (London, Edward Thomas, 1966).

21 See Wasserman, *The Finer Tone*, p. 66: 'in the introductory stanzas images and human values are gradually blended stereoscopically until at length the reader's mode of poetic vision has been adjusted to see the symbolized value as the third-dimensional projection of the image'.

22 Kelley, 'Poetics and the Politics of Reception', p. 347, has noted the syntactical confusion here.

23 Simpson, *Irony and Authority*, p. 15.

24 Kroeber, *Romantic Narrative Art*, pp. 37ff. Wasserman (*The Finer Tone*, p. 67) also defines the technique as symbolic: 'Keats must entice a pursuit of his images by the reader, whose ardour will transform them into symbols'; see also Waldoff, *Keats and the Silent Work of Imagination*, p. 91: 'the relationship between action and motive is blurred, the logic of transitions is elided, much of the meaning is encoded in indeterminate symbols'; and Van Ghent, *The Myth of the Hero*, p. 126, who also explains the effect in a vocabulary sympathetic to my own: 'Keats's plot appears as sheer enactment, stripped, as in a dream, of any rationalization or convention of causality'.

25 See Robert Jamieson, ed., *Popular Ballads and Songs* (2 vols., Edinburgh, 1806), vol. II, pp. 7f. See also the use of the expression 'manna-dew' in *Endymion*, Book I, line 766. In the draft version of 'La Belle Dame sans Merci' (reproduced in *Letters*, vol. II, p. 95, and the notes to Stillinger's edition, p. 358) the word was first 'honey-dew', which is also found in *Endymion*, Book 2, line 7 and appears in both Coleridge's 'The Rime of the Ancient Mariner' (line 407) and his 'Kubla Khan' (line 53), both strongly implicated as intertexts for 'La Belle Dame sans Merci'.

26 This is similar to Kroeber's argument that we 'are not expected to believe literally in the wight's experience. We do not have to, because unmistakeable contrasts in imagery...create an aesthetic reality, a purposeful coherence not dependent on literal credulity' (*Romantic Narrative Art*, pp. 40–41).

27 As Leon Waldoff says 'the demonstrative pronoun becomes one of the most overdetermined words in all of Keats's poetry, suddenly bearing the burden of meaning for the entire poem and at the same time frustrating efforts to interpret it' (*Keats and the Silent Work of Imagination*, p. 86).

7: THE SPRING ODES

1 Barnard, *John Keats*, p. 98, for example, argues that it is precisely to their denial of audience that the odes owe their greatness: 'Not only were the spring odes and the later ode "To Autumn" written with no immediate sense of an audience, but their form gives Keats an uninhibited freedom denied him by narrative'.

2 Vendler, *The Odes of John Keats*, passim.

3 See David Lindley, *Lyric* (London, Methuen, 1985), pp. 1–4, for a concise summary of definitions of the lyric. Lindley describes four defining features: 1. musical accompaniment/'poetry that sings'; 2. the poet's own voice; 3. the use of present tense; 4. brevity.

4 M. H. Abrams, *A Glossary of Literary Terms*, 4th edn. (New York, Holt, Rinehart and Winston, 1981), p. 99. For a study of ways in which the concept of lyric developed in the eighteenth century, and ways in which 'plot' came to be seen as 'external' to poetry (*contra* Aristotle, who describes it as the 'soul' of poetry), see Norman Maclean, 'From Action to Image: Theories of the Lyric in the Eighteenth Century', in R. S. Crane, ed., *Critics and Criticism: Ancient and Modern* (University of Chicago Press, 1952), pp. 408–60, esp. p. 439. The idea of the narrativity of lyric is not uncommon in theoretical considerations of the form, however: see, for example, Jonathan Culler's discussion, after Paul de Man, of the inevitable tendency of language, even in the lyric, towards narrative, in 'Changes in the Study of the Lyric', in Chaviva Hošek and Patricia Parker, eds., *Lyric Poetry: Beyond New Criticism* (Ithaca, Cornell University Press, 1985), pp. 53–4. There have also been recent arguments for the narrativity of the Romantic lyric in particular: see, for example, Tilottama Rajan's idea that the Romantic lyric is 'inter-textual' or 'dialogic' and therefore moves towards a form which 'is quite different from the pure lyric', in 'Romanticism and the Death of Lyric Consciousness', in Hošek and Parker, *Lyric Poetry*, p. 206; and Sharon Cameron's idea, in *Lyric Time: Dickinson and the Limits of Genre* (Baltimore, The Johns Hopkins University Press, 1979), p. 217, that 'the Romantics often frame their lyrics in narrative settings; they show a resistance to the full temporal disembodiment exemplified in more modern poems'.

5 Cameron, *Lyric Time*, p. 206.
6 Lindley, *Lyric*, p. 72.
7 R. Potter, *An Inquiry into some Passages in Dr Johnson's 'Lives of the Poets'* (London, 1783), p. 14.
8 See Paul de Man, 'Lyrical Voice in Contemporary Theory: Riffaterre and Jauss', in Hošek and Parker, eds., *Lyric Poetry*, p. 55: 'The principle of intelligibility in lyric poetry, depends on the phenomenalization of poetic voice. Our claim to understand the text coincides with the actualization of a speaking voice, be it (monologically) that of the poet or (dialogically) that of the exchange that takes place between author and reader in the process of comprehension'.
9 Anne Williams, *Prophetic Strain: The Greater Lyric in the Eighteenth Century* (University of Chicago Press, 1984), p. 16.
10 *Ibid.*, pp. 13, 14.
11 Clayton, *Romantic Vision*, p. 75. On the odes and narrative, see Patricia Parker's notion of the assimilation of the romance quest into the ode in *Inescapable Romance*, p. 173, an idea which Waldoff develops in *Keats and the Silent Work of Imagination*, pp. 102, 111–12; on the odes from the point of view of reader-response, see Susan J. Wolfson's comment in *The Questioning Presence*, p. 332, that the odes require 'negotiation through the questioning presence of a reader' and that Keats's poetry 'achieves its fullest imaginative value in the poetics of cooperation so engendered'.
12 *The Examiner* (23 March 1817), p. 190. On the tensions between 'narrative' and 'language' in 'Ode to Psyche', see Geoffrey H. Hartman, 'Reading Aright: Keats's "Ode to Psyche"', in Eleanor Cook *et al.*, eds., *Centre and Labyrinth: Essays in Honour of Northrop Frye* (University of Toronto Press, 1983), pp. 217, 222; and see Wolfson, *The Questioning Presence*, pp. 307–8, on some of the narrative strategies employed in the poem.
13 Vendler, *The Odes of John Keats*, p. 62, speaks of the 'sacrifice' of 'audience for a putative, though scarcely realized, solipsism', and comments that in this poem Keats 'still conceived of art as ... directed to no audience except Psyche, the poet's own soul' (p. 77): such comments would seem to ignore the convoluted complexities of reception in the poem.
14 *Ibid.*, pp. 81, 109.
15 *Ibid.*, p. 95.
16 Waldoff, *Keats and the Silent Work of Imagination*, p. 128; compare Wasserman's idea, in *The Finer Tone*, p. 189, of the instability created by the opening stanza.
17 Indeed, critics often write about 'Ode to a Nightingale' in terms of narrative: see, for example, William Dodd, 'Keats's "Ode to a Nightingale" and "On a Grecian Urn"[*sic*]: Two Principles of Organization', *Lingua e Stile*, 6 (1971), p. 250, on the 'sequential, narrative type of development' in the ode; Wasserman, *The Finer Tone*,

p. 180, on the ode's 'sequentiality'; R. H. Fogle, 'Keats's *Ode to a Nightingale*', *PMLA*, 68 (1953), p. 219, on the poem's 'controlled complexity of movement based upon a crucial suspense'; Van Ghent, *The Myth of the Hero*, p. 257, on the 'plot' and the 'action' of the poem; Vendler, *The Odes of John Keats*, p. 83, on the '"events" of the ode, as it unfolds in time'. For a study of the tense-changes in the poem, see Francis Berry, *Poets' Grammar: Person, Time, and Mood in Poetry* (London, Routledge and Kegan Paul, 1958), pp. 135–9; and Vendler, *The Odes of John Keats*, p. 97. As I have argued elsewhere, the strangely incongruous reference to Ruth as weeping and homesick may be understood to be doubly imbued with temporality from its reference to the alienation of gleaners in 1818–19 – a retelling of an old tale with pressing contemporary relevance ('The Politics of Gleaning in Keats's "Ode to a Nightingale" and "To Autumn"', *KSJ*, 39, 1990, pp. 34–8; and see my discussion of the gleaner figure in 'To Autumn' in Chapter 9, below).

18 But see Waldoff, *Keats and the Silent Work of Imagination*, p. 151, on the way that the stanza deleted from 'Ode on Melancholy' reveals 'a narrative structure in the idea of the quest that underlies the more obviously declamatory and argumentative style of the poem'.

19 The pleasure of this text would then be what Roland Barthes describes as 'writing aloud': 'what it searches for (in a perspective of bliss) are the pulsional incidents, the language lined with flesh, a text where we can hear the grain of the throat, the patina of consonants, the voluptuousness of vowels, a whole carnal stereophony' (*The Pleasure of the Text*, tr. Richard Miller, New York, Farrar, Strauss and Giroux, 1975, pp. 66–7).

20 Tilottama Rajan, 'Death of Lyric Consciousness', p. 196.

21 Recently, A. W. Phinney, 'Keats in the Museum: Between Aesthetics and History', *JEGP*, 90 (1991), pp. 208–29, has made a similar point: the ode 'anticipates the very confrontation that has emerged in the history of its reading' (p. 210), and encodes 'in itself an allegory of its own reading' (p. 218). It should be noted, though, that this reading – Phinney's and mine – is itself also figured by the poem and that this is far from the *only* response. That is, to say that the poem produces its own self-reflexive response is a problem of, rather than a solution to, reading. Various other critics have commented on the poem's self-reflexivity: see, for example, Douglas B. Wilson, 'Reading the Urn: Death in Keats's Arcadia', *SEL*, 25 (1985), p. 826; Leo Spitzer, 'The "Ode on a Grecian Urn", or Content vs Metagrammar', *Comparative Literature*, 7 (1955), pp. 203–25; Murray Krieger, 'The Ekphrastic Principle and the Still Movement of Poetry; or "Laokoön" Revisited', in *The Play and Place of Criticism* (Baltimore, The Johns Hopkins University Press, 1967), pp. 124–5; Michael Hinden, 'Reading the Painting, Seeing the Poem: Vermeer and Keats', *Mosaic*, 17 (1984), pp. 17–34; Barnard, *John Keats*, p. 105; and Philip Fisher, 'A Museum with One Work Inside: Keats's "Ode on a Grecian Urn" and the Finality of Art', in J. H.

Smith, ed., *Brandeis Essays in Literature* (Waltham, Mass., Department of English and American Literature, Brandeis University, 1983), p. 72.

22 Stillinger, *The Hoodwinking of Madeline*, pp. 167–73.

23 See Stillinger, *ibid.*, for a discussion of this problem.

24 On the contemporary *ut pictura poesis* debate in relation to Keats's ode, see James O'Rourke, 'Persona and Voice in "Ode on a Grecian Urn"', *SiR*, 26 (1987), pp. 31–2; Phinney, 'Keats in the Museum', pp. 211–18; and James A. W. Heffernan, 'Ekphrasis and Representation', *NLH*, 22 (1991), pp. 297–316, esp. pp. 302–9.

25 Chambers, *Story and Situation*, p. 6.

26 Prince, 'Notes on the Text as Reader'.

27 *Ibid.*, p. 230.

28 Marcel Proust, *On Reading*, trs. Jean Autret and William Burford (London, Souvenir Press, 1972), pp. 35–7. Although Proust's word is *incitations*, I shall employ the (etymologically related) word 'enticements'.

29 See Smith, *Poetic Closure*, p. 195.

30 See Wolfson, *The Questioning Presence*, p. 320.

31 As Geoffrey Hartman says, in 'History Writing as Answerable Style', in *The Fate of Reading and Other Essays* (University of Chicago Press, 1975), p. 102, the urn's 'mystery is in danger of being dissolved, its form broken for the sake of a message'; see also O'Rourke ('Persona and Voice', p. 39), who speaks of narrative failure and of the necessity to generate new material at this point; and Vendler, *The Odes of John Keats*, p. 129.

32 Benjamin Robert Haydon, 'On the Cartoon of the Sacrifice at Lystra', *Annals of the Fine Arts*, 4, 13 (1820), pp. 238–9. For considerations of the influence of this essay on the poem, see Robert Gittings, *The Odes of Keats and Their Earliest Known Manuscripts in Facsimile*, (London, Heinemann, 1970), p. 70; and J. R. MacGillivray, Letter to the *Times Literary Supplement* (July 1938), pp. 465–6.

33 *CN*, 3557–8 and 4422; Keats, *Letters*, vol. I, p. 218.

34 For other conflations of 'happy' with 'chance', see *Endymion*, I, 891, 'The Eve of St Agnes', line 91, and *Otho the Great*, III.ii.252. Keats's letters suggest a very real sense of the relationship between happiness and chance (his word for such chance or fate tends to be 'circumstances'): there is a repeated concern in his letters with the 'continual struggle against the suffocation of accidents' (*Letters*, vol. I, p. 179), and the way that 'Man is propell'd to act and strive and buffet with Circumstance' (*Letters*, vol. I, p. 210), in the context of the possibility of happiness. See Stuart Peterfreund, 'The Truth about "Beauty" and "Truth": Keats's "Ode on a Grecian Urn"', Milton, Shakespeare, and the Uses of Paradox', *KSJ*, 35 (1986), pp. 62–82: 'the numerous repetitions of the word happy suggest a lexical foregrounding calculated to push the word beyond its commonly accepted (and limited) meaning and into the realm of paronomasia and paradox' (pp. 69–70). Vendler

(*The Odes of John Keats*, p. 138) calls these repetitions 'babble, in which what is being said is palpably subordinated to the effect of incoherent envy'. More generally, for the idea of the estranging effect of verbal repetition, see Paul Valéry, 'Poetry and Abstract Thought', in *The Art of Poetry*, tr. Denise Folliot (London, Routledge and Kegan Paul, 1958), p. 55.

35 According to Dwight E. Robinson, 'Ode on a "New Etrurian" Urn, A Reflection of Wedgwood Ware in the Poetic Imagery of John Keats', *KSJ*, 12 (1963), p. 13, the stanza was 'a kind of sub-plot or caesura to its major orgiastic action'; Douglas Bush points out that the stanza is 'logically a digression', in 'Keats and His Ideas', in M. H. Abrams, ed., *English Romantic Poets: Modern Essays in Criticism* (New York, Oxford University Press, 1960), p. 335; and Cleanth Brooks, *The Well Wrought Urn: Studies in the Structure of Poetry* (London, Methuen, 1968), p. 131, says that stanza 4 'forms a contrast with the earlier scenes ... it constitutes another chapter in the history that the "Sylvan Historian" has to tell'.

36 'Beyond the Pleasure Principle', in *Works*, vol. xviii, pp. 7–64, esp. pp. 62ff. Again, Keats's letters, written around the time of the 'Urn', record such concerns: writing of the possibility of human happiness on 21 April 1819, Keats says: 'I can imagine such happiness carried to an extreme – but what must it end in? – Death' (*Letters*, vol. ii, p. 101; see also, vol. ii, p. 123). The curious repetition of 'happy' may also be said to originate, paronomastically, in the most prolonged and most influential eighteenth-century meditation on death and posterity, Edward Young's *Night Thoughts*, Keats's lines 'More happy love! more happy, happy love!' seeming to repeat Young's repetitions in 'Lovely in Death the beauteous Ruin lay; / And if in Death still lovely, Lovelier There; / Far lovelier! Pity swells the Tide of Love' (*Night Thoughts*, ed. Stephen Cornford, Cambridge University Press, 1989, Night iii, lines 104–6).

37 See Jack, *Keats and the Mirror of Art*, p. 219.

38 There is, admittedly, something of an ambiguity in the punctuation of the stanza which affects this reading: Miriam Allott's (apparently arbitrary) replacement of the semi-colon by a dash at the end of line 27 (in *The Poems of John Keats*), seems to make the figures on the urn 'above', but there seems to be no authority for this punctuation (Stillinger's edition of the poem, taken from the 1820 published version, gives a semi-colon; the *Annals* version gives a colon; while George Keats's fair-copy, reproduced in Gittings, *Manuscripts*, gives a comma). See Wolfson, *The Questioning Presence*, pp. 322–3, for a fuller discussion of the grammatical ambiguities involved in line 28.

39 See Stillinger, *The Hoodwinking of Madeline*, p. 101; and Wasserman, *The Finer Tone*, pp. 14 and 59.

40 As various critics have pointed out, within the terms of the *ut pictura poesis* debate, Keats is also, especially in stanzas three and four, showing what poetry can do – through irony, ambiguity, puns, etc. – which painting

cannot: see O'Rourke, 'Persona and Voice', p. 41; John J. Teunissen and Evelyn J. Hinz, '"Ode on a Grecian Urn": Keats's "Laocoön"', *English Studies in Canada*, 6 (1980), p. 178; Heffernan, 'Ekphrasis and Representation', pp. 301–8. As Heffernan comments (p. 305), 'part of what teases us out of thought in this poem is precisely its narrativity'.

41 See, for example, William Empson, *The Structure of Complex Words* (London, Hogarth, 1985), p. 374.

42 John Bayley, 'The Heroine on the Urn', *SiR*, 24 (1985), p. 562. Vendler, too, claims to see 'no evidence for puns here' (*The Odes of John Keats*, p. 311, note 14), although what 'evidence' is possible is problematic: puns, again, are subject to the contingency of reader-response. The function of puns/coincidences here is, like the function of the narrator, to make the arbitrary seem motivated (see Jonathan Culler, ed., *On Puns: The Foundation of Letters*, Oxford, Basil Blackwell, 1988, pp. 12–15). But the question which we might, uneasily, ask is: who provides such motivation, the writer or the reader? Is there, for example, a further pun on 'overwrought', such that it signifies not only 'excited' and 'drawn over', but also 'over-written', a self-parody of stanza four? (*Endymion* provides possible semantic parallels of 'wrought' as 'written' at 1, 557, 'had wrought this flowery spell', and 3, 198, 'o'erwrought with symbols'; see Simpson, *Irony and Authority*, p. 8, on another parallel from the letters; and see also Wolfson, *The Questioning Presence*, pp. 324–5.) In 1817, J. H. Reynolds had criticized Keats's 1817 *Poems* in a review because 'he is apt to make his descriptions overwrought' (*Heritage*, p. 49). But is this 'over-reading' the 'Urn'? Are we being overwrought?

43 See William F. Zak, '"To Try that Long Preserved Virginity": Psyche's Bliss and the Teasing Limits of the Grecian Urn', *KSJ*, 31 (1982), p. 99, for a comparable reading.

8: THE 'HYPERION' POEMS

1 Despite the profusion of epic poems written in the early years of the nineteenth century, the very possibility of epic was itself often questioned during the period: see, for example, the opening to an anonymous essay, 'Thoughts on Novel Writing' in *Blackwood's Edinburgh Magazine*, 4 (January 1819), p. 394: 'Since, in modern times, the different modes of national existence are no longer capable of being represented in epic poems, it has become the task of the novelist to copy, in an humbler style, the humbler features exhibited by human life'. On the 'proliferation' of epics in the early nineteenth century, see Curran, *Poetic Form and British Romanticism*, pp. 158–79.

2 For the text of the Advertisement and Keats's reaction to it, see John Barnard, ed., *John Keats: The Complete Poems*, 2nd edn. (Harmondsworth, Penguin, 1980), p. 514. Both John Middleton Murry, *Keats and Shakespeare* (London, Oxford University Press, 1926), pp. 81–2, and de

Sélincourt, *The Poems of John Keats*, p. 487, point to the chronological impossibility of Keats having *given up* the poem because of the critical reviews.

3 See, especially, Lockhart in *Blackwood's Edinburgh Magazine* (*Heritage*, pp. 97–110) and an anonymous review in *The British Critic* (*Heritage*, pp. 91–6), as well as the attacks on Hunt and the 'Cockney' poets, such as 'Letter from Z. to Leigh Hunt, King of the Cockneys' in *Blackwood's*, 3 (1818), pp. 196–201, and the series of attacks under the title 'The Cockney School of Poetry' in *Blackwood's* (1817–19). For a recent discussion of these attacks, see Kim Wheately, 'The *Blackwood's* Attacks on Leigh Hunt', *Nineteenth-Century Literature*, 47 (1992), pp. 1–31. The question of the extent to which the criticisms of *Endymion* were effective (and, indeed, even the question of the extent of the criticisms themselves) is somewhat controversial. As John O. Hayden points out, in *The Romantic Reviewers: 1802–24* (London, Routledge and Kegan Paul, 1969), p. 190, the majority of the reviews of *Endymion* were, in fact, positive; Lewis M. Schwartz, 'Keats's Critical Reception in Newspapers of His Day', *KSJ*, 21–2 (1972–3), p. 170, however, disagrees, and claims that the attacks were 'devastating' and that 'despite a numerical preponderance of favorable reviews for that year, *Endymion* was not well received' (see also Briggs, 'Conscious and Unconscious Reactions', pp. 1106–29, for a similar analysis); but for less decisive opinions see Robert Gittings, *The Living Year*, p. 13, and Bate, *John Keats*, pp. 366–73. The generally overwrought tone of the reviews at the time, together with the fact that Keats's friends Hunt, Hazlitt, and Haydon were embroiled in such polemics, and the fact that the rhetoric in the criticism of *Endymion* was so overtly political in motivation, suggest that 'devastating' might be overstating the case. Indeed, Keats's reaction was to say that 'I think I shall be among the English Poets after my death' (*Letters*, vol. I, p. 394). Nevertheless, Keats's comments on *Endymion* and his subsequent anxieties about 'mawkishness' and his poems being 'smokeable', together with his often virulent attacks on reviewers, all suggest that the effect should not be ignored.

4 On the relationship between the narrative form of 'Hyperion' and *Endymion*, see Aske, *Keats and Hellenism*, pp. 73–4; Michael Ragussis, *The Subterfuge of Art: Language and the Romantic Tradition* (Baltimore, The Johns Hopkins University Press, 1978), pp. 39–41, also comments on the 'implicit distinction' between the two poems.

5 The politics of 'Hyperion' are, in fact, a matter of some controversy: see, for example, Barnard, *John Keats*, pp. 59–60; Morris Dickstein, 'Keats and Politics', *SiR*, 25 (1986), pp. 179–80; Kenneth Muir, 'The Meaning of "Hyperion"', in *Reassessment*, pp. 104–5; Butler, *Romantics, Rebels, and Reactionaries*, pp. 151–4; Alan J. Bewell, 'The Political Implications of Keats's Classical Aesthetics', *SiR*, 25 (1986), pp. 220–29; Vincent Newey, '"Alternate uproar and sad peace": Keats, Politics, and the

Idea of Revolution', *The Yearbook of English Studies*, 19 (1989), pp. 265–89; Daniel P. Watkins, *Keats's Poetry and the Politics of the Imagination* (New Jersey, Associated University Presses, 1989), ch. 4. The poem is not exactly a call to revolution, however – indeed, the plot of revolution is a primary locus of narrative failure – and Keats's inability to go beyond Apollo's deification might be read in connection with such anti-revolutionary politics. For Keats, as for many of his contemporaries, revolution is figured as an agent of reaction: the French Revolution 'put a temporry stop to this ... change, the change for the better' (*Letters*, vol. II, pp. 193–4).

6 Of course the reductions in Keatsian excess in 'Hyperion' may be explained by the fact that many of the criticisms in the reviews of *Endymion* were recognized by Keats himself to be justified in substance if not in tone: as he said of one of the reviews, 'J. S. is perfectly right in regard to the slipshod Endymion' (*Letters*, vol. I, p. 374).

7 On the silence of the opening to 'Hyperion', see, for example, Ragussis, *The Subterfuge of Art*, p. 42, who also comments on the 'insistently negative syntax and diction', p. 43; see also Wolfson, *The Questioning Presence*, pp. 253–4; Aske, *Keats and Hellenism*, pp. 94–5; and Anya Taylor 'Superhuman Silence: Language in *Hyperion*', *SEL*, 19 (1979), pp. 673–87.

8 As Michael Ragussis comments, the Naiad figure 'symbolizes the silence of the whole scene' (*The Subterfuge of Art*, p. 43).

9 On the 'Hyperion' poems and narrative form, see Little, *Keats as a Narrative Poet*, who comments on the lack of 'action' compared to the memorable 'static images' in 'Hyperion' (pp. 129–33); similarly, Muir, 'The Meaning of "Hyperion"', in *Reassessment*, p. 109, comments that in 'Hyperion', 'Keats's narrative power is only intermittently displayed'; see also Ragussis, *The Subterfuge of Art*, p. 43, on the poem's lack of 'action'. The poem's narrative is usually described as fragmentary: see, for example, Tilottama Rajan, *Dark Interpreter*, p. 183, and Aske, *Keats and Hellenism*, pp. 84–5; alternatively, 'Hyperion' is described as a series of *tableaux* in Douglas Bush, *John Keats: His Life and Writings* (London, Weidenfeld and Nicolson, 1966), p. 100 (on Book One), and Gradman, *Metamorphosis in Keats*, p. 52. 'The Fall of Hyperion', by contrast, tends to be described as 'lyric' in mode due to its lack of 'action', and to its first-person narrator – Helen Vendler (*The Odes of John Keats*, p. 208) claims that 'For all its pretensions to epic narrative ... its import is lyric'. As Marjorie Levinson comments in *The Romantic Fragment Poem: A Critique of a Form* (Chapel Hill, University of North Carolina Press, 1986), p. 167, '"Hyperion"'s mode is typically characterized as objective, dramatic, Miltonic, and Greek, while "The Fall" is described as subjective, lyrical, Dantesque, and Romantic'. On the other hand, Wolfson, *The Questioning Presence*, p. 259, and Geoffrey H. Hartman, 'Spectral Symbolism and Authorial Self in Keats's "Hyperion"', in *The*

Fate of Reading, p. 60, both discern a specifically lyric force behind 'Hyperion', and, similarly, Paul A. Cantor, *Creature and Creator: Myth-Making and English Romanticism* (Cambridge University Press, 1984), p. 167, comments that 'Keats shapes his epic material in *Hyperion* so that it becomes ... a vehicle for the essentially lyric purpose of self-examination'. Some critics, however, have attempted to plot distinctly narratorial forces in the poems: Pierre Vitoux, 'Keats's Epic Design in *Hyperion*', *SiR*, 14 (1975), pp. 165–83, attempts to recreate the unfinished narrative; and Mark Edmundson, 'Keats's Mortal Stance', *SiR*, 26 (1987), p. 97, discerns the conventional plot of a 'progress from ignorance to wisdom' in 'The Fall'.

10 Gerald Prince, 'The Disnarrated', *Style*, 22 (1988), p. 2.

11 Prince, *ibid.*, p. 8, note 1, suggests, as an alternative to 'disnarrated', the term 'alternarrated', which would explicitly express this alterity.

12 Whenever we come across a Keatsian foregrounding of voice – an elaboration of the materiality of voice   we might read such moments as a kind of disnarration or, rather, a refusal of narration, a refusal of meaning. On the question of voice in 'Hyperion', see Anya Taylor, 'Superhuman Silence', pp. 673–87, and Aske, *Keats and Hellenism*, pp. 94–6.

13 See James Kissane, 'The Authorization of John Keats', p. 70: 'The Fall' is 'a parasitic engrafting upon the original, a kind of palimpsest'.

14 For studies of these alterations, see Baker, *John Keats and Symbolism*, p. 108, who argues that 'Keats' use of direct address and exposition is disastrous rather than effective'; conversely, Paul D. Sheats, in 'Stylistic Discipline in *The Fall of Hyperion*', *KSJ*, 17 (1968), pp. 85–7, argues that the structural alterations allowed Keats to reposition the theme of the birth of the poet and produce a 'disinterestedness' which would (potentially) allow a full epic development; and Robert D. Wagner, 'Keats's "Ode to Psyche" and the Second "Hyperion"', *KSJ*, 13 (1964), pp. 35–6, goes so far as to suggest that in 'The Fall' the 'dual role' of the narrator as 'engaged protagonist and redeemed narrator' allows a 'double view of reality' without which there can be 'no tangible evidence of growth, of progress beyond the immediate'; see also Muir, 'The Meaning of "Hyperion"', in *Reassessment*, pp. 114–20, who argues that 'Keats was right to print the first version. It was more likely to be acceptable to the public taste' (p. 120).

15 The logical incoherence of the distinctions (made in the Induction and in the dialogue between the narrator and Moneta later in the poem) have been widely discussed: see, for example, Bate, *John Keats*, pp. 598–600; Jones, *John Keats's Dream of Truth*, p. 99; Sperry, *Keats the Poet*, pp. 328–9; Stillinger, *The Hoodwinking of Madeline*, pp. 62–4; Brian Wicker, 'The Disputed Lines in *The Fall of Hyperion*', *Essays in Criticism*, 7 (1957), pp. 28–41; Baker, *John Keats and Symbolism*, pp. 108–16; Wolfson, *The Questioning Presence*, p. 352.

16 In fact, this is the kind of pragmatic definition of 'literature' produced by, for example, Costanzo Di Girolamo, in *A Critical Theory of Literature* (Madison, University of Wisconsin Press, 1981), p. 65.
17 On the lack of point in 'Hyperion', William C. Stephenson, 'The Performing Narrator in Keats's Poetry', *KSJ*, 26 (1977), p. 63, comments that the poem 'lacks a center of reference', a problem which 'stems partly from its undeveloped plot; the isolated fragments are not organized around a specific set of circumstances'; see Balachandra Rajan, *The Form of the Unfinished: English Poetics from Spenser to Pound* (New Jersey, Princeton University Press, 1985), p. 231, on the internal contradictions which undermine the poem.
18 'Faulture' is Keats's neologism in 'The Fall' (1, 70).
19 On Keats and framing, see Robert M. Adams '*Trompe l'Oeil* in Shakespeare and Keats', *Sewanee Review*, 61 (1953), pp. 245–6.
20 In terms of narrative level in a technical sense, this should be reduced to three levels: the Induction (extradiegetic), the poet-narrator's tale (diegetic), and the *histoire* of Hyperion (metadiegetic) (see Gérard Genette, *Narrative Discourse*, tr. Jane E. Lewin, Oxford, Basil Blackwell, 1986, pp. 228–9): but these levels are complicated by the narrator's increasing percipience, which involves other layerings of narrative.
21 Through the use of the first-person narrator, there is, of course, a strong sense of narratorial intimacy: see F. K. Stanzel, *A Theory of Narrative*, 2nd edn., tr. Charlotte Goedsche (Cambridge University Press, 1984), pp. 79–110, on the choice of first- and third-person narrators. Barnard, *John Keats*, p. 129, comments on the way in which 'The Fall' 'paradoxically attain[s] a severe impersonality through intense subjectivity'.
22 Vendler, *The Odes of John Keats*, pp. 216, 222, 224.
23 Indeed, there has been a concerted and apparently unwarranted effort by critics and editors (starting with Richard Woodhouse in his copy of Keats's draft) to exclude a number of crucial lines from the poem (1, 187–210), in which the narrator is defined as a dreamer precisely in opposition to the desire to be a poet. For the textual details of these lines, see Stillinger, *The Poems of John Keats*, p. 672.
24 Rzepka, *The Self as Mind*, p. 204.
25 *Ibid.*, pp. 203–4.

9: 'TO AUTUMN'

1 Quoted in G. S. Fraser, ed., *John Keats: Odes, A Casebook* (London, Macmillan, 1971), p. 48.
2 Bate, *John Keats*, p. 581; Aileen Ward, *John Keats: The Making of a Poet* (London, Secker and Warburg, 1963), p. 321; Bush, *John Keats: His Life and Writings*, p. 176.
3 McGann, *The Beauty of Inflections*, p. 61. See Paul H. Fry, 'History, Existence, and "To Autumn"', *SiR*, 25 (1986), pp. 211–19, for a

response to McGann's reading which argues for an understanding of the poem as concerned with 'the ontology of the lyric moment': while McGann argues that Keats suppresses history, Fry asserts its irrelevance, but both read the poem in terms of the *exclusion* of the historical.

4 Vincent Newey, '"Alternate uproar and sad peace"', p. 288. William Keach's political reading of the bees in stanza one of 'To Autumn' is, perhaps, the nearest that critics have come to a 'political' reading of the poem ('Cockney Couplets: Keats and the Politics of Style', *SiR*, 25, 1986, pp. 193–6). For recent more general considerations of Keats and politics, see Levinson, *Keats's Life of Allegory*; Paul Hamilton, 'Keats and Critique', in Marjorie Levinson *et al.*, *Rethinking Historicism: Critical Readings in Romantic History* (Oxford, Basil Blackwell, 1989); and Watkins, *Keats's Poetry and the Politics of Imagination*.

5 See Heinzelman, *The Economics of the Imagination*, for illuminating chapters on both Wordsworth and Blake in relation to the economics of writing: as Heinzelman argues, 'the tension between aesthetic and economic processes erupts whenever the artist attempts to describe the dynamics of his own labor, but the modern (i.e., post-eighteenth-century) artist has acquired a singularly pressing need to resolve that tension' (p. 156).

6 See also 'Sleep and Poetry', lines 290–93, and 'The Fall of Hyperion', 1, 467; and see *Letters*, vol. II, p. 211.

7 Vendler, *The Odes of John Keats*, p. 276.

8 See John Creaser, 'From "Autumn" to Autumn in Keats's Ode', *Essays in Criticism*, 38 (1988), pp. 190–214, for an analysis of the disruptive implications of the use of apostrophe in the poem.

9 See Jack, *Keats and the Mirror of Art*, p. 236; Annabel M. Patterson, '"How to load and … bend": Syntax and Interpretation in Keats's "To Autumn"', *PMLA*, 94 (1979), pp. 449–58; McGann, *The Beauty of Inflections*, p. 54; Vendler, *The Odes of John Keats*, ch. 7; Macksey, 'Keats and the Poetics of Extremity', pp. 875, 879; Creaser, 'From "Autumn" to Autumn', pp. 201–2; Karla Alwes, 'Moneta and Ceres: The Final Relationship Between Keats and the Imagination', *Nineteenth Century Literature*, 43 (1988), pp. 212–19.

10 In a sense it might be argued that the solecism is that of the critical tradition, in that Keats does not explicitly mention the cornucopia and it is various annotated editions of Keats's poems that gloss the line in terms of the equation of Ceres and cornucopia: see, for example, M. Robertson, ed., *Keats: Poems Published in 1820* (Oxford University Press, 1980), p. 209; Roger Sharrock, ed., *Keats: Selected Poems and Letters* (Oxford University Press, 1964), p. 212; D. G. Gillham, ed., *John Keats: Poems of 1820* (London, Collins, 1969), p. 141; Allott, ed., *The Poems of John Keats*, p. 642; Barnard, *John Keats*, p. 702 (but see Douglas Bush, ed., *John Keats: Selected Poems and Letters*, Boston, Houghton Mifflin, 1959, p. 354: 'The horn of plenty is usually associated with Amalthea').

Annotators tend to give similar glosses to 'The Fall of Hyperion', 1, 35–7, where Proserpine and 'the fabled horn' are mentioned together. The absence of any connection between Ceres and the cornucopia in the mythology or the iconography of Ceres (she is generally described as having a crown made from ears of corn and as holding a lighted torch in one hand and poppies in the other) seems to suggest that it was Keats's own invention, and one which involves a significant redescription of the figure: Ceres taught men how to work in order to gain abundance, whereas the horn of plenty simply produces abundance without the need for work. On the importance of Ceres for Keats, see Helen Vendler's comment that 'Keats's mind was never far from Ceres' (*The Odes of John Keats*, p. 234).

11 Andrew Tooke, *The Pantheon, Representing the Fabulous Histories of the Heathen Gods and Most Illustrious Heroes* (1698), 31st edn. (London, 1803), p. 162: this is only the most convenient of the formulations provided by a number of classical dictionaries available in the early nineteenth century, all of which provide similar descriptions. Significantly, Jean-Jacques Rousseau makes a very similar analysis in *A Discourse Upon the Origin and Foundation of the Inequality among Mankind* (London, 1761): 'To the tilling of the Earth the Distribution of it necessarily succeeded, and to Property once acknowledged the first Rules of Justice: for to secure every Man his own, every Man must have something... The Ancients, says *Grotius*, by giving to *Ceres* the Epithet Legislatrix, and to a Festival celebrated in her Honour the Name of *Thesmophoria*, insinuated that the Distribution of Lands produced a new kind of Right; that is, the Right of Property different from that which results from the Law of Nature' (pp. 124–6).

12 See Arnold Davenport, 'A Note on "To Autumn"', in Kenneth Muir, ed., *Reassessment*, p. 96, on autumn as a boundary season.

13 Tooke's mythological explanation of the origins of private property, agriculture, and law, should be read in the context of other eighteenth-century explanations of the origins of property, such as that of Rousseau, quoted above, note 11. For accounts of the enclosures movement in the late eighteenth and early nineteenth centuries, see W. A. Armstrong, 'Rural Population Growth, Systems of Employment and Incomes', ch. 7 in G. E. Mingay, ed., *The Agrarian History of England and Wales: Volume VI, 1750–1850* (Cambridge University Press, 1989), pp. 721–8; Raymond Williams, *The Country and the City* (London, Chatto and Windus, 1973), pp. 96–107; Michael Turner, *Enclosures in Britain, 1750–1830* (London, Macmillan, 1984); Pamela Horn, *Life and Labour in Rural England, 1760–1850* (London, Macmillan, 1987), pp. 46–51, and *The Rural World, 1780–1850: Social Change in the English Countryside* (London, Hutchinson, 1980), pp. 51–7.

14 See, for example, Bate, *John Keats*, pp. 546–7, on Keats's use of Dryden in 'Lamia'.

15 *The Twickenham Edition of the Poems of Alexander Pope*, ed. John Butt (7 vols., London, Methuen, 1961), vol. III, part 2, p. 107.

16 On the importance and significance of lines 155–78, see, for example, Earl R. Wasserman, Pope's *Epistle to Bathurst: A Critical Reading with an Edition of the Manuscripts* (Baltimore, The Johns Hopkins University Press, 1960), p. 40; and John Barrell and Harriet Guest, 'On the Use of Contradiction: Economics and Morality in the Eighteenth-Century Long Poem', in *The New Eighteenth Century: Theory, Politics, English Literature*, eds. Felicity Nussbaum and Laura Brown (New York, Methuen, 1987), p. 124.

17 See Patterson, 'Syntax and Interpretation', pp. 454–6.

18 The most recent example of this usage given by the *OED* is from a 1599 poem by the poet Alexander Hume: 'Throw all the land great is the gild / Of rustik folks that crie'.

19 See Gittings, *Manuscripts*, pp. 58–9, which shows that in the first draft Keats drew a line through 'gold' and 'gilds', and then wrote 'barred' and 'blooms' just above.

20 For examples of Clare on enclosures, see 'Helpston Green', 'The Lamentations of Round-Oak Waters', 'The Lament of Swordy Well' (esp. lines 183–91), 'The Fens' (lines 69–116), 'Remembrances' (lines 41–50): quotations from *The Oxford Authors: John Clare*, eds. Eric Robinson and David Powell (Oxford University Press, 1984). On Clare and enclosures, see John Barrell, *The Idea of Landscape and the Sense of Place, 1730–1840: An Approach to the Poetry of John Clare* (Cambridge University Press, 1972), pp. 110–20, 189–215; and Bob Heyes 'John Clare and Enclosures', *John Clare Society Journal*, 6 (1987), pp. 10–19.

21 Robert W. Malcolmson, *Life and Labour in England 1700–1780* (London, Hutchinson, 1981), pp. 34, 144, 166, note 30; see also Heyes, 'Enclosures', p. 16.

22 E. P. Thompson, *The Making of the English Working Class* (London, Victor Gollancz, 1964), p. 218. Compare Williams's comment on enclosures as 'a form of legalised seizure enacted by representatives of the beneficiary class' (*The Country and the City*, p. 98). Both comments are somewhat controversial, but have the advantage of echoing contemporary (radical) opposition to enclosures – expressed, for example, by Clare. For a more 'balanced' recent analysis of the evidence, see, for example, Armstrong, 'Rural Population Growth', pp. 721–8.

23 See my article, 'The Politics of Gleaning', pp. 34–8, in which I attempt to show, through reference to a very specific articulation of the discourse of gleaning in the early nineteenth century, the engagement of 'To Autumn' in the debate. For biblical references to gleaning and charity, see Ruth ii, 9–17; Leviticus xix, 9–10, xxiii, 22; Deuteronomy xxiv, 19–21. On the history of gleaning in the nineteenth century, see W. A. Armstrong, 'Food, Shelter and Self-Help, The Poor Law, and the Position of the Labourer in Rural Society', ch. 8 in Mingay, *Agrarian*

History, pp. 734–5; and David Hoseason Morgan, *Harvesters and Harvesting, 1840–1900: A Study of the Rural Proletariat* (London, Croom Helm, 1982), pp. 151–61.

24 See, for example, John Constable's 'The Gleaners: Brighton' (1823), Samuel Palmer's 'The Gleaning Field' (*c.*1833), Jean-François Millet's 'Des glaneuses' (1857), and Jules Breton's 'Le rappel des glaneuses (Artois)' (1859).

25 See Ivy Pinchbeck, *Women Workers and the Industrial Revolution, 1750–1850* (London, George Routledge, 1930), p. 103.

26 M. M. Bakhtin 'Discourse in the Novel', in *The Dialogic Imagination: Four Essays*, trs. Caryl Emerson and Michael Holquist (Austin, University of Texas Press, 1981), pp. 259–422; Julia Kristeva, *The Kristeva Reader*, ed. Toril Moi (London, Blackwell, 1986), p. 111; Michael Riffaterre, *Semiotics of Poetry* (Bloomington, Indiana University Press, 1978); Roland Barthes, 'Theory of the Text', in *Untying the Text: A Post-Structuralist Reader*, ed. Robert Young (London, Routledge and Kegan Paul, 1981), pp. 31–47. See Culler 'Presupposition and Intertextuality', in *The Pursuit of Signs*, pp. 169–87, on the ambivalent status of intertextual referents.

27 *Selected Prose of T. S. Eliot*, ed. Frank Kermode (London, Faber and Faber, 1975), p. 153.

28 Barthes, 'Theory of the Text', p. 39.

EPILOGUE: ALLEGORIES OF READING ('LAMIA')

1 See Keats's comments on Brown in a letter of August 1819: 'I like his society as well as any Man's, yet regretted his return – it broke in upon me like a Thunderbolt – I had got in a dream among my Books – really luxuriating in a solitude and silence' (*Letters*, vol. II, p. 138); and see Bate, *John Keats*, pp. 345–8.

2 A similar drama may be discerned behind Keats's comment of 27 October 1818, that 'I feel assured I should write from the mere yearning and fondness I have for the Beautiful even if my night's labours should be burnt every morning and no eye ever shine upon them' (*Letters*, vol. I, p. 388); McGann argues for such an analysis of the construction of subjectivity in Romantic aesthetics in *Social Values and Poetic Acts*, p. 76.

3 Richard Harter Fogle, 'Keats's *Lamia* as Dramatic Illusion', in Clyde De L. Ryals, ed., *Nineteenth-Century Literary Perspectives: Essays in Honor of Lionel Stevenson* (Durham, N.C., Duke University Press, 1974), p. 66; Garrett Stewart, '*Lamia* and the Language of Metamorphosis', *SiR*, 15 (1976), p. 3.

4 On the inevitability and the reductiveness of allegorical readings of 'Lamia', see Bernstein, 'Keats' "Lamia"', pp. 176, 190–2: 'it defies any schematic allegorical reading. "Lamia" is a lamia, but it is ... [also] a maze and a trap, a verbal web, a labyrinth, a gordian knot'; see also

Stewart, 'Language of Metamorphosis', p. 3, and Neff, 'Overdetermination and Ambiguity', pp. 139–40. These all take part in an alternative tradition of reading, in which 'Lamia' is understood to be resistant to allegory: such readings, however, tend to provide their own allegory – of textual indeterminacy or unreadability.

5 Murry, *Keats and Shakespeare*, p. 157.

6 Bush, *John Keats: His Life and Writings*, p. 161; Bate, *John Keats*, p. 557.

7 Finney, *The Evolution of Keats's Poetry*, p. 700; Fogle, 'Dramatic Illusion', p. 72 (Apollonius is the 'insensitive reader').

8 Bernice Slote, *Keats and the Dramatic Principle* (University of Nebraska Press, 1958), p. 153; Perkins, *The Quest for Permanence*, pp. 263–76; Rzepka, *The Self as Mind*, pp. 216–20.

9 Morris Dickstein, *Keats and His Poetry* (University of Chicago Press, 1974), p. 234.

10 Wolfson, *The Questioning Presence*, pp. 333–43. Bernstein, 'Keats's "Lamia"', pp. 190–91, provides a similar analysis of allegorical readings of 'Lamia' based on binary oppositions and suggests that 'They usually fall under some variation of the Apollonian-Dionysian conflict with Lycius caught between the two and Keats (according to the critics) reluctantly or wholeheartedly embracing the one side or the other' (p. 190): Bernstein suggests oppositions between poetic imagination and reality; ideal and real; fatal illusion and vital reality; visionary poet and philosopher; feeling/sensuousness and knowledge/thought; poetry and medicine.

11 Waldoff, *Keats and the Silent Work of Imagination*, p. 170; Bruce Clarke, 'Fabulous Monsters of Conscience: Anthropomorphosis in Keats's Lamia', *SiR*, 23 (1984), p. 562; Terence Allan Hoagwood, 'Keats and Social Context: Lamia', *SEL*, 29 (1989), p. 679; Levinson, *Keats's Life of Allegory*, p. 261.

12 Rzepka, *The Self as Mind*, p. 219. When 'the herd' enter the palace they enter 'marveling' because they have known 'the street... / ... from childhood all complete / Without a gap' (2, 152–4): in the same way, poetry might be understood to be constructed within the non-existent interstices of language, an opening of gaps within the homogeneous surface of the literary tradition. By creating a poem out of nothing and placing it in the public domain, the poet takes up an intertextual space which was not previously perceived. For discussions of 'Lamia' in terms of its contemporary audience, see Wolfson, *The Questioning Presence*, p. 335; Joseph C. Sitterson, 'Narrator and Reader in Lamia', *SP*, 79 (1982), pp. 304–7; Finney, *The Evolution of Keats's Poetry*, pp. 649, 667–8; Barnard, *John Keats*, p. 119. And see Kroeber, *British Romantic Art*, p. 200: Keats 'persistently returns to the difficulty dramatized as the pivotal event of "Lamia": Lycius precipitates the destructive conclusion by insisting on a public display of his infatuation with Lamia. The plot device exemplifies a spurring contradiction that troubled Keats from

early in his career. To make public the pleasure of sensory experience is to violate the privacy that is a condition of the pleasure'.

13 See, for example, Watkins, *Keats's Poetry and the Politics of Imagination*, p. 136, on these questions.

14 For a brilliant account of the rhetorical *trompe l'oeil* of this figure, see Eugenio Donato, 'The Writ of the Eye: Notes on the Relationship of Language to Vision in Critical Theory', *MLN*, 99 (1984), pp. 971–2.

15 See, for example, Stewart, 'Language of Metamorphosis', pp. 6, 10–13, and *passim*.

16 In this respect, Levinson's claim, in *Keats's Life of Allegory*, p. 291, that 'the name Lamia nowhere appears in the poem … neither Lycius nor Apollonius discovers Lamia's identity. It is *Keats* alone who names Lamia and he does so only outside the text, in the title' is incomprehensible (the name appears eighteen times in the poem, three times on the lips of Lycius himself, and the *dénouement* is usually read as the discovery by Apollonius not only of Lamia's name but also her identity): but it is certainly suggestive in terms of the name's uncanny status.

17 See Paul de Man's description of allegory in 'The Rhetoric of Temporality', in *Blindness and Insight: Essays in the Rhetoric of Contemporary Criticism*, 2nd edn. (London, Methuen, 1983), p. 207: 'allegory designates primarily a distance in relation to its own origin, and, renouncing the nostalgia and the desire to coincide, it establishes its language in the void of this temporal difference. In so doing, it prevents the self from an illusory identification with the non-self, which is now fully, though painfully, recognised as a non-self'. And we might end with a repetition of the words with which we began this study, from de Man, *Allegories of Reading*, p. 77: 'The allegory of reading narrates the impossibility of reading'.

Bibliography

Abraham, Nicolas, 'The Shell and the Kernel', *Diacritics*, 9 (1979), pp. 16–28.
'Notes on the Phantom: A Complement to Freud's Metapsychology', *Critical Inquiry*, 13 (1987), pp. 287–92.
'The Phantom of Hamlet or the Sixth Act: Preceded by the Intermission of "Truth"', *Diacritics*, 18 (1988), pp. 2–19.
Abraham, Nicolas and Maria Torok, *The Wolf Man's Magic Word: A Cryptonymy*, tr. Nicholas Rand, Minneapolis, University of Minnesota Press, 1986.
Abrams, M. H., *The Mirror and the Lamp: Romantic Theory amd the Critical Tradition* (1953), Oxford University Press, 1971.
Natural Supernaturalism: Tradition and Revolution in Romantic Literature, London, Oxford University Press, 1971.
A Glossary of Literary Terms, 4th edn., New York, Holt, Rinehart and Winston, 1981.
Adams, Robert M., '*Trompe-l'Oeil* in Shakespeare and Keats', *Sewanee Review*, 61 (1953), pp. 238–255.
Adelman, Clifford, 'The Dangers of Enthrallment', in Allan Danzig, ed., *Twentieth Century Interpretations of 'The Eve of St Agnes'*, Englewood Cliffs, Prentice-Hall, 1971.
Allott, Miriam, '"Isabella", "The Eve of St Agnes", and "Lamia"', in Muir, ed., *Reassessment*.
Altick, Richard D., *The English Common Reader: A Social History of the Mass Reading Public, 1800–1900* (1957), University of Chicago Press, 1963.
Alwes, Karla, 'Moneta and Ceres: The Final Relationship Between Keats and the Imagination', *Nineteenth Century Literature*, 43 (1988), pp. 212–19.
Armstrong, W. A., 'Rural Population Growth, Systems of Employment and Incomes' and 'Food, Shelter and Self-Help, The Poor Law, and the Position of the Labourer in Rural Society', in G. E. Mingay, ed., *The Agrarian History of England and Wales: Volume VI, 1750–1850*, Cambridge University Press, 1989.
Aske, Martin, 'Magical Spaces in "The Eve of St Agnes"', *Essays in Criticism*, 31 (1981), pp. 196–209.

Keats and Hellenism: An Essay, Cambridge University Press, 1985.

Bahti, Timothy, 'Ambiguity and Indeterminacy: The Juncture', *Comparative Literature*, 38 (1986), pp. 218–23.

Baker, Jeffrey, *John Keats and Symbolism*, Brighton, Harvester, 1986.

Bakhtin, M. M., *The Dialogic Imagination: Four Essays*, trs. Caryl Emerson and Michael Holquist, Austin, University of Texas Press, 1981.

Banfield, Ann, *Unspeakable Sentences: Narration and Representation in the Language of Fiction*, Boston, Routledge and Kegan Paul, 1982.

'Ecriture, Narration and the Grammar of French', in Jeremy Hawthorn, ed., *Narrative: From Malory to Motion Pictures*, London, Edward Arnold, 1985.

Barnard, John, *John Keats*, Cambridge University Press, 1987.

'Keats's Tactile Vision: "Ode to Psyche" and the Early Poetry', *KSMB*, 33 (1982), pp. 1–24.

Baron, Michael, 'Speaking and Writing: Wordsworth's "Fit Audience"', *English*, 32 (1983), pp. 217–50.

Barrell, John, *The Idea of Landscape and the Sense of Place, 1730–1840: An Approach to the Poetry of John Clare*, Cambridge University Press, 1972.

The Political Theory of Painting from Reynolds to Hazlitt: 'The Body of the Public', New Haven, Yale University Press, 1986.

Barrell, John and Harriet Guest, 'On the Use of Contradiction: Economics and Morality in the Eighteenth-Century Long Poem', in Felicity Nussbaum and Laura Brown, eds., *The New Eighteenth Century: Theory, Politics, English Literature*, New York, Methuen, 1987.

Barthes, Roland, *S/Z*, Paris, Seuil, 1970.

S/Z, tr. Richard Miller (1974), Oxford, Basil Blackwell, 1990.

The Pleasure of the Text, tr. Richard Miller, New York, Farrar, Strauss and Giroux, 1975.

'Theory of the Text', in Robert Young, ed., *Untying the Text: A Post-Structuralist Reader*, London, Routledge and Kegan Paul, 1981.

The Rustle of Language, tr. Richard Howard, Oxford, Basil Blackwell, 1986.

The Semiotic Challenge, tr. Richard Howard, Oxford, Basil Blackwell, 1988.

Bate, W. Jackson, *The Stylistic Development of Keats* (1945), New York, Humanities Press, 1962.

John Keats, Cambridge, Mass., Harvard University Press, 1963.

The Burden of the Past and the English Poet, London, Chatto and Windus, 1971.

Bayley, John, *The Uses of Division: Unity and Disharmony in Literature*, London, Chatto and Windus, 1976.

'The Heroine on the Urn', *SiR*, 24 (1985), pp. 551–65.

'Sexist', *London Review of Books*, 9, 22 (10 December 1987), pp. 22–3.

Beaujour, Michel, 'Some Paradoxes of Description', *Yale French Studies*, 61 (1981), pp. 27–59.

Behrendt, Stephen C., *Shelley and His Audiences*, Lincoln, University of Nebraska Press, 1989.

Bell, Arthur H., '"The Depth of Things": Keats and Human Space', *KSJ*, 23 (1974), pp. 77–94.

Belt, Debra, 'The Poetics of Hostile Response, 1575–1610', *Criticism*, 33 (1991), pp. 419–59.

Bennett, Andrew J., 'The Politics of Gleaning in Keats's "Ode to a Nightingale" and "To Autumn"', *KSJ*, 39 (1990), pp. 34–8.

'"Fragment of Castle-builder" and Keats's Use of Sexual Slang', *English Language Notes*, 28, 2 (1990), pp. 39–50.

'"Devious Feet": Wordsworth and the Scandal of Narrative Form', *ELH*, 59 (1992), pp. 145–73.

'Shelley in Posterity', in Stuart Curran and Betty T. Bennett, eds., *Shelley: Poet and Legislator of the World*, Baltimore, The Johns Hopkins University Press, forthcoming.

Benveniste, Emile, *Problems in General Linguistics* (1966), tr. Mary Elizabeth Meek, Florida, University of Miami Press, 1971.

Bernstein, Gene M., 'Keats' "Lamia": The Sense of A Non-Ending', *Papers on Language and Literature*, 15 (1979), pp. 175–192.

Berry, Francis, *Poets' Grammar: Person, Time, and Mood in Poetry*, London, Routledge and Kegan Paul, 1958.

Bewell, Alan J, 'The Political Implications of Keats's Classical Aesthetics', *SiR*, 25 (1986), pp. 220–29.

Bialostosky, Don H., *Making Tales: The Poetics of Wordsworth's Narrative Experiments*, University of Chicago Press, 1984.

Bloom, Harold, *The Ringers in the Tower: Studies in the Romance Tradition*, University of Chicago Press, 1971.

Poetry and Repression: Revisionism from Blake to Stevens, New Haven, Yale University Press, 1976.

Briggs, Harold E., 'Keats's Conscious and Unconscious Reactions to Criticism of *Endymion*', *PMLA*, 60 (1945), pp. 1106–29.

Bromwich, David, 'Keats's Radicalism', *SiR*, 25 (1986), pp. 197–210.

ed., *Romantic Critical Essays*, Cambridge University Press, 1987.

Bronson, Bertrand Harris, *Facets of the Enlightenment: Studies in English Literature and Its Contexts*, Berkeley, University of California Press, 1968.

Brooks, Cleanth, *The Well Wrought Urn: Studies in the Structure of Poetry* (1949), London, Methuen, 1968.

Brooks, Peter, *Reading for the Plot: Design and Intention in Narrative*, Oxford University Press, 1984.

Bundy, Murray W., '"Invention" and "Imagination" in the Renaissance', *JEGP*, 29 (1930), pp. 535–45.

Burgess, C. F., '"The Eve of St Agnes": One Way to the Poem', *English Journal*, 54 (1965), pp. 389–94.

Burke, Edmund, *A Philosophical Enquiry into the Origin of Our Ideas of the Sublime and Beautiful*, ed. J. T. Boulton, London, Routledge and Kegan Paul, 1958.

Bush, Douglas, 'Keats and His Ideas', in M. H. Abrams, ed., *English*

234　　　　　　　　　　　　　*Bibliography*

   Romantic Poets: Modern Essays in Criticism, New York, Oxford University Press, 1960.
   John Keats: His Life and Writings, London, Weidenfeld and Nicolson, 1966.
Butler, Marilyn, *Peacock Displayed: A Satirist in His Context*, London, Routledge and Kegan Paul, 1979.
   Romantics, Rebels, and Reactionaries: English Literature and its Background, 1760–1830, Oxford University Press, 1981.
Byron, George Gordon, *Lord Byron: The Complete Poetical Works*, ed. Jerome J. McCann, 7 vols., Oxford University Press, 1980–1993.
Camaiora, Luisa Conti, '"Idle Fever" and "Diligent Indolence": Opposing Principles in Keats', *Rivista di Letteratura Moderne e Comparate*, 28 (1975), pp. 165–84.
Cameron, Sharon, *Lyric Time: Dickinson and the Limits of Genre*, Baltimore, The Johns Hopkins University Press, 1979.
Cantor, Paul A., *Creature and Creator: Myth-Making and English Romanticism*, Cambridge University Press, 1984.
Chambers, Ross, 'Narrative Point', *Southern Review*, 16 (1983), pp. 60–73.
   Story and Situation: Narrative Seduction and the Power of Fiction, Manchester, Manchester University Press, 1984.
Chatman, Seymour, *Story and Discourse: Narrative Structure in Fiction and Film*, Ithaca, Cornell University Press, 1978.
   'On Deconstructing Narratology', *Style*, 22 (1988), pp. 9–17.
   'What Can We Learn From Contextualist Narratology', *Poetics Today*, 11 (1990), pp. 309–28.
Chilcott, Tim, *A Publisher and His Circle: The Life and Work of John Taylor, Keats's Publisher*, London, Routledge and Kegan Paul, 1972.
Clare, John, *The Oxford Authors: John Clare*, eds. Eric Robinson and David Powell, Oxford University Press, 1984.
Clark, Timothy, *Derrida, Heidegger, Blanchot: Sources of Derrida's Notion and Practice of Literature*, Cambridge University Press, 1992.
Clarke, Bruce, 'Fabulous Monsters of Conscience: Anthropomorphosis in Keats's Lamia', *SiR*, 23 (1984), pp. 555–79.
Clayton, Jay, *Romantic Vision and the Novel*, Cambridge University Press, 1987.
Coleridge, Samuel Taylor, *The Friend*, ed. Barbara E. Rooke, 2 vols., New Jersey, Princeton University Press, 1969.
   Lectures 1808–1819 on Literature, ed. R. A. Foakes, 2 vols., London, Routledge and Kegan Paul, 1987.
   Samuel Taylor Coleridge, Biographia Literaria, eds. W. Jackson Bate and James Engell, 2 vols., London, Routledge and Kegan Paul, 1983.
   Collected Letters of Samuel Taylor Coleridge, 6 vols., ed. Earl Leslie Griggs, Oxford University Press, 1956–71.
   The Notebooks of Samuel Taylor Coleridge, 6 vols. to date, ed. Kathleen Coburn, London, Routledge and Kegan Paul, 1957– .

Collins, A. S., *The Profession of Letters: A Study of the Relation of Author to Patron, Publisher, and Public, 1780–1832*, London, Routledge, 1928.

Coser, Lewis A., *Men of Ideas: A Sociologist's View* (1965), New York, The Free Press, 1970.

Creaser, John, 'From "Autumn" to Autumn in Keats's Ode', *Essays in Criticism*, 38 (1988), pp. 190–214.

Cronin, Richard, *Colour and Experience in Nineteenth-Century Poetry*, London, Macmillan, 1988.

Cross, Nigel, *The Common Writer: Life in Nineteenth-Century Grub Street*, Cambridge University Press, 1985.

Cruse, Amy, *The Englishman and His Books in the Early Nineteenth Century*, London, Harrap, 1930.

Culler, Jonathan, *The Pursuit of Signs: Semiotics, Literature, Deconstruction*, London, Routledge and Kegan Paul, 1981.

'The Identity of the Literary Text', in Mario J. Valdés and Owen Miller, eds., *Identity of the Literary Text*, University of Toronto Press, 1985.

'Changes in the Study of the Lyric', in Hošek and Parker, eds., *Lyric Poetry*.

ed., *On Puns: The Foundation of Letters*, Oxford, Basil Blackwell, 1988.

Curran, Stuart, *Poetic Form and British Romanticism*, New York, Oxford University Press, 1986.

Dällenbach, Lucien, 'Reflexivity and Reading', *NLH*, 11 (1980), pp. 435–449.

The Mirror in the Text, tr. Jeremy Whiteley, Cambridge, Polity, 1989.

D'Avanzo, Mario L., *Keats's Metaphors for the Poetic Imagination*, Durham, N. C., Duke University Press, 1967.

Davenport, Arnold, 'A Note on "To Autumn"', in Kenneth Muir, ed., *John Keats: A Reassessment*.

de Almeida, Hermione, ed., *Critical Essays on John Keats*, Boston, G. K. Hall, 1990.

de Bolla, Peter, *The Discourse of the Sublime: Readings in History, Aesthetics and the Subject*, Oxford, Basil Blackwell, 1989.

de Man, Paul, 'Keats and Hölderlin', *Comparative Literature*, 8 (1956), pp. 28–45.

Blindness and Insight: Essays in the Rhetoric of Contemporary Criticism, 2nd edn., London, Methuen, 1983.

Allegories of Reading: Figural Language in Rousseau, Nietzsche, Rilke, and Proust, New Haven, Yale University Press, 1979.

'Hypogram and Inscription: Michael Riffaterre's Poetics of Reading', *Diacritics*, 11, 4 (1981), pp. 17–35.

The Resistance to Theory, Manchester University Press, 1986.

'Lyrical Voice in Contemporary Theory: Riffaterre and Jauss', in Hošek and Parker, eds., *Lyric Poetry*.

Derrida, Jacques, *Margins of Philosophy*, tr. Alan Bass, Brighton, Harvester, 1982.

'Foreword: *Fors*: The Anglish Words of Nicolas Abraham and Maria Torok', in Abraham and Torok, *The Wolf Man's Magic Word*.

The Post Card: From Socrates to Freud and Beyond, tr. Alan Bass, University of Chicago Press, 1987.

Mémoires for Paul de Man, revised edn., New York, Columbia University Press, 1989.

'Telepathy', tr. Nicholas Royle, *The Oxford Literary Review*, 10 (1988), pp. 3–41.

Acts of Literature, ed. Derek Attridge, New York, Routledge, 1992.

Devlin, D. D., *Wordsworth and the Poetry of Epitaphs*, London, Macmillan, 1980.

Dickstein, Morris, *Keats and His Poetry: A Study in Development* (1971), University of Chicago Press, 1974.

'Keats and Politics', *SiR*, 25 (1986), pp. 175–81.

Dodd, William Nigel, 'Keats's "Ode to a Nightingale" and "On a Grecian Urn"[*sic*]: Two Principles of Organization', *Lingua e Stile*, 6 (1971), pp. 241–61.

Dodsley, Robert, *An Essay on Fable* (1764), Los Angeles, William Andrews Clark Memorial Library, 1965.

Donato, Eugenio, 'The Writ of the Eye: Notes on the Relationship of Language to Vision in Critical Theory', *MLN*, 99 (1984), pp. 959–78.

Draper, John W., 'The Metrical Tale in XVIII-Century England', *PMLA*, 52 (1937), pp. 390–97.

Easson, Angus, 'Statesman, Dwarf and Weaver: Wordsworth and Nineteenth-Century Narrative', in Jeremy Hawthorn, ed., *The Nineteenth-Century British Novel*, London, Edward Arnold, 1986.

Eaves, Morris, 'Romantic Expressive Theory and Blake's Idea of the Audience', *PMLA*, 95 (1980), pp. 784–801.

Edmundson, Mark, 'Keats's Mortal Stance', *SiR*, 26 (1987), pp. 85–104.

Ehrenpreis, Anne Henry, ed., *The Literary Ballad*, London, Edward Thomas, 1966.

Eisenstein, Elizabeth L., *The Printing Press as an Agent of Change: Communications and Cultural Transformations in Early-Modern Europe*, 2 vols., Cambridge University Press, 1979.

Eliot, T. S., *Selected Prose of T. S. Eliot*, ed. Frank Kermode, London, Faber and Faber, 1975.

Empson, William, *The Structure of Complex Words* (1951), London, Hogarth, 1985.

Ende, Stuart A., *Keats and the Sublime*, New Haven, Yale University Press, 1976.

Erickson, Lee, 'The Poets' Corner: The Impact of Technological Changes in Printing on English Poetry, 1800–1850', *ELH*, 52 (1985), pp. 893–911.

Robert Browning: His Poetry and His Audiences, Ithaca, Cornell University Press, 1984.

Feather, John, *A History of British Publishing*, London, Croom Helm, 1988.

Ferguson, Frances, *Wordsworth: Language as Counter-Spirit*, New Haven, Yale University Press, 1977.

Fields, Beverly, 'Keats and the Tongueless Nightingale: Some Unheard Melodies in "The Eve of St Agnes"', *The Wordsworth Circle*, 14 (1983), pp. 246–50.

Finch, G. J., 'Wordsworth, Keats, and "the language of the sense"', *Ariel*, 11, 2 (1980), pp. 23–36.

Fineman, J., 'Shakespeare's "Perjur'd Eye"', *Representations*, 7 (1984), pp. 59–86.

Finney, Claude Lee, *The Evolution of Keats's Poetry*, 2 vols., Cambridge, Mass., Harvard University Press, 1936.

Fischer, Hermann, 'Metre and Narrative Rhetoric in Byron', *The Byron Journal*, 10 (1982), pp. 38–53.

Romantic Verse Narrative: The History of a Genre (1964), tr. Sue Bollans, Cambridge University Press, 1991.

Fisher, Philip, 'A Museum with One Work Inside: Keats's "Ode on a Grecian Urn" and the Finality of Art', in J. H. Smith, ed., *Brandeis Essays in Literature*, Waltham, Mass., Department of English and American Literature, Brandeis University, 1983.

Fogle, Richard Harter, 'A Reading of Keats's "The Eve of St Agnes"', *College English*, 6 (1945), pp. 325–28.

'Keats's *Ode to a Nightingale*', *PMLA*, 68 (1953), pp. 211–22.

'Keats's *Lamia* as Dramatic Illusion', in Clyde De L. Ryals, ed., *Nineteenth-Century Literary Perspectives: Essays in Honor of Lionel Stevenson*, Durham, N.C., Duke University Press, 1974.

Forster, E. M., *Aspects of the Novel* (1927), Harmondsworth, Penguin, 1982.

Foscolo, Ugo, 'Narrative and Romantic Poems of the Italians', *Quarterly Review*, 21 (1819), pp. 486–556.

Fraser, G. S., ed., *John Keats: Odes, A Casebook*, London, Macmillan, 1971.

Freud, Sigmund, *The Standard Edition of the Complete Psychological Works of Sigmund Freud*, trs. James Strachey *et al.*, 24 vols. (1955), London, Hogarth, 1981.

Fried, Michael, *Absorption and Theatricality: Painting and Beholder in the Age of Diderot*, Berkeley, University of California Press, 1980.

Courbet's Realism, University of Chicago Press, 1990.

Friedman, Albert B., *The Ballad Revival: Studies in the Influence of Popular on Sophisticated Poetry*, University of Chicago Press, 1961.

Fry, Paul H., 'History, Existence, and "To Autumn"', *SiR*, 25 (1986), pp. 211–19.

Frye, Northrop, *Anatomy of Criticism: Four Essays* (1957), New Jersey, Princeton University Press, 1973.

Gelley, Alexander, *Narrative Crossings: Theory and Pragmatics of Prose Fiction*, Baltimore, The Johns Hopkins University Press, 1987.

Genette, Gérard, *Figures II: Essais*, Paris, Seuil, 1969.

'Boundaries of Narrative', *NLH*, 8 (1976), pp. 1–13.

Narrative Discourse, tr. Jane E. Lewin (1980), Oxford, Basil Blackwell, 1986.

Girolamo, Costanzo Di, *A Critical Theory of Literature*, Madison, University of Wisconsin Press, 1981.

Gittings, Robert, *John Keats: The Living Year* (1954), London, Heinemann, 1978.

The Keats Inheritance, London, Heinemann, 1964.

John Keats (1968), Harmondsworth, Penguin, 1985.

Godfrey, Clarice, '"Endymion"', in Muir, ed., *Reassessment*.

Goellnicht, Donald C., 'Keats on Reading: "Delicious Diligent Indolence"', *JEGP*, 88 (1989), pp. 190–210.

Goodman, Paul, *The Structure of Literature*, University of Chicago Press, 1954.

Gradman, Barry, *Metamorphosis in Keats*, Brighton, Harvester, 1980.

Greenblatt, Steven, *Shakespearean Negotiations: The Circulation of Social Energy in Renaissance England*, Oxford University Press, 1988.

Hagstrum, Jean H., *The Romantic Body: Love and Sexuality in Keats, Wordsworth, and Blake*, Knoxville, University of Tennessee Press, 1985.

Halévy, Eric, *England in 1815* (1913), 2nd edn., trs. E. I. Watkin and D. A. Barker, London, Ernest Benn, 1949.

Hamilton, Paul, 'Keats and Critique', in Marjorie Levinson *et al.*, *Rethinking Historicism: Critical Readings in Romantic History*, Oxford, Basil Blackwell, 1989.

Hamon, Philippe, 'Rhetorical Status of the Descriptive', *Yale French Studies*, 61 (1981), pp. 1–26.

'What is a Description?', in Tzvetan Todorov, ed., *French Literary Theory Today: A Reader*, Cambridge University Press, 1982.

Harding, Anthony John, 'Speech, Silence, and the Self-Doubting Interpreter in Keats's Poetry', *KSJ*, 35 (1986), pp. 83–103.

Hartman, Geoffrey H., *The Fate of Reading and Other Essays*, University of Chicago Press, 1975.

'Reading Aright: Keats's "Ode to Psyche"', in Eleanor Cook, *et al.*, eds., *Centre and Labyrinth: Essays in Honour of Northrop Frye*, University of Toronto Press, 1983.

Haworth, Helen E., 'Keats and the Metaphor of Vision', *JEGP*, 67 (1968), pp. 371–94.

Hayden, John O., *The Romantic Reviewers: 1802–24*, London, Routledge and Kegan Paul, 1969.

Haydon, Benjamin Robert, 'On the Cartoon of the Sacrifice at Lystra', *Annals of the Fine Arts*, 4, 13 (1820), pp. 226–47.

Hazlitt, William, *The Complete Works of William Hazlitt*, ed. P. P. Howe, 21 vols., London, Dent, 1932.

Heffernan, James A. W., 'Ekphrasis and Representation', *NLH*, 22 (1991), pp. 297–316.

Heinen, Hubert, 'Interwoven Time in Keats's Poetry', *Texas Studies in Literature and Language*, 3 (1961), pp. 382–8.

Heinzelman, Kurt, *The Economics of the Imagination*, Amherst, University of Massachusetts Press, 1980.

'Self-interest and the Politics of Composition in Keats's *Isabella*', *ELH*, 55 (1988), pp. 159–93.

Heyes, Bob, 'John Clare and Enclosures', *John Clare Society Journal*, 6 (1987), pp. 10–19.

Hill, John Spencer, ed., *Keats: The Narrative Poems*, London, Macmillan, 1983.

Hinden, Michael, 'Reading the Painting, Seeing the Poem: Vermeer and Keats', *Mosaic*, 17 (1984), pp. 17–34.

Hoagwood, Terence Allan, 'Keats and Social Context: *Lamia*', *SEL*, 29 (1989), pp. 675–97.

Homans, Margaret, 'Keats Reading Women, Women Reading Keats', *SiR*, 29 (1990), pp. 341–70.

Hopkins, Brooke, 'Keats and the Uncanny: "This living hand"', *The Kenyon Review*, n.s., 11, 4 (1989), pp. 28–40.

Horn, Pamela, *Life and Labour in Rural England, 1760–1850*, London, Macmillan, 1987.

The Rural World, 1780–1850: Social Change in the English Countryside, London, Hutchinson, 1980.

Hošek, Chaviva and Patricia Parker, eds., *Lyric Poetry: Beyond New Criticism*, Ithaca, Cornell University Press, 1985.

Hungerford, Edward B., *Shores of Darkness*, New York, Columbia University Press, 1941.

Hunt, Leigh, *The Story of Rimini*, London, 1816.

ed., *Classic Tales, Serious and Lively, with Critical Essays on the Merits and Reputations of the Authors*, 2 vols., London, 1807.

ed., *The Indicator*, 2 vols., London, 1820.

Iser, Wolfgang, *The Act of Reading: A Theory of Aesthetic Response*, Baltimore, The Johns Hopkins University Press, 1978.

Jack, Ian, *Keats and the Mirror of Art*, Oxford University Press, 1967.

The Poet and His Audience, Cambridge University Press, 1984.

Jackson, Geoffrey, 'Nominal and Actual Audiences: Some Strategies of Communication in Wordsworth's Poetry', *The Wordsworth Circle*, 12 (1981), pp. 226–31.

Jackson, J. R. de J., ed., *Coleridge: The Critical Heritage*, London, Routledge and Kegan Paul, 1970.

Jamieson, Robert, ed., *Popular Ballads and Songs*, 2 vols., Edinburgh, 1806.

Johnson, Samuel, *A Dictionary of the English Language*, 2 vols. (1755), New York, Ams Press, 1967.

Rasselas, Poems, and Selected Prose (1952), ed. Bertrand H. Bronson, 3rd edn., New York, Holt Rinehart and Winston, 1971.

Jones, John, *John Keats's Dream of Truth* (1969), London, Chatto and Windus, 1980.

Keach, William, 'Cockney Couplets: Keats and the Politics of Style', *SiR*, 25 (1986), pp. 182–96.

Keats, John, *The Poems of John Keats*, ed. Ernest de Sélincourt (1905), 7th edn., London, Methuen, 1951.

Keats: Poems Published in 1820, ed. M. Robertson (1909), Oxford University Press, 1980.

The Letters of John Keats: 1814–1821, 2 vols., ed. Hyder Edward Rollins, Cambridge, Mass., Harvard University Press, 1958.

John Keats: Selected Poems and Letters, ed. Douglas Bush, Boston, Houghton Mifflin, 1959.

Keats: Selected Poems and Letters, ed. Roger Sharrock, Oxford University Press, 1964.

Selected Poetry, ed. Paul de Man, New York, The New American Library, 1966.

John Keats: Poems of 1820, ed. D. G. Gillham, London, Collins, 1969.

The Poems of John Keats, ed. Miriam Allott, London, Longman, 1970.

The Odes of Keats and Their Earliest Known Manuscripts in Facsimile, ed. Robert Gittings, London, Heinemann, 1970.

Letters of John Keats, ed. Robert Gittings, Oxford University Press, 1970.

John Keats: The Complete Poems, 2nd edn., ed. John Barnard, Harmondsworth, Penguin, 1980.

The Poems of John Keats, ed. Jack Stillinger, London, Heinemann, 1978.

Kelley, Theresa M., 'Poetics and the Politics of Reception: Keats's "La Belle Dame sans Merci"', *ELH*, 54 (1987), pp. 333–62.

Kellman, Stephen, *Loving Reading: Erotics of the Text*, Hamden, Conn., The Shoe String Press-Archon Books, 1985.

Kermode, Frank, *Essays on Fiction*, London, Routledge and Kegan Paul, 1983.

Kernan, Alvin, *Printing, Technology, Letters and Samuel Johnson*, New Jersey, Princeton University Press, 1987.

Kerrigan, John, 'Keats and *Lucrece*', *Shakespeare Survey*, 41 (1989), pp. 103–18.

Kissane, James, 'The Authorization of John Keats', *KSJ*, 37 (1988), pp. 58–74.

Klancher, Jon P., *The Making of English Reading Audiences, 1790–1832*, Madison, University of Wisconsin Press, 1987.

Knight, Richard Payne, *An Analytical Inquiry into the Principles of Taste*, 4th edn., London, 1808.

Krieger, Murray, *The Play and Place of Criticism*, Baltimore, The Johns Hopkins University Press, 1967.

Kristeva, Julia, *The Kristeva Reader*, ed. Toril Moi, London, Blackwell, 1986.

Kroeber, Karl, *Romantic Narrative Art* (1960), Madison, University of Wisconsin Press, 1966.

'Trends in Minor Romantic Narrative Poetry', in James V. Logan, *et al.*, eds., *Some British Romantics: A Collection of Essays*, Ohio State University Press, 1966.

British Romantic Art, Berkeley, University of California Press, 1986.

Labov, William, *Language in the Inner City: Studies in the Black English Vernacular*, Oxford, Basil Blackwell, 1972.

Lamb, Charles, *The Letters of Charles and Mary Lamb*, ed. Edwin W. Marrs, 3 vols., Ithaca, Cornell University Press, 1975.

Lamb as Critic, ed. Roy Park, London, Routledge and Kegan Paul, 1980.

Le Comte, Edward S., *Endymion in England: The Literary History of a Greek Myth*, New York, Columbia University Press, 1944.

Lemprière, John, *A Classical Dictionary* (1788), 8th edn., London, 1812.

Leoff, Eve, *A Study of John Keats's Isabella*, Universität Salzburg, 1972.

Levinson, Marjorie, *The Romantic Fragment Poem: A Critique of a Form*, Chapel Hill, University of North Carolina Press, 1986.

Keats's Life of Allegory: The Origins of a Style, Oxford, Basil Blackwell, 1988.

Lévi-Strauss, Claude, *The Elementary Structures of Kinship*, revised edn., trs. James Harle Bell and John Richard von Sturmer, Boston, Beacon, 1969.

Leyda, Seraphia D., 'The Structure of Keats's "I stood tip-toe upon a little hill"', in M. L. Johnson and S. D. Leyda, eds., *Reconciliations: Studies in Honor of Richard Harter Fogle*, Universität Salzburg, 1983.

Lindley, David, *Lyric*, London, Methuen, 1985.

Lipking, Lawrence, *The Life of the Poet: Beginning and Ending Poetic Careers*, University of Chicago Press, 1981.

Little, Judy, *Keats as a Narrative Poet: A Test of Invention*, Lincoln, University of Nebraska Press, 1975.

Liu, Alan, *Wordsworth and the Sense of History*, Stanford University Press, 1989.

Lovell, Terry, *Consuming Fiction*, London, Verso, 1987.

Lyotard, Jean-François, *The Différend: Phrases in Dispute*, tr. G. Van den Abbeele, Minneapolis, University of Minnesota Press, 1988.

The Lyotard Reader, ed. Andrew Benjamin, Oxford, Basil Blackwell, 1989.

Lyotard, Jean-François and Jean-Loup Thébaud, *Just Gaming*, tr. Wlad Godzich, Manchester University Press, 1985.

McGann, Jerome J., *The Romantic Ideology: A Critical Investigation*, University of Chicago Press, 1983.

The Beauty of Inflections: Literary Investigations in Historical Method and Theory, Oxford University Press, 1985.

Social Values and Poetic Acts: The Historical Judgment of Literary Work, Cambridge, Mass., Harvard University Press, 1988.

MacGillivray, J. R., Letter to the *Times Literary Supplement* (July 1938), pp. 465–6.

McKendrick, Neil, John Brewer and J. H. Plumb, *The Birth of a Consumer Society: The Commercialization of Eighteenth-Century England*, London, Europa Publications, 1982.

McKeon, Michael, *The Origins of the English Novel: 1600–1740*, Baltimore, The Johns Hopkins University Press, 1987.

Macksey, Richard, 'Keats and the Poetics of Extremity', *MLN*, 99 (1984), pp. 845–84.

Maclean, Marie, *Narrative as Performance: The Baudelairean Experiment*, London, Routledge, 1988.

Maclean, Norman, 'From Action to Image: Theories of the Lyric in the Eighteenth Century', in R. S. Crane, ed., *Critics and Criticism: Ancient and Modern*, University of Chicago Press, 1952.

Malcolmson, Robert W., *Life and Labour in England 1700–1780*, London, Hutchinson, 1981.

Mangin, Edward, *An Essay on Light Reading, As it May be Supposed to Influence Moral Conduct and Literary Taste*, London, 1808.

Mann, Paul, 'Apocalypse and Recuperation: Blake and the Maw of Commerce', *ELH*, 52 (1985), pp. 5–10.

Marston, John, *The Fawn*, ed. Gerald A. Smith, London, Edward Arnold, 1965.

Martin, Philip W., *Byron: A Poet Before His Public*, Cambridge University Press, 1982.

Martin, Wallace, *Recent Theories of Narrative*, Ithaca, Cornell University Press, 1986.

Matthews, G. M., ed. *Keats: The Critical Heritage*, London, Routledge and Kegan Paul, 1971.

Matthey, François, *The Evolution of Keats's Structural Imagery*, Berne, Francke, 1974.

Meisenhelder, Susan Edwards, *Wordsworth's Informed Reader: Structures of Experience in His Poetry*, Nashville, Vanderbilt University Press, 1988.

Mermin, Dorothy, *The Audience in the Poem: Five Victorian Poets*, New Brunswick, Rutgers University Press, 1983.

Metzger, Lore, *One Foot in Eden: Modes of Pastoral in Romantic Poetry*, Chapel Hill, University of North Carolina Press, 1986.

Mill, John Stuart, *Essays on Poetry*, ed. F. Parvin Sharpless, Columbia, University of South Carolina Press, 1976.

Miller, D. A., *Narrative and Its Discontents: Problems of Closure in the Traditional Novel*, New Jersey, Princeton University Press, 1981.

Milton, John, *The Poems of John Milton*, eds. John Carey and Alastair Fowler, London, Longman, 1968.

Morgan, David Hoseason, *Harvesters and Harvesting, 1840–1900: A Study of the Rural Proletariat*, London, Croom Helm, 1982.

Moses, Henry, *A Collection of Antique Vases, Altars, Paterae, Tripods, Candelabra, Sarcophagi, [etc]*, London, 1814.

Muir, Kenneth, ed., *John Keats: A Reassessment*, Liverpool University Press, 1958.

Mulvey, Laura, 'Visual Pleasure and Narrative Cinema', *Screen*, 16, 3 (1975), pp. 6–18.

Munday, Michael, 'The Novel and its Critics in the Early Nineteenth Century', *SP*, 79 (1982), pp. 205–26.

Murray, Hugh, *Morality of Fiction; or, an Inquiry into the Tendency of Fictitious Narratives, with Observations on Some of the most Eminent*, Edinburgh, 1805.

Murry, John Middleton, *Keats and Shakespeare*, London, Oxford University Press, 1926.

Keats (1930), London, Jonathan Cape, 1955.

Nabholtz, John R., '*My Reader, My Fellow Labourer*': *A Study of English Romantic Prose*, Columbia, University of Missouri Press, 1986.

Neff, D. S., 'Overdetermination and Ambiguity: Narrative Strategies in Keats's *Lamia*', *Research Studies*, 52 (1983), pp. 138–45.

Nellist, Brian, 'Shelley's Narratives and "The Witch of Atlas"', in Miriam Allott, ed., *Essays on Shelley*, Liverpool University Press, 1982.

Nelson, Beth, *George Crabbe and the Progress of Eighteenth-Century Narrative Verse*, Lewisburg, Bucknell University Press, 1976.

Newbery, John, *The Art of Poetry on a New Plan*, 2 vols., London, 1762.

Newey, Vincent, '"Alternate uproar and sad peace": Keats, Politics, and the Idea of Revolution', *The Yearbook of English Studies*, 19 (1989).

Newman, Beth, 'Narratives of Seduction and the Seductions of Narrative: The Frame Structure of *Frankenstein*', *ELH*, 53 (1986), pp. 141–63.

Nystrand, Martin, *The Structure of Written Communication: Studies in Reciprocity Between Writers and Readers*, New York, Academic Press, 1986.

ed., *What Writers Know: The Language, Process, and Structure of Written Discourse*, New York, Academic Press, 1982.

O'Reid, John Charles, [Josiah Conder], *Reviewers Reviewed: Including an Enquiry into the Moral and Intellectual Effects of Habits of Criticism*, Oxford, 1811.

O'Rourke, James, 'Persona and Voice in "Ode on a Grecian Urn"', *SiR*, 26 (1987), pp. 27–48.

Owen, W. J. B., *Wordsworth as Critic*, University of Toronto Press, 1969.

Parker, Patricia A., *Inescapable Romance: Studies in the Poetics of a Mode*, New Jersey, Princeton University Press, 1979.

'Dilation and Delay: Renaissance Matrices', *Poetics Today*, 5 (1984), pp. 519–35.

'Shakespeare and Rhetoric: "Dilation" and "Delation" in *Othello*', in Patricia Parker and Geoffrey Hartman, eds., *Shakespeare and the Question of Theory*, New York, Methuen, 1985.

Parrinder, Patrick, *Authors and Authority: A Study of English Literary Criticism and its Relation to Culture, 1750–1900*, London, Routledge and Kegan Paul, 1977.

Partridge, Eric, *A Dictionary of Slang and Unconventional English*, 8th edn., ed. Paul Beale, London, Routledge, 1984.

Patterson, Annabel M., '"How to load and...bend": Syntax and Interpretation in Keats's To Autumn', *PMLA*, 94 (1979), pp. 449–58.

Patterson, Charles I., 'The Monomyth in the Structure of Keats's *Endymion*', *KSJ*, 31 (1982), pp. 64–81.

Pavel, Thomas G., *The Poetics of Plot: The Case of English Renaissance Drama*, Manchester University Press, 1985.

Peacock, Thomas Love, *Memoirs of Shelley and Other Essays and Reviews*, ed. Howard Mills, London, Rupert Hart-Davis, 1970.

Pearsall, D. A., 'Introduction', in Pearsall, ed., *The Floure and the Leafe and the Assembly of Ladies*, London, Thomas Nelson, 1962.

Perkins, David, *The Quest for Permanence: The Symbolism of Wordsworth, Shelley and Keats*, Cambridge, Mass., Harvard University Press, 1959.

Wordsworth and the Poetry of Sincerity, Cambridge, Mass., Harvard University Press, 1964.

Peterfreund, Stuart, 'The Truth about "Beauty" and "Truth": Keats's "Ode on a Grecian Urn"', Milton, Shakespeare, and the Uses of Paradox', *KSJ*, 35 (1986), pp. 62–82.

Phinney, A. W., 'Keats in the Museum: Between Aesthetics and History', *JEGP*, 90 (1991), pp. 208–29.

Pinchbeck, Ivy, *Women Workers and the Industrial Revolution*, 1750–1850, London, George Routledge, 1930.

Pope, Alexander, *The Twickenham Edition of the Poems of Alexander Pope*, ed. John Butt, 7 vols. (1951), London, Methuen, 1961.

Epistle to Bathurst: A Critical Reading with an Edition of the Manuscripts, ed. Earl R. Wasserman, Baltimore, The Johns Hopkins University Press, 1960.

Porter, Roy, *English Society in the Eighteenth Century*, 2nd ed., Harmondsworth, Penguin, 1990.

Potter, R., *An Inquiry into some Passages in Dr Johnson's 'Lives of the Poets'*, London, 1783.

Prendergast, Christopher, *The Order of Mimesis: Balzac, Stendhal, Nerval, Flaubert*, Cambridge University Press, 1986.

Price, Martin, *Forms of Life: Character and Moral Imagination in the Novel*, New Haven, Yale University Press, 1983.

Prince, Gerald, 'Notes on the Text as Reader', in Suleiman and Crosman, eds., *The Reader in the Text*.

Narratology: The Form and Functioning of Narrative, Berlin, Mouton, 1982.

'Introduction to the Study of the Narratee', in Jane P. Tompkins, ed., *Reader-Response Criticism*.

'Narrative Pragmatics, Message, and Point', *Poetics*, 12 (1983), pp. 527–36.

'The Disnarrated', *Style*, 22 (1988), pp. 1–8.

Proctor, B. W. [Barry Cornwall], *A Sicilian Story with Diego De Mantilla, and Other Poems*, London, 1820.

Proust, Marcel, *On Reading*, trs. Jean Autret and William Burford, London, Souvenir Press, 1972.

Rabinowitz, Peter J., *Before Reading: Narrative Conventions and the Politics of Interpretation*, Ithaca, Cornell University Press, 1987.

Ragussis, Michael, 'Narrative Structure and the Problem of the Divided Reader in *The Eve of St Agnes*', *ELH*, 42 (1975), pp. 378–94.

The Subterfuge of Art: Language and the Romantic Tradition, Baltimore, The Johns Hopkins University Press, 1978.

Railo, Eino, *The Haunted Castle: A Study of the Elements of English Romanticism*, London, George Routledge, 1927.

Rajan, Balachandra, *The Form of the Unfinished: English Poetics from Spenser to Pound*, New Jersey, Princeton University Press, 1985.

Rajan, Tilottama, *Dark Interpreter: The Discourse of Romanticism*, Ithaca, Cornell University Press, 1980.

'Romanticism and the Death of Lyric Consciousness', in Hošek and Parker, eds., *Lyric Poetry*.

The Supplement of Reading: Figures of Understanding in Romantic Theory and Practice, Ithaca, Cornell University Press, 1990.

'The Erasure of Narrative in Post-Structuralist Representations of Wordsworth', in Kenneth R. Johnston *et al.*, eds., *Romantic Revolutions: Criticism and Theory*, Bloomington, Indiana University Press, 1990.

Rashkin, Esther, 'Tools for a New Psychoanalytic Literary Criticism: The Work of Abraham and Torok', *Diacritics*, 18 (1988), pp. 31–52.

Reid, Ian, 'Prospero Meets Adam Smith: Narrative Exchange and Control in *The Prelude*', *Textual Practice*, 1 (1987), pp. 169–91.

Reiman, Donald H., ed., *The Romantics Reviewed: Contemporary Reviews of British Romantic Writers*, 9 vols., New York, Garland Publishing, 1972.

Review of *Patronage, A Poem* (anon.), *The London Magazine* (Baldwin's), 2, 12 (December 1820), p. 628.

Reynolds, John Hamilton, *The Garden of Florence and Other Poems*, London, 1821.

Ricardou, Jean, 'Belligérance du texte', in Claudine Gothot-Mersch, ed., *La production du sens chez Flaubert*, Paris, Union Générale d'Editions, 1975.

Ricks, Christopher, *Keats and Embarrassment* (1974), Oxford University Press, 1976.

Ricoeur, Paul, *Time and Narrative*, trs. Kathleen McLaughlin and David Pellauer, 3 vols., University of Chicago Press, 1984–88.

Ridley, M. R., *Keats' Craftsmanship: A Study in Poetic Development* (1933), London, Methuen, 1965.

Riffaterre, Michael, *Semiotics of Poetry*, Bloomington, Indiana University Press, 1978.

'Descriptive Imagery', *Yale French Studies*, 61 (1981), pp. 107–25.

'Relevance of Theory/Theory of Relevance', *Yale Journal of Criticism*, 1, 2 (1988), pp. 163–76.

Robinson, Dwight E., 'Ode on a "New Etrurian" Urn, A Reflection of Wedgwood Ware in the Poetic Imagery of John Keats', *KSJ*, 12 (1963), pp. 11–35.

Rollins, Hyder Edward, ed., *The Keats Circle: Letters and Papers and More Letters and Poems of the Keats Circle*, 2nd edn., 2 vols., Cambridge, Mass., Harvard University Press, 1965.

Rousseau, Jean-Jacques, *A Discourse Upon the Origin and Foundation of the Inequality among Mankind*, London, 1761.

Royle, Nicholas, *Telepathy and Literature: Essays on the Reading Mind*, Oxford, Basil Blackwell, 1991.

Ruoff, Gene W., 'Wordsworth on Language: Towards a Radical Poetics for English Romanticism', *The Wordsworth Circle*, 3 (1972), pp. 204–11.

'The Sense of a Beginning: *Mansfield Park* and Romantic Narrative', *The Wordsworth Circle*, 10 (1979), pp. 174–86.

Ruthven, K. K., 'Keats and Dea Moneta', *SiR*, 15 (1976), pp. 445–59.

Ryals, Clyde De L., 'The Nineteenth Century Cult of Inaction', *Tennessee Studies in Literature*, 4 (1959), pp. 51–60.

Rzepka, Charles J., *The Self as Mind: Vision and Identity in Wordsworth, Coleridge, and Keats*, Cambridge, Mass., Harvard University Press, 1986.

Salvaggio, Ruth, 'Time, Space, and the Couplet', *PQ*, 62 (1983), pp. 95–108.

Saunders, J. W., *The Profession of English Letters*, London, Routledge and Kegan Paul, 1964.

Schwartz, Lewis M., 'Keats's Critical Reception in Newspapers of His Day', *KSJ*, 21–2 (1972–3), pp. 170–187.

Scott, Walter, *Sir Walter Scott on Novelists and Fiction*, ed. Ioan Williams, London, Routledge and Kegan Paul, 1968.

The Prefaces to the Waverley Novels, ed. M. A. Weinstein, Lincoln, University of Nebraska Press, 1978.

Sharpe, Charles Kirkpatrick, *Metrical Legends*, Oxford, 1807.

Sheats, Paul D., 'Stylistic Discipline in *The Fall of Hyperion*', *KSJ*, 17 (1968), pp. 75–88.

Shelley, Percy Bysshe, *The Letters of Percy Bysshe Shelley*, ed. Frederick L. Jones, 2 vols., Oxford University Press, 1964.

Shelley's Critical Prose, ed. Bruce R. McElderry, Lincoln, University of Nebraska Press, 1967.

Shelley's Poetry and Prose, eds. Donald H. Reiman and Sharon B. Powers, New York, Norton, 1977.

Simpson, David, *Irony and Authority in Romantic Poetry*, London, Macmillan, 1979.

Siskin, Clifford, *The Historicity of Romantic Discourse*, New York, Oxford University Press, 1988.

Sitterson, Joseph C., 'Narrator and Reader in *Lamia*', *SP*, 79 (1982), pp. 297–310.

Slote, Bernice, *Keats and the Dramatic Principle*, University of Nebraska Press, 1958.

Smith, Barbara Herrnstein, *Poetic Closure: A Study of How Poems End*, University of Chicago Press, 1968.

'Narrative Versions, Narrative Theories', in W. J. T. Mitchell, ed., *On Narrative*, University of Chicago Press, 1981.

Smith, Louise Z., 'The Material Sublime: Keats and *Isabella*', *SiR*, 13 (1974), pp. 299–311.

Sperry, Stuart M., *Keats the Poet*, New Jersey, Princeton University Press, 1973.

Spiegelman, Willard, *Wordsworth's Heroes*, Berkeley, University of California Press, 1985.

Spitzer, Leo, 'The "Ode on a Grecian Urn"', or Content vs Metagrammar', *Comparative Literature*, 7 (1955), pp. 203–25.

Stanzel, F. K., *A Theory of Narrative*, 2nd ed., tr. Charlotte Goedsche, Cambridge University Press, 1984.

Steiner, Wendy, *Pictures of Romance: Form Against Context in Painting and Literature*, University of Chicago Press, 1988.

Stephenson, William C., 'The Performing Narrator in Keats's Poetry', *KSJ*, 26 (1977), pp. 51–71.

Stevenson, Lionel, 'The Mystique of Romantic Narrative Poetry', in W. Paul Elledge and Richard L. Hoffman, eds., *Romantic and Victorian*, Rutherford, Fairleigh Dickinson University Press, 1971.

Stewart, Garrett, '*Lamia* and the Language of Metamorphosis', *SiR*, 15 (1976), pp. 3–41.

Reading Voices: Literature and the Phonotext, Berkeley, University of California Press, 1990.

Stillinger, Jack, *The Hoodwinking of Madeline and Other Essays on Keats's Poems*, Urbana, University of Illinois Press, 1971.

'The Plots of Romantic Poetry', *College Literature*, 12 (1985), pp. 97–112.

Sturgess, Philip J. M., 'A Logic of Narrativity', *NLH*, 20 (1989), pp. 763–83.

Suleiman, Susan and Inge Crosman, eds., *The Reader in the Text: Essays on Audience and Interpretation*, New Jersey, Princeton University Press, 1980.

Swartz, Richard G., 'Wordsworth, Copyright, and the Commodities of Genius', *Modern Philology*, 89 (1992), pp. 482–509.

Swingle, L. J., *The Obstinate Questionings of English Romanticism*, Baton Rouge, Louisiana State University Press, 1987.

Talbot, Norman, 'Porphyro's Enemies', *Essays in Criticism*, 38 (1988), pp. 215–32.

Talfourd, T. N., 'An Attempt to Estimate the Poetical Talent of the Present Age', *The Pamphleteer*, 5 (London, 1815).

Taylor, Anya, 'Superhuman Silence: Language in *Hyperion*', *SEL*, 19 (1979), pp. 673–87.

Taylor, John Tinnon, *Early Opposition to the English Novel: The Popular Reaction from 1760–1830*, New York, Columbia University Press, 1943.

Teunissen, John J. and Evelyn J. Hinz, '"Ode on a Grecian Urn": Keats's "Laocoön"', *English Studies in Canada*, 6 (1980), pp. 176–201.

Thomas, Edward, *Keats*, London, T. C. and E. C. Jack, 1916.

Thompson, E. P., *The Making of the English Working Class* (1963), London, Victor Gollancz, 1964.

'Thoughts on Novel Writing' (anon.), *Blackwood's Edinburgh Magazine*, 4 (January 1819), pp. 394–6.

Tompkins, Jane P., ed., *Reader-Response Criticism: From Formalism to Post-Structuralism*, Baltimore, The Johns Hopkins University Press, 1980.

Tooke, Andrew, *The Pantheon, Representing the Fabulous Histories of the Heathen Gods and Most Illustrious Heroes* (1698), 31st edn., London, 1803.

Turner, Michael, *Enclosures in Britain, 1750–1830*, London, Macmillan, 1984.

Valéry, Paul, *The Art of Poetry*, tr. Denise Folliot, London, Routledge and Kegan Paul, 1958.

Van Ghent, Dorothy, *Keats: The Myth of the Hero*, New Jersey, Princeton University Press, 1983.

Vendler, Helen, *The Odes of John Keats*, Cambridge, Mass., Harvard University Press, 1983.

Vitoux, Pierre, 'Keats's Epic Design in *Hyperion*', *SiR*, 14 (1975), pp. 165–83.

Wagner, Robert D., 'Keats's "Ode to Psyche" and the Second "Hyperion"', *KSJ*, 13 (1964), pp. 29–41.

Waldoff, Leon, *Keats and the Silent Work of Imagination*, Urbana, University of Illinois Press, 1985.

Ward, Aileen, *John Keats: The Making of a Poet*, London, Secker and Warburg, 1963.

'"That Last Infirmity of Noble Mind": Keats and the Idea of Fame', in Donald H. Reiman, *et al.*, eds., *The Evidence of the Imagination: Studies in the Interaction Between Life and Art in English Romantic Literature*, New York University Press, 1978.

Wasserman, Earl R., *The Finer Tone: Keats' Major Poems*, Baltimore, The Johns Hopkins University Press, 1953.

Watkins, Daniel P., *Keats's Poetry and the Politics of Imagination*, New Jersey, Associated University Presses, 1989.

Wheately, Kim, 'The *Blackwood's* Attacks on Leigh Hunt', *Nineteenth-Century Literature*, 47 (1992), pp. 1–31.

White, R. S., *Keats as a Reader of Shakespeare*, London, Athlone, 1987.

Whiteside, Anna, 'The Double Bind: Self-referring Poetry', in Anna Whiteside and Michael Issacharoff, eds., *On Referring in Literature*, Bloomington, Indiana University Press, 1987.

Wicker, Brian, 'The Disputed Lines in *The Fall of Hyperion*', *Essays in Criticism*, 7 (1957), pp. 28–41.

Williams, Anne, *Prophetic Strain: The Greater Lyric in the Eighteenth Century*, University of Chicago Press, 1984.

Williams, Ioan, ed., *Novel and Romance 1700–1800*, London, Routledge and Kegan Paul, 1970.

Williams, Raymond, *The Country and the City*, London, Chatto and Windus, 1973.

Wilson, Douglas B., 'Reading the Urn: Death in Keats's Arcadia', *SEL*, 25 (1985), pp. 823–44.

Wolfson, Susan J., 'Keats the Letter-Writer: Epistolary Poetics', *Romanticism Past and Present*, 6, 2 (1982), pp. 43–61.

'The Language of Interpretation in Romantic Poetry: "A Strong Working of the Mind"', in Arden Reed, ed., *Romanticism and Language*, London, Methuen, 1984.

The Questioning Presence: Wordsworth, Keats, and the Interrogative Mode in Romantic Poetry, Ithaca, Cornell University Press, 1986.

Wordsworth, William, *The Letters of William and Dorothy Wordsworth*, 7 vols., ed. Ernest de Sélincourt, 2nd edn., rev. Chester L. Shaver, Mary Moorman and Alan G. Hill, Oxford University Press, 1967–1988.

William Wordsworth: The Poems, 2 vols., ed. John O. Hayden, Harmondsworth, Penguin, 1977.

The Prelude 1799, 1805, 1850, eds. Jonathan Wordsworth *et al.*, New York, Norton, 1979.

Selected Prose, ed. John O. Hayden, Harmondsworth, Penguin, 1988.

Wordsworth, William and S. T. Coleridge, *Lyrical Ballads*, eds. R. L. Brett and A. R. Jones (1963), London, Methuen, 1968.

Wright, Herbert G., *Boccaccio in England from Chaucer to Tennyson*, London, Athlone, 1957.

Yost, George, 'Keats's Halfway Zone', *PQ*, 60 (1981), pp. 95–103.

Young, Edward, *Night Thoughts*, ed. Stephen Cornford, Cambridge University Press, 1989.

Z, 'Letter from Z. to Leigh Hunt, King of the Cockneys', *Blackwood's Edinburgh Magazine*, 3 (May 1818), pp. 196–201.

Zak, William F., 'The Confirmation of Keats's Belief in Negative Capability: The "Ode on Indolence"', *KSJ*, 25 (1976), pp. 55–64.

'"To Try that Long Preserved Virginity": Psyche's Bliss and the Teasing Limits of the Grecian Urn', *KSJ*, 31 (1982), pp. 82–104.

Zeff, Jaqueline, 'Strategies of Time in Keats's Narratives', *SEL*, 17 (1977), pp. 621–37.

Zionkowski, Linda, 'Bridging the Gulf Between: The Poet and the Audience in the Work of Gray', *ELH*, 58 (1991), pp. 331–50.

Index

250

DH

821.
7
BEN

Printed in the United Kingdom
by Lightning Source UK Ltd.
131994UK00002B/33/A